MW00824823

IN SEARCH OF PIPE DREAMS

PRAISE FOR IN SEARCH OF PIPE DREAMS ...

"This is not only a book about pipes and dreams, this is a book about life, freedom and enjoying the pleasures of being alive."

Miguel Narciso, Lisbon, Portugal

"*In Search Of Pipe Dreams* is the birth of a genre classic, combining memoir, pipe lore and opinion, written in an intimate, conversational tone that goes by all too swiftly. Of course, this will make for many re-readings. It is a real treat. I think it a genuinely creative stroke to have the book 'bookended' by the brilliant Albert Mendez, a real iconoclast, and excellent writer."

John F. McGahen, Calumet City, IL

"What a wonderful book, full of interesting information, and written with zest and a love of pipes and the people associated with them."

Tom Colwell, Ph.D., W. Nyack, NY

"This book never ceased to amaze me, because it is so informative and interesting."

Leslie Ng, Guangzhou (Canton), China

"I recommend this book highly to everyone interested in all aspects of pipes and pipe collecting."

Bill Unger, Columbus, OH

"What a fine book ... it's going to have a place of honor on the table by my 'pipe' chair in the living room."

Regis McCafferty, Albuquerque, NM

"Highly informative and thoroughly entertaining, you'll read it, as I did, more than once."

Leonard Fogel, Scarsdale, NY

"Thanks for your passion."

Kelly Crow, Atlanta, GA

"I've read a lot of books, and this is the first time that I've enjoyed a book so much that I wanted to go right back and read it again."

Joe Lankford, Enumclaw, WA

"It is a great book."

George Amrom, M.D., Philadelphia, PA

"A real 'tour de force' ... "

Ed Lehman, Chicago, IL

"I think it's fantastic! I've never known as much about pipes as I do now -- as a result of reading this book."

Peter Stokkebye, Corral de Tierra, CA

"*In Search of Pipe Dreams* is a thoroughly enjoyable book ... Rick writes with an infectious enthusiasm and a style which draws the reader into the joys of pipe smoking."

Fred Heim III, Menomonee Falls, WI

"It is great fun and very well written."

Fred Hanna, Ph.D., Cockeysville, MD

"This book would be enjoyable if read in sections, but I could not put it down after beginning it and intend to read it again (and again)."

Gordon Soladar, Sherman Oaks, CA

"This book deserves a special place in the library of all pipe enthusiasts."

Steve Johnson, Los Angeles, CA

"Rick Newcombe has put together a fantastic book. Not only is it very interesting, but it makes a person feel comfortable and relaxed while reading it."

Frank Burla, Downers Grove, IL

"What an outstanding book!!!! I can't seem to put it down and I have read it twice already."

Steve Rowland, Plymouth, MN

"I like your very personal and entertaining approach to vital subjects that are of interest to all pipe collectors."

Lars Kiel, Mørke, Denmark

"This book is magnificent ... persuasive ... unsurpassed ... liquid prose."

Mark Shropshire, Atlanta, GA

"Love your book!!!"

Mike Kaupp, Los Angeles, CA

"It's really a wonderful, wonderful book!"

Rob Cooper, Moorestown, NJ

"Congratulations for a book well written, well presented, and a balanced approach to the pursuit of pipe enjoyment."

Ben Rapaport, Reston, VA

"It's a pleasure to travel a journey of the senses through the pages in which the art of pipe smoking is elevated to the level of sophistication that it deserves."

Lalo Schifrin, Beverly Hills, CA

"I would HIGHLY recommend this book to anyone. I thoroughly enjoyed it. Your passion for pipes and travel comes through loud and clear. Your writing style is smooth and easy. It feels as though I am having a conversation with you."

Bruce Harris, Scotch Plains, NJ

"I bought *In Search of Pipe Dreams* at the Kansas City Pipe Show last weekend, and my wife agreed to drive the four hours to our home so I could read it -- and I can't put the thing down! FANTASTIC!!!!"

Mark Schloemer, Rozel, KS

"Your book was a pleasure to read, and I couldn't put it down for quite a stretch. Thank you, Rick, for a great book. It's worth it and will get several reads."

Matt Guss, Lakewood, WA

"I must express my compliments to you for your most interesting and touching book ... it is quite amazing."

Holger Frickert, Hamburg, Germany

"This book contains a mother lode of information for pipe smokers. It is simply a wonderful resource that I will return to again and again. Your writings have greatly influenced my pipe smoking pleasure."

B. Michael Williams, Ph.D., Rock Hill, SC

"The book is a tremendous achievement and chronicles Rick's travels around the world in search of high grade pipes ... The foreword and epilogue by Albert Mendez are a brilliantly written, acerbic view of the pipe world, and the world in general for that matter."

Mark Beale, M.D., Charleston, SC

"It was like sipping a fine wine. I enjoyed it a little bit at a time."

Fred Janusek, Green Bay, WI

"It is a wonderful book that I couldn't put down -- well worth the small price."

John Goldberg, Chicago, IL

"Thank you very much for writing this fantastic book -- it was a great pleasure to read."

Uli, Woehrle, M.D., Stuttgart, Germany

"Rick's book belongs in every pipe collector's library."

Rich Esserman, New York, NY

"I loved the book. It was so easy to follow, and the interviews are very informative and entertaining. I believe that every pipe shop, and every pipe lover, needs this book."

Art Karounos, Cologne, Germany

"I can truly say I love your book."

James Logan, Phoenixville, PA

"When I got to the end, I felt a sense of disappointment -- that there was no more to read."

Gene Umberger, Green Bay, WI

"I have groaned and yawned my way though many, many pipe books. Rick's book is different; it is by far the best I have ever read on the subject ... It rivets your attention from cover to cover. Albert Mendez' introduction and epilogue are priceless."

Ken Campbell, Wheeling, WV

"I could not easily put it down. It was so good, in fact, that I forced myself to 'sip' the pages rather than visually 'gulp' them down. I have personally read this book twice in three weeks time and have learned something new with each read."

Steve Fallon, Waco, TX

"Thanks so much for writing this book ... we indeed live in the 'Golden Age' of smoking pipes and tobaccos. Oh, by the way, the forward and ending thoughts by Albert Mendez were pure genius."

Arley Curty, Salt Lake City, UT

"This is the first pipe book I couldn't put down until I was finished with it, very much like a good work of fiction in the reading but factual in its accounts."

Ted Weidner, Omaha, NE

"Congratulations on such a wonderful, outstanding book, which for all pipe lovers must be 'THE BIBLE' of the future."

Lars Bernth, Assens, Denmark

IN SEARCH OF PIPE DREAMS

Rick Newcombe

Sumner Books
Los Angeles

Copyright © 2003, 2006, 2010 by Rick Newcombe

All rights reserved. No part of this book may be reproduced or transmitted in any form or by any means, electronic or mechanical, including photocopying, recording or by any information storage and retrieval system, without permission in writing from the Publisher.

Sumner Books
5777 W. Century Blvd., Suite 700
Los Angeles, CA 90045
ISBN 0-966-62391-6

SIXTH PRINTING

Rick Newcombe's e-mail address: rnewcombe@creators.com

Printed in the United States of America

To Carole, whose love of travel is contagious, and to Sara and Jack, who made our trips, and our world, so special.

~ ~ ~ ~ ~

CONTENTS

Acknowledgments and Credits……………………………………....I

Somewhat Introductory……………………………………….. i

Preface……………………………………………………… 1

Pipe Dreams Around the World…………………………….... 4

Chapter 1
Put That in Your Pipe……………………………………….. 7

Chapter 2
Pipe Shops and Pipe Makers in Europe………………….…..23

Chapter 3
Jess Chonowitsch: Character Counts………………………..... 34

Chapter 4
The Best Bargain Imaginable………………………………… 46

Chapter 5
Estate Pipes…………………………………………………..53

Chapter 6
Sixten Ivarsson -- The Thomas Edison of Pipe Making………... 62

Chapter 7
Lars Ivarsson, One in a Million………………………………66

Chapter 8
Your Pipes Should Have an Easy Draw………………………. 80

Chapter 9
S. Bang -- Ulf and Per, Two of the Greatest Ever……………….93

Chapter 10
Breaking in a New Pipe………………………………………. 99

Chapter 11
Keeping the Inside of Your Pipe Clean............................ 108

Chapter 12
Bo Nordh: In a League of His Own..................................116

Chapter 13
An Answer to Mr. Robert Schrire....................................130

Chapter 14
Coloring Your Meerschaum Pipe Easily........................... 140

Chapter 15
Paul Perri: Quiet Dignity.. 143

Chapter 16
Peterson Pipes... 149

Chapter 17
Too Many Pipes? Never!... 154

Chapter 18
Bertram: The Nation's Pipe Maker.................................. 164

Chapter 19
Germany: A Gold Mine for Great Pipes............................173

Chapter 20
Castello's Tradition of Excellence...................................195

Chapter 21
Paolo Becker -- An Expert Craftsman.............................. 201

Chapter 22
Two Types of Pipe Collectors.......................................206

Chapter 23
Random Reflections.. 221

Chapter 24
Pipe Smoking as an Antidote to Stress............................. 233

Epilogue.. 247

"As concerns tobacco, there are many superstitions. And the chiefest is this – that there is a *standard* governing the matter, whereas there is nothing of the kind. Each man's own preference is the only standard for him, the only one which he can accept, the only one which can command him."

Mark Twain
"Concerning Tobacco" (1893)

~ ~ ~

A PERSONAL NOTE FOR THE FIFTH PRINTING

It is hard to believe that after less than two years we are already on the Fifth Printing of this book. I want to offer my profound thanks to all the enthusiastic pipe collectors who have made it possible.

I also want to mention a handful of truly gifted pipe makers who were not included in the original draft -- only because of oversights on my part. For instance, I remember once looking up something I had written in the book, while enjoying a beautiful Peter Hedegaard "chimney" pipe, and it occurred to me that I completely forgot to mention Hedegaard of Denmark, who is one of the finest pipe makers in the world.

Other great pipe makers who were not mentioned include Baldo Baldi of Italy, who makes unusual pipes; Les Wood of England, whose silver work on pipes is among the best in the world, and the very talented David Jones of America.

In addition, I forgot to mention GBD, an excellent old English factory pipe. I have a 1960s-era GBD "author" that is superb. Also, Ascorti and the old Caminetto are two of my favorite Italian pipe brands. Davidoff and Porsche both make unique pipes.

I have no doubt there are dozens of other pipe makers -- individuals and factories -- I am forgetting, but please remember that this was never intended to be an encyclopedic pipe book. It is primarily a book offering my opinions, such as they are.

If you want a truly comprehensive book on pipes, I'd suggest *Pipes: Artisans and Trademarks* by José Manuel Lopes of Portugal. The English edition came out in 2005, and it is a fantastic book that is beautifully illustrated.

There is one other point I want to make concerning my personal taste in pipes. I mention this because many readers have told me they bought pipes that are sculptures to be admired, and they said they did so on my advice. I cringe when I hear this, because I prefer classical shaped pipes, and I judge a pipe primarily by how well it smokes and not whether it is a beautiful museum piece.

Of course, I write extensively about pipe makers who make beautifully artistic pieces. But the ones I write about, and the ones whose pipes I buy, such as Bo Nordh and the Ivarssons, are the ones whose pipes are great smokers, even if they also are works of art.

To me, the most important thing is that the pipe be a great smoker. All else is secondary.

As pipe smokers, we should be proud of our hobby and willing to defend the deep-rooted art of relaxed pipe smoking -- a practice that started centuries ago.

We must resist the anti-tobacco hysteria sweeping the world by pointing out the stress-reducing benefits of moderate pipe smoking. Always remember the words of Ed Kolpin (from P. 235), "You live longer with a pipe." Ed will soon be 100 years old.

Many people have inquired about my favorite shape, and that's easy: it is the apple/pot/billiard, similar to the gold banded Jess Chonowitsch pipe on the front cover of this book, and the silver banded S. Bang pipe on the back cover. Both are stunningly beautiful, and these types of pipes (after my special opening) are as good as it gets ... in my opinion.

Rick Newcombe
Los Angeles, California
January 2006

ACKNOWLEDGMENTS AND CREDITS

This book would not have been possible without the assistance of many individuals. First and foremost, there is Albert Mendez, who provided a long distance sounding board, editorial suggestions and just the right encouragement to motivate me to complete the task. Also, I want to offer special thanks to Marianne Sugawara, who figured out how to format the text on her computer, and how to scan the photos, so that I could see my articles as a book long before it was published. She also willingly tolerated my never-ending series of changes and rewrites. Christina Lee helped a great deal, and Julia Suits drew the wonderful illustration of Hitler lecturing Einstein.

I want to thank Peter Stokkebye, Dayton Matlick and Bill Nunnelly, all successful entrepreneurs whom I genuinely admire, for making it easy for American collectors to find high grade pipes and tobaccos, and I want to thank the magazine editors who ran many of the articles in the first place. They are Virginia Postrel of *Reason,* Chuck Stanion of *Pipes and tobaccos*, Joel Farr of *Pipe Friendly*, Bill Unger of *The Pipe Collector*, and Tom Dunn of *The Pipe Smoker's Ephemeris.*

The cover photograph of an S. Bang pipe was taken by Robert Gardner, and the photos on the back cover were provided by Uptown's and Music City, Tabak-Lädeli, S. Bang and Castello. The photos inside the book were provided by Carole Newcombe, Tessie Pablo, Uptown's, Tabak-Lädeli, Iwan Ries, Tinder Box, *Pipes and tobaccos*, Catherine Patnode, Rainer Barbi, Karl Heinz Joura, David Field, Dan Pipe, Brian McNulty, Joy Pulvers and Bonnie Chonowitsch. Lars Ivarsson provided the photo of the Sixten Ivarsson pipe that is reproduced in triplicate, as seen below, and at the end of each chapter.

SOMEWHAT INTRODUCTORY

by Albert Mendez

Put That In Your Pipe is the very first thing by Mr Richard Newcombe which I ever read (in the Summer, 1994–Spring, 1995 number of *The Pipe Smoker's Ephemeris*), and I was greatly impressed with this good-natured examination of the seemingly irrational and demonstrably malicious conduct of those who are—for reasons best known to themselves—resolutely opposed to the use of tobacco. [1]

Amongst the many excellent observations in this piece, is one about the ridicule and contempt directed against pipe-smokers by the scribblers and demagogues. This isn't surprising when you consider that in the past, pipe smoking attracted mostly sober, respectable, and rational men; precisely the sort of person you want to discredit at the outset, when attacking an institution.

The somewhat misleadingly titled *Pipe Shops and Pipe Makers in Europe* (except for a brief stop in England, it deals primarily with Danish and German pipe-shops and pipe-makers) is an early, concise look at the great Danish craftsmen, pervaded with the sort of profound insight that alone can flesh out mere names into living men.

When this piece was written, the Danish pipes available in the United States were mostly pedestrian, factory-made items, and (as Mr Newcombe points out) smokers and collectors, reluctant to pay large sums of money for makes that they were unfamiliar with, quite naturally gravitated towards the well-established triumvirate of Barling, Charatan and Dunhill.

Mr Newcombe rightly praises the tolerance of Danish society for pipe-smoking (and many other things), but notes that high taxes are a problem, as the lowest level of personal taxation is fifty percent, and the national VAT (value added tax) is nearly twenty-five percent. What prince of bygone days, ruling *Dei Gratia,* no matter how cynical, or mad, would have dared to demand half of his subjects' incomes? The low-born apparatchiki who have everywhere usurped rule, have no qualms about perpetrating this and similar enormities.

Jess Chonowitsch: Character Counts is a forthright, effective, and pertinent duologue between Mr Newcombe and the craftsman. Anyone who can read this chapter and not be seized by a strong desire to own one of Mr Chonowitsch's pipes must have ice water in his veins.

'Brief but tidy' is the best description of *The Best Bargain Imaginable*, an appreciation of second-hand pipes by American makers, which serves as a perfect aperitif to the following essay, *Estate Pipes*. In the latter, Mr Newcombe's admirable style—free of pedantic verbosity, or what is far more objectionable, the parroting of 'news media' illiteracies (e.g., the use of 'resonate' in connexion with anything other than acoustics, electrical engineering, or bad Victorian poetry)—is displayed to its very best advantage. I was particularly interested in his examination of a topic that is usually avoided by other commentators: cleanliness.

I grew up in a society that was (then-a-days) obsessed with cleanliness. Boiling water and powerful disinfectants were liberally applied to everything before use, and this was often carried to what foreigners viewed as somewhat absurd extremes. Mrs Mary Urrutia Randelmann, in her superb cookery book, *Memories of a Cuban Kitchen*, relates the tale of a friend's

'...plastic Howdy Doody and Peter Pan dolls, which had been sterilized in boiling water by his zealous mother and deformed for life.' Our first residence in this country was an antediluvian flat in Brooklyn's Park Slope, where my mother was horrified to find floors made of *wood*, with crevices that could potentially harbour entire colonies of bacteria. She promptly boiled huge buckets of water, added ammonia, and strong brown soap, and poured them on to the floors. Naturally, the water found its way into the flats below.... In my family, one always uses the same china, glasses and silverware; back home, these were engraved with a small initial, to ensure that each person's place was set with their own pieces. Obviously, the notion of smoking someone else's pipe was entirely unthinkable.

My introduction to the smoking of second-hand pipes came through my father-in-law, who had a very handsome Dunhill bulldog dating from the mid-thirties. This pipe had been damaged during the war, and upon his return to England, he had the pipe mended with a long silver sleeve around the stem. The pipe fascinated me, mostly, I think, because it was an honourably wounded veteran. One day, in a genial humour over the port, he (my father-in-law) declared that I should have it. Naturally, I thought he meant that I should keep it as a memento, and I was appalled (to say the least) when he made it clear that he expected me to smoke it. Some of this must have shown on my face, because he added that he would flush it clean with whisky.

A few days later, under the uneasy gaze of my poor wife (who was all too familiar with my fastidiousness), I was handed the pipe and an open tin of *Three Nuns*. What could I do? I filled the bowl and smoked a pipe with the man.

Following this metaphorical plunge into icy water, and the confirmation of my suspicions—by means of simple comparison—that the affordable new pipes from reputable makers were distinctly inferior to those which were available from them only ten years before, I began to buy second-hand pipes on a regular basis. I developed my own routine for cleaning these, beginning with the alcohol treatment favoured by my father-in-law (although I substituted inexpensive vodka for whisky), followed by the use of a small cabinet-maker's scraper to clean the interior of the bowl down to the bare wood. I cleaned the draught holes by passing machinists' parallel reamers (known here as straight flute reamers, I believe) of gradually increasing diameter through them.

Mr Newcombe is also a clean-it-down-to-the-bare-wood man, and in addition, he has—following lengthy consultation with some of the most distinguished names in pipe making, and quite extensive (and expensive) experimentation—developed some simple, but indisputably effective procedures to enhance the smoking qualities of second-hand (or new) pipes. It would be pointless for me to expound upon these, as Mr Newcombe has already done so most admirably here and elsewhere in the book.

This chapter also examines the somewhat thorny question of whether it is socially acceptable (for logically there can be no other hindrance to a man doing as he wishes with his own property) to alter a pipe to suit one's preferences. Personally, I find that it depends—as do so many other things in life—upon the observance of good taste. If some gentleman wants to increase the flue diameter of his pipe, what harm is there in it? There is no outward sign of the pipe being any different and after all, the exterior is what most collectors are primarily interested in. On the other hand, if some odious *mequetrefe* buys a nice old Barling and has a gold cowboy hat fitted to it as a bowl cover, then he should be slain most vilely and his remains committed to unconsecrated ground.

My father disliked 'plastics' (a word used by us generically, to include Bakelite, vulcanite, etc.) and after purchase, his Barlings were sent to an artificer, to be fitted with replacement bits made of horn. These 'taste' better and are easier on the teeth. Did this substitution 'ruin' the pipes? In my opinion and (I think) in that of any man of discernment, the pipes were enhanced, rather than marred.

It seems to me that this entire business has more to do with the getting of money, than with the preservation of historically significant objects, inasmuch as a certain type of person is always

iv

willing to pay far more for a second-hand article of quality, if it doesn't bear any marks of previous ownership.

Another extraordinarily interesting question examined by Mr Newcombe in this chapter, is that of the service life of a briar pipe. I don't think I have previously read anything on this subject, and I found the various opinions absolutely fascinating. I have owned some nineteenth-century pipes that smoked well, and others (of identical quality) that were unsmokable, so I am inclined to agree with Mr René Wagner, who feels that many different factors—including the quality of the tobacco smoked in the pipe—contribute towards diminishing, or prolonging, the life of a briar.

The two Ivarssons—father and son—are the subject of *Sixten Ivarsson–The Thomas Edison of Pipe Making* and *Lars Ivarsson, One in a Million*. In the final third of the nineteenth century, Victorian men of business, anxious to meet the overwhelming demand from the newly affluent middle classes for trumpery trappings, increasingly turned to standard patterns designed to facilitate the mass production of 'quality' articles. This had an irrefragably destructive effect on the æsthetic qualities of such things as sporting guns, watches, and tobacco-pipes, all of which were reduced to repetitive examples of mechanical mediocrity. Collectable as they are today, the popular BBB pipes of the late nineteenth century are perfect examples of this kind of goods. As is so often the case with the assertions of low tradesmen, 'best briar' meant exactly the opposite thing, since most of these pipes were made from markedly inferior briar. Nearly a hundred years would pass before one man, Ivarsson *père* (partly from artistic vision, and partly from absolute economic necessity), reintroduced the creative element into pipe-making by allowing the characteristics of the *ébauchon* to determine the form of the finished pipe.

Few sons are as good as their fathers, and most are worse, but the Gods granted Mr Sixten Ivarsson the double boon of skill in his craft and a son capable of matching—and even surpassing—the father's achievements. Mr Lars Ivarsson is a master of the pipe-making craft yet, as Mr Newcombe points out, there is no mention of him in the first volume of *The Pipe Smoker's Ephemeris*, and only one brief reference in the second. Other works on the subject give him equally short shrift, and these omissions are uncomfortably indicative of the somewhat limited horizons of many pipe-smokers in the United States.

Mr Newcombe offers us many absorbing glimpses of this gentleman's opinions, procedures, and techniques, and he mentions in passing that—like so many other Scandinavian craftsmen—Mr Lars Ivarsson still uses hand-made, razor-sharp knives for a lot of his work. I once spent an afternoon watching the great Swedish wood-carver, Mr Wille Sundqvist, teaching a group of trendy-lefties how to make simple treen spoons with a knife, and I concluded that the proper use of this oldest of man's tools requires more acumen, strength, and discipline than most men can now command.

Invariably, when two men from different countries discuss technical details, minor confusions will arise, and when Mr Newcombe questions Mr Ivarsson *fils* about the age of briar, the latter assures him that '...the myth of hundred-year-old briar is just that—a myth'. As one reads on, it becomes apparent that the craftsman mistakenly believes that they are talking about how long briar should be stored before making it into pipes. When one-hundred-year-old briar is spoken of, what is meant is that the rhizome[2], from which the *ébauchon* was cut, was taken from a mature *bruyère* (the *Erica Arborea*, or white heath, which grows to the aspect and dimensions of a small tree), seventy-five to two hundred and fifty years old.

Your Pipes Should Have an Easy Draw marks the beginning of Mr Newcombe's efforts to acquaint his fellow pipe-smokers with the results of his researches into the physics of pipe-making, and here he makes an excellent case for opening the flues (or draught holes) of pipes to a larger diameter than is commonly used.

Unlike some of the other names in this book, Mr S. Bang's is one that I was familiar with, admittedly only because a German friend mentioned the man and his pipes to me in the early eighties. We were discussing the military rifles of the early twentieth century, and we speculated about this gentleman's possible connection to another S. Bang, the designer of the singularly silly, but felicitously named, Bang semiautomatic rifle.

From *S. Bang–Ulf and Per, Two of the Greatest Ever* we learn that Mr S. Bang, the pipe-maker, was a far wiser man than his namesake. Early in his career, he decided that he was not a particularly skilful workman and chose to concern himself with the mundane activities of business (until his retirement in 1984), employing two master craftsmen—Mr Per Hansen and Mr Ulf Noltensmeier—to make the pipes that bear his name.

In *Breaking in a New Pipe,* Mr Newcombe presents us with a very comprehensive overview of the different techniques employed by pipe-smokers for this mysterious (and reportedly unavoidable) process of tempering a new pipe. These range from the sublime to the ridiculous, including the use of various liquids—some unexpected (water) and others repulsive (saliva)—to coat the interior before the ritual lighting of the crucial First Bowl.

Personally, I have never found it necessary to do anything to a new pipe, other than to completely smoke a full bowl of properly packed tobacco. To me the first pipeful tastes just as good (or as bad) as the fiftieth, and it has been my experience that a *good* new pipe will smoke well from the start. Second-hand pipes are another matter altogether. These may begin by smoking very badly indeed and come to smoke superbly, once one has 'sweated out' the lingering effluvia of the previous owner's revolting mixture.

One of the most important things I've learned, during thirty-eight years of pipe smoking, is that the taste and burning qualities of even the finest tobacco are greatly enhanced in a properly cleaned pipe. Sadly, most pipe-smokers are somewhat careless in this respect, and either allow foul-tasting residues to accumulate unchecked, or follow an abbreviated routine which removes only the most superficial of unwholesome deposits.

Mr Newcombe gives us a detailed description of his quite thorough cleaning technique in *Keeping the Inside of Your Pipe Clean*, and any new (or old) pipe-smoker could do far worse than to read this essay closely and adopt some—or all—of the measures described herein.

One of my great foibles is that of not being able to separate the man from his work, hence my favourite books are those written by men whose lives and opinions are agreeable to me. This caprice extends even unto waiters and barbers. I prefer to be attended by silent, elderly men, and cannot abide the supercilious buggers who insist on inflicting their histrionics on the hapless diners. Similarly, I will not suffer any man to touch my head, except he be a sober, aged fellow, well seasoned by the cares of life.

I suppose this is why I am genuinely sorry that my straitened circumstances do not permit me to acquire one or two examples of Mr Bo Nordh's work. The vibrant portrait painted in *Bo Nordh: In a League of His Own* made a powerful impression upon me; under Mr Newcombe's candid, delicate, and affectionate treatment, Mr Nordh, the master craftsman, emerges as an eminently likeable man, the sort of chap that one would be proud to have as a friend. I will not dilute the colours on Mr Newcombe's canvas by selecting highlights and prosing on about them, as the pseuds and *cognoscenti* are wont to do, but simply point out that the warmth, depth, and deceptively simple composition make this a most satisfying study and a fitting tribute to Mr Nordh's artistry.

An Answer to Mr. Robert Schrire was penned by Mr Newcombe in an attempt to dispel any false conclusions inadvertently drawn by pipe-smokers, after reading *Bo Nordh: The Wizard of Briar*, an article by Mr Schrire, which contained some lines capable of misinterpretation.

In *Coloring Your Meerschaum Pipe Easily,* Mr Newcombe acquaints us with his system for imparting that attractive amber colouring to the venerable meerschaum pipe. The simple process combines the three favourite, tried-and-true methods, successfully employed by smokers since Victorian times.

I have never owned, smoked, or even seen a Paul Perri pipe, but after reading *Paul Perri: Quiet Dignity*, I feel certain that I should enjoy his work. Mr Newcombe had one of this gentleman's pipes re-styled, re-stained, and fitted with a new bit. Upon completion, he showed Mr Perri the finished product. Did the craftsman leap at him with a sharp scalpel, determined to inflict grave bodily injury, or die in the attempt? No, he expressed his admiration for the re-worked pipe, and said that he had no objection to its modification, provided Mr Newcombe enjoyed the result. Such compassion and forbearance is rarely found outside of the *Lives of the Saints*.

'I have a soft spot for Peterson pipes', writes Mr Newcombe in his introduction to *Peterson Pipes*. So do I. Two of the best smokers I have are Petersons; a thirty-year old full-bent 'Standard' and an even older 'Kildare' saddle-bit Liverpool. These two extremely humble pipes are completely reliable, indoors or outdoors, wet or fine, their only limitation being that they require two or three days rest after use.

Elsewhere in the book (in *Too Many Pipes? Never!*) Mr Newcombe recalls a sad experience with the Dunhill shop in *Beverly Hills*, where some insolent shop-assistant asked him if the pipe he was smoking was a Peterson's and, upon Mr Newcombe replying that this was so, this *crapaud* informed him that '...if you're into Peterson, you really don't belong at Dunhill'. This goes a long way towards explaining something that I heard, when I was dining as a guest at the Guards' in London, on a mild April evening in 1969. The club was in some turmoil over its finances, and the other persons at the table were inveighing against the members who wanted to alleviate these difficulties, by allowing businessmen to use the premises for 'functions'. When one of that party entered the room, wearing a modish, wide-lapelled suit in place of a dinner jacket, one of the guardees said 'bloody ponce,' and my host whispered loudly to me, 'just like a demned floor-walker at Dunhill's.'

In the introductory lines to *Too Many Pipes? Never!* Mr Newcombe informs us that this essay was written as a response to a gratuitous diatribe directed against him by the editor of a now-defunct periodical. Apparently this fellow believed that Mr Newcombe's preference for bespoke Danish pipes stigmatizes him as an 'elitist' who doesn't feel comfortable with ordinary goods and will have only 'luxury' items—like Rolls-Royce motorcars—about him.

When people are attempting to forcibly persuade one to accept ideas, or products, which they are hoping to get a great deal of money from, and one refuses to acquiesce, expressing a desire to stick with what one knows intimately and feels comfortable with, they invariably accuse one of being 'prejudiced' and an 'elitist'.

As far as 'luxury' goods are concerned, for the past forty years or so, these have been mostly intended for the *arrivistes* and *poseurs*. Rolls-Royce long ago declined into an ostentation for pop singers, politicians and the like. And those expensive, trendy watches and fountain pens (usually carried by illiterate twisters, who can't write legibly with *any* sort of pen), along with the debased gold[3] gimcrack worn by the spenders of our depreciated notes, merely serve to mark the owners as vulgarians or confidence tricksters.

The answers to the questions of how many pipes a man should own, or how much he should spend on them, are purely subjective. Twenty-five years ago, when I occasionally purchased Charatans, I could easily afford the higher-grade Coronations and Supremes, yet I always bought the Specials, a dozen at a time. Why? Because I liked them and I didn't have to worry about losing them or breaking them, and having plenty of them allowed me to rest them after smoking only one bowl, which kept them sweet and dry.

Mr Newcombe also expresses here his scepticism of the amusing nonsense about pipe tobacco having a shelf life of only two years. No doubt, the manufacturers of the new, inferior blends, who spend far more money on advertising and packaging than on good leaf, are well pleased that this yarn has acquired some currency.

The capital cities of great countries are themselves great only when they have grown naturally. Artificially contrived capitals rarely ever capture men's imaginations, thus Bonn never achieved the legitimacy of Berlin, and planned capitals remain nothing more than embarrassing experiments. So it is with Brasilia, and with Washington, D.C., which—even during those years when it was the political capital of the world—has never been a great city.

Bertram: The Nation's Pipe Maker, a superbly well-written essay, briefly examines the rise and fall of this renowned American establishment, and touches lightly in passing upon the physical and moral decline of our nation's capital.

Americans tend to think of England as the place where the pipe is most popular; they are mistaken, of course, and the title properly belongs to Germany. The Germans are, and always have been, great smokers. They consume huge quantities of cigars and cigarettes every year, but in the past, pipe smoking was always far and away the most widespread form of tobacco use amongst them. Curiously, we never thought of Germany as a source of quality pipes, and indeed most Germans of my acquaintance smoked Dunhills or Charatans. Happily this situation is now somewhat altered. During a recent trip to Germany, Mr Newcombe had occasion to meet Wolfgang Becker, Karl Heinz Joura, and Rainer Barbi—three of the German pipe-makers whose work rivals that of the Danish masters—and his many excellent observations and impressions of that visit are contained in *Germany: A Gold Mine for Great Pipes.*

My encounters with Italian pipes have been mostly with those low-grade pieces in stock shapes, marked 'Genuine Italian Briar', which were to be found in any tobacconist's shop of about thirty-five years ago. These, and the occasional Savinelli *Giubileo d'Oro*, found their way into my hands as gifts from well-meaning acquaintances. I am willing to go to any lengths to avoid giving pain to a kindly person, so I smoked these pipes with every indication of enjoyment, until such a time as the giver was satisfied with my delight. These experiences were excruciating.

So it was that I read Mr Newcombe's *Castello's Tradition of Excellence* with great interest, and was very pleased to learn that the Castello pipes are reportedly every bit as good as the acclaimed English makes. This is hardly surprising; after all, Italy enjoys an abundant supply of some of the best briar available, and a long tradition of skilled workmanship.

Whereas Castello is a relatively large operation, the subject of *Paolo Becker–an Expert Craftsman* is a Roman shop operated by two partners, Paolo Becker and Giorgio Musicò, who specialize in highly-finished pipes, some following the traditional English shapes, and others freehands which are undeniably inspired by Danish design.

There are two completely different and apparently irreconcilable schools of thought about pipe collectors. The Absolutists maintain that the very sun shines forth in its fiery glory from a certain portion of their anatomy, and proclaim them the saviours of pipe smoking, and the life-blood that keeps the whole business alive. To set against this, The Unconformables believe that they are a troublesome lot of wretches who stir up strife, and bring discredit and trouble upon the decent sort of pipe-smokers. They (The Unconformables) strongly feel that pipe collectors should be transported *en masse* to some desolate and unpleasant locale, and abandoned there without any tobacco. Both of these views are much too extreme for a reasonable man to be comfortable with, and whilst I agree that pipe collectors can be very tiresome indeed, Justice should always be tempered with Mercy. This seems to me the better way: let us by all means strand them in some inhospitable spot, but let us leave them *some* tobacco.

Two Types of Pipe Collectors looks at some of the polemics that have been exercising the pipe-smoking ideologues for the past few years. One of these is the question of whether a pricey pipe from a celebrated shop is necessarily better than a modestly priced one from a humble maker. I have found that this depends almost entirely upon the nature and extent of the pipe-maker's clientele. An establishment that depends upon a limited number of discerning customers, who know what a first-rate pipe should be, and are willing to pay (and wait) for it, will undoubtedly produce a better pipe than one which is relying on a long-established reputation, and a highly-recognizable name, to 'market' the largest number of indifferent pipes to the sort of persons who equate pretentiousness with superior quality.

Then there is this silly business of 'flaws' and what precisely constitutes a 'first' or a 'second'. As Mr Newcombe points out, there is no such thing as an entirely unblemished pipe, and when someone says they have one, it simply means that they haven't taken the pipe into the bright sunlight and closely examined the briar surfaces with a high-quality, ten-power *loupe*. If one does that, one will find—even in the highest grades of the best makes—minute pits caused by grains of sand becoming trapped in the living wood, and imperceptible dints of varying depths, where the softer matter has shrunk away from the canals.

Finally, there is the *querelle* about altering one's pipes to suit one's taste. I will recast what I wrote earlier in this commentary; a man may do as he wishes with his own property, unless society doesn't countenance it and he is solicitous to remain socially acceptable (admittedly, not one of my great ambitions). It is very difficult for me to understand why the collectors grow wroth over harmless modifications like enlarging the draught-hole, yet remain relatively complacent about such things as replacement bits that are carefully reproduced to be indistinguishable from the originals, and newly cut dies intended to perfectly duplicate the original maker's markings. Surely these practices are much more likely to cause confusion for future collectors, to prove harmful to preservation, and quite possibly to be abused for fraudulent ends.

As a lifelong bibliophile and collector, I have been forced to associate with second-hand booksellers a great deal, and these fellows are quite adamant about the absolute necessity of keeping books in the exact condition in which they were purchased. No repairs, no binding, no marks of ownership, no excessive reading; nothing is allowed to indicate that the book once belonged to a human being who held it dear, and turned to it for solace in times of sorrow, or to dispel the ennui of modern life. I find this extremely distasteful. It smacks too much of the pawnbroker's preference for unmarked articles, which are easier to sell when the pledge goes unredeemed, and—in the case of elderly clients—easier to replace with an inferior piece of similar appearance. Strangely enough, books that were 'improved' by other booksellers, then sold and later repurchased by them, are not under this interdiction and fetch a considerable premium when resold to some university in Texas, where they sit—unseen and unloved—with fourteen other identical examples, on hygienic, air-conditioned shelves.

At the risk of offending many perfectly decent chaps, I must be honest and admit that if altering a pipe eliminates the possibility of getting more money for it than I originally paid, then I am all for it. To my chagrin, I was brought up to look upon the pursuit of riches as morally injurious and decidedly vulgar, and it was impressed upon me that poverty was infinitely preferable to even the slightest dishonesty. These undoubtedly noble precepts have made life extremely difficult for me, but one cannot easily put aside the habits of a lifetime, and the thought that my pipes will not be the object of unseemly wrangling after my demise is one of considerable comfort to me.

To my great satisfaction, I find myself unreservedly in agreement with Mr Newcombe's closing remarks where he urges pipe-smokers to stand fast against intimidation from collectors, and where he observes that pipe-collecting is unique, because pipes (like books) are constantly used by—and in intimate contact with—the owner during his lifetime. 'I am a pipe collector because I am a pipe smoker—and for no other reason.' This averment *du fond du coeur* of Mr Newcombe's perfectly coincides with my avowed tenets.

Random Reflections is a pleasant miscellany of opinions, helpful suggestions, and a clarification of some of Mr Newcombe's views that have been unjustly assailed as 'pernicious' and even 'unmutual' (which is a capital crime in any democracy). Base-minded persons have even suggested that Mr Newcombe's praise of top-grade pipes is motivated by pecuniary considerations; that he has been bribed by the makers to cry up their products. If we didn't live in a time remarkable for its turpitude, and corruption had not permeated the fabric of our society so thoroughly, such a ludicrous accusation would scarcely merit notice. So for brevity's sake, let us eschew detail and merely pause to consider that a craftsman's margin is not sufficiently ample to allow subornation, especially on the magnificent scale required to tempt a quite comfortable man. Only corporations have those kinds of resources, as any politician could testify, if he, or she, were so inclined. A man does not turn to craftsmanship because he wishes to grow rich, but to avoid placing himself in the power of churls, and to satisfy that natural yearning to create things that are both functional and beautiful. Far from being in a position to offer bribes, most of the makers that these essays treat of are dependent upon the custom of men like Mr Newcombe, for a significant portion of their income.

And so we come to the final chapter, *Pipe Smoking as an Antidote to Stress*, an essay dealing primarily with health and the preservation of it, which opens with a very good anecdote about the English philosopher, Bertrand Russell, an inveterate pipe-smoker who lived ninety-eight years.

De gustibus et coloribus non disputandum. 'There is no arguing about tastes and colours.' This hoary maxim, so beloved of the mediæval scholars, perfectly defines the core idea of Mr Newcombe's philosophy. Throughout his essays, we find reiterated the proviso that the preferences he champions are just that, preferences. He has found them personally agreeable, but he does not insist that they are for everyone, and he is perfectly willing to accept that they may only be suitable for him. To this I might add a more recent motto of my own coinage: *accept no limitations.* Mr Newcombe constantly stresses that one should not allow any other person, including the writer, to dictate what one should or should not do with one's pipes and tobacco, and that one should find by personal trial what is most personally satisfying.

In closing, I must say that the strongest impression I have received from the estimable Mr Newcombe's collected essays, is that he is a man who tremendously enjoys everything connected with his passion for pipes, especially travelling with his wife and children. Mr Newcombe has contrived to keep his family close to him in everything that he does. Surely this, and not the possession of the 'best' pipes, is the most remarkable thing that he has accomplished, and certainly the most desirable thing in life.

[1] I could, however, wish that he had chosen someone other than Albert Einstein as the exemplar of a great and admirable pipe-smoker; I know entirely too much about this fellow's activities to have any high regard for him. He too was a fanatic, perfectly willing to sacrifice the happiness and well-being of his fellow human beings, to further his particular brand of 'ism'. His legacy to the entire planet, of a permanent State of Emergency—with its associated anxieties, repressions and privations—based upon the threat of a future nuclear horror, is more reprehensible and inimical to humanity, than anything done by the legions of tyrants that have plagued the race of man.

[2] Rhizome is the correct word, in both English and French, for what American writers refer to as a 'burl' (a burl, or burr, is actually an excrescence on the trunk of a tree, from which cabinetmakers can slice small, thin, highly-figured sheets for veneer). This rhizome, also known as a *souche* (stock) in French, is a large subterranean bulb of a striking red colour, from which both the roots and the main stem of the tree spring. Sometimes called the 'root-ball' by English woodworkers, this extremely hard growth is very fire-resistant, and is the source of the wood used in briar pipes. Only about twenty-five percent of the rhizome can be cut into *ébauchons* for this purpose; the balance provides an excellent and highly prized firewood for the rustics who harvest it.

[3] The actual gold content of fourteen-carat gold (the most commonly used alloy) is only 58.33%.

PREFACE

This is not a definitive book about pipes but rather a series of essays on pipe-related subjects, offering my philosophical musings and highly opinionated comments. Some are conventional and others controversial, and all are offered in a spirit of optimism and fun.

I stress this because pipes, and everything to do with them -- collecting, smoking, modifying, cleaning, trading, reading and writing about them -- have literally changed my life, at least the spare time in my life when I am not at work or with my family. I can identify with the late Dr. George Sheehan, the running doctor, who said that the discovery of jogging in middle age was a life-changing experience. "At the age of reason, I was placed on a train, the shades drawn, my life's course and destination already determined," he wrote in his book, *Dr. Sheehan on Running.* "At the age of 45, I pulled the emergency cord and ran into the world. It was a decision that meant no less than a new life, a new course, a new destination."

In the same way, without a conscious "archetype," as Carl Jung might have put it, or "role model," as we say today, I carved my own path as a pipe collector in search of the perfect pipe, which is of course an impossibility, and have settled for the more easily obtainable pipe dreams; meaning, anything to do with pipes that I find relaxing, pleasurable and exciting. I have traveled around the world in search of these pipe dreams, and I have swapped stories and shared tobacco with enthusiastic collectors and Old World craftsmen in Denmark, Italy, Germany, England, Ireland, Switzerland, South Africa and China, not to mention my friends in New York, Chicago, Philadelphia, Atlanta and a dozen other American cities.

During my first 10 years as a pipe smoker, I was content with a collection of pipes mostly accumulated on Father's Days,

Christmases and birthdays thanks to the generosity of my wife, Carole, and with an occasional visit to a local tobacconist to make a purchase here and there, so that I had about 50 or 60 pipes when I became a serious -- some would say fanatical -- collector. At about the same time, as I became more and more interested in the study of what makes a great pipe, my taste buds changed almost from one day to the next. The blue packages of Captain Black, which had been so mild and sweet for so many years, suddenly gave me tongue bite and tasted as if I were sipping straight syrup. I switched to English and Oriental blends with latakia, especially Dunhill tobaccos, and have been content ever since.

I wrote my first pipe article back in the 1970s, which was a profile of Bill Fader for UPI that was reprinted in dozens of newspapers. I selected Bill, who was president of the Retail Tobacco Dealers Association for many years, because he sold me my first pipe. If I had not switched from cigarettes to a pipe, I suspect my health would have been impaired dramatically at this point in my life; in fact, at the rate I was smoking cigarettes, I probably would be writing these words with the assistance of an oxygen tank! So in that context, and in others as well, I believe that pipe smoking *saved* my life.

Collecting pipes can become even more important than smoking pipes. In fact, many of the pipe collectors I know do not actually smoke pipes at all. For them, it is the thrill of the chase -- and the beauty of Old World craftsmanship -- that keeps them enthusiastic about the hobby.

The vast majority of chapters in this book are reprints of magazine articles that I have written since the early 1990s. Some are reprinted verbatim while others have been modified slightly to reflect my changing views. I wrote about the subjects that interested me, and there is no topic that has captured my imagination more than the artistic skill and craftsmanship of the individuals who make what I consider the most beautiful and best smoking pipes ever made -- but only after they have been modified to my precise specifications. I hope you enjoy the stories, and I hope my suggestions and enthusiasm enhance your enjoyment of this very special and unique hobby that we call pipe collecting.

Rick Newcombe
Los Angeles, California
August 2003

PIPE DREAMS AROUND THE WORLD

The author, relaxing on a park bench in England, in 1981.

Back in England, 1995, with his wife, Carole.

AFRICA

On a very cold photo safari hunt in South Africa, kept warm by a blanket and a Jess Chonowitsch pipe.

ASIA

With collector Andy Chan, in Beijing, China. We had met at a Chicago Pipe Show.

EUROPE

From left to right, René Wagner of Tabak-Lädeli in Zurich, Switzerland, Jess Chonowitsch, me and Bo Nordh in Bo's backyard near Malmö, Sweden.

SOUTH AMERICA

Relaxing on a park bench with Carole and a pipe in Santiago, Chile.

~~~~~

PUT THAT IN YOUR PIPE

The anti-smoking movement has continued to gather strength since this first chapter appeared as an article in Reason *magazine in June 1994, and many of the restrictions that I feared, such as not being allowed to smoke in my office in Los Angeles, have been passed as laws. The same is true for the proposed taxes; in fact, there are always new proposals for new tobacco taxes. Why doesn't someone write about the fact that politicians profit more from smoking than tobacco company executives?*

In 1994 the anti-tobacco movement was largely confined to California and Washington, D.C., and it was just starting to spread across the country. Since then, it has become a worldwide phenomenon.

When I wrote about the cigar boom of the mid-nineties, I mentioned three cigar smokers who have all since died: George Burns at age 100; Milton Berle at age 93, and W. Clement Stone at age 100. So much for secondhand smoke.

* * * * *

The end of the last century saw the birth of two Germans who will be famous for eternity: Adolf Hitler, the bloodthirsty dictator, and Albert Einstein, the peace-loving genius scientist. Both men held strong views on the subject of smoking, and it is worth examining their opinions as we approach the end of the current century. This is especially true because there are proposals in Congress to ban smoking in the workplace, to raise tobacco taxes by astronomical percentages and to have the federal government regulate tobacco as a drug.

Hitler was a zealot about many things, so it is not surprising to discover that he was an extremist on the subject of smoking. He was a militant anti-smoker. He regarded smoking as vile and disgusting. According to *Time* magazine, "Adolf Hitler was a fanatical opponent of tobacco." He was fond of proclaiming that women of the Third Reich did not smoke at all, even though many of them did. Richard Klein, a professor of French literature at Cornell University, in his fascinating book *Cigarettes Are Sublime*, wrote that Hitler was "a fanatically superstitious hater of tobacco smoke."

THE ANTI-SMOKER   THE PIPE SMOKER

Einstein, on the other hand, was very passionate about his pipe smoking. According to *The Ultimate Pipe Book*, during one lecture, Einstein ran out of pipe tobacco and borrowed some cigarettes from his students so he could crumple the tobacco into his pipe. "Gentlemen," he said, "I believe we've made a great discovery!" But later, he decided that his conclusion was premature. He learned firsthand that cigarette tobacco is quite different from pipe tobacco. It lacks the aroma, the fullness and the taste of pipe tobacco. However, what appealed most to the great scientist was the entire ritual -- carefully choosing from a variety of pipes and tobaccos, delicately loading the briar, puffing and tamping, and the associated contemplation. He said pipe smoking helped him relax and gain perspective. "I believe that pipe smoking contributes to a somewhat calm and objective judgment in all human affairs," he said in 1950 at age 71 when he became a lifetime member of the Montreal Pipe Smokers Club.

I offer this contrast between Hitler the militant anti-smoker and Einstein the moderate pipe smoker for two reasons: first, to encourage the crusading anti-smokers in America to become a little more tolerant; and second, to encourage cigarette smokers to take up moderate pipe smoking of one to three bowls a day as a relaxing and healthier alternative.

The current political pressure to ban all smoking from the workplace, even from designated smoking areas, is symptomatic of an attitude in our society that is distressing to those of us who value freedom. This attitude degenerates into a movement to prohibit for everyone what some of us don't like. If you're in a minority and the majority wants to pass a law against you, God help you. The majority will do it. Even a few scientists will attempt to prove whatever it is they want to prove, regardless of the evidence. A good example is the fact that many scientists have questioned the Environmental Protection Agency's conclusions about secondhand smoke. Going back to our Hitler/Einstein comparison, it is easy to see that fanatical intolerance, as opposed to moderation and consideration, are at the heart of the smoking debate in America today.

I am speaking out as a private citizen because I am a successful entrepreneur who is responsible for sending millions of tax dollars to the state and federal governments each year -- from my own taxes, from my company, from our shareholders, from our employees, from our clients and from our vendors. It is frustrating beyond belief to know that my tax money finances politicians seeking to pass laws banning me from smoking a pipe in my own office. (Incidentally, I have a large private office with a powerful air purifier, and I keep the doors closed.)

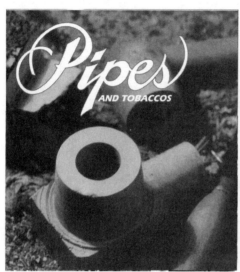 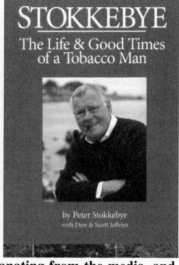

Despite all the anti-tobacco noises emanating from the media, and the increasing amount of censorship of tobacco advertising, we still have a free press in America, as seen in the superb publications shown above. *Pipes and tobaccos* **is a wonderful magazine, well written and full of interesting photos. The autobiography of tobacco legend Peter Stokkebye (right) is absolutely fascinating and a must-read for all serious pipe smokers. Both can be purchased through www.pt-magazine.com.**

California Rep. Henry Waxman is proposing what he calls the "Smoke-Free Environment Act," which would prohibit smoking in any public facility. By "public facility," he means not just government buildings but *any* building that is entered by 10 or more people at least one day per week (except residences, this time). But what if the building is privately owned and its owner wants to smoke? Too bad. His private building will be classified as a "public facility." Labor Secretary Robert Reich has threatened to use the Occupational Safety and Health Administration to support a ban on smoking in the workplace.

Besides seeking to ban smoking in "public" buildings, the Clinton health plan proposes raising the tax on some cigars by more than 3,000 percent and the tax on pipe tobacco by nearly 2,000 percent. The Clinton plan also wants to raise the tax on chewing tobacco by more than 10,000 (!) percent. Talk about targeting the poor. The militant anti-smokers should read history. King James I of England hated smoking as much as Henry Waxman and raised tobacco taxes by 4,000 percent. King James was wholly unsuccessful and, of course, created a huge black market for tobacco. Fortunately, 400 years after his death, England is known for some of the finest pipes in the world, including Ashton, Dunhill, Charatan, Comoy, Sasieni and Upshall, just to name a few.

The latest assault on all forms of tobacco comes from Dr. David Kessler, head of the Food and Drug Administration, who wants to regulate nicotine as a drug. The fact that nicotine gum requires a prescription is ridiculous. It is another example of making life more difficult for the poor. [That law, fortunately, has since been changed.] Anna Quindlen of *The New York Times* recently praised Kessler and used the words "courageous" and "brave" to describe those members of Congress who were eager to suspend the First Amendment by restricting tobacco advertising.

I'd suggest that Kessler and Quindlen read *John Barleycorn* by Jack London, in which London confessed that he was a hopeless alcoholic. He wrote that he favored women's suffrage because he was convinced that the women would pass Prohibition and thus he would be forced by government decree to stop drinking. In fact, he said, by passing a law, alcohol would no longer be a problem for the nation.

Well, the country did pass Prohibition. Whether it was because of women's suffrage or not, I don't know. What we know for sure is that it did not wipe out alcohol, to say the least. As for Jack London, he stopped drinking because he suffered an early death, not because of government decree. And Carry Nation, the woman who led the fight for the prohibition of all alcohol, was mentally ill. This last fact does not come as a complete surprise to those of us who have first-hand experience in dealing with the tobacco prohibitionists.

The anti-smoking movement has been gaining momentum for decades, but it is only in the last year or so that it has really become Gestapo-like in its enforcement. I believe I know why. The reason is cigarettes, plain and simple. Cigarette smokers are reluctant to speak out. It is extremely difficult to be a moderate cigarette smoker, and heavy (i.e., normal) cigarette smokers are clearly at risk of suffering heart attacks, lung cancer or emphysema. We all have friends and relatives who have suffered from lifetimes of cigarette smoking. Most cigarette smokers want to quit and thus feel no enthusiasm in defending their habit.

Despite these health hazards, however, all attempts to prohibit cigarette smoking represent a dangerous threat to freedom. Alcohol also carries considerable health risks, but attempts to prohibit it ultimately backfired by provoking Mafia wars and turning ordinary citizens into criminals.

While I am not advocating cigarette smoking, I am advocating freedom. In fact, my hope is that if you smoke cigarettes, you will consider switching to a pipe. The difference between chain-smoking cigarettes and moderate pipe smoking is the difference between drinking a case of beer or a bottle of vodka a day versus having a glass of wine with lunch or dinner.

There is an enormous amount of anecdotal evidence that pipe smoking offers *psychological* benefits, yet these are never considered in the debate. Ask any pipe smoker about the joy of his hobby! It is incredibly relaxing. It is fun. It is pleasurable. It tastes good. It feels good. It helps us unwind. It helps us cope with stress. It enhances objectivity. It facilitates contemplation.

All of these psychological factors contribute positively to good physical health, but when are they mentioned in the discussions led by Waxman, Kessler and Reich? Never.

Long after King James I, Dunhill and other British companies make some of the best smoking pipes in the world.

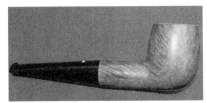 

Two gorgeous old Dunhills: a patent number root briar from 1950 (left) and an ODA bruyere from 1972 (right).

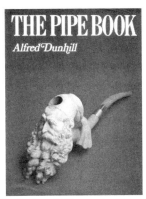

Alfred Dunhill wrote *The Pipe Book* in 1924, and it is still in print today.

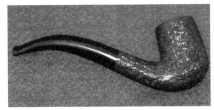 

A bent 1940 black sandblast patent number Dunhill shell.

An unusual Dunhill churchwarden, made in 1989, but modeled after the old clay churchwarden pipes.

England has a long tradition of making some of the best smoking pipes anywhere, including these straight grained Upshalls (above).

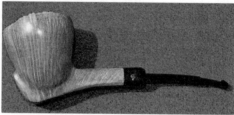

A stunning Charatan coronation -- one of the first imported to the United States, in 1965.

Barry Jones (left), who worked at Charatan for many years, was one of the founders of James Upshall Pipes and currently oversees the company's pipe making operations. On his right is enthusiastic collector and owner of Upshall, Moty Ezrati.

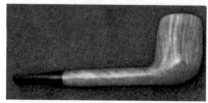

A beautiful Ashton Canadian.   A pre-transition Barling apple.

They don't want to know about such intangible issues as enjoyment, relaxation, fun, pleasure or reward. The starting point of their thinking is the simple question: Is this activity good for you or not in a strict biological sense? If it is not good for you, or if we *think* it is bad for you, then we will attempt to outlaw it. But if that is the starting point of their thinking, then the end result logically would be to outlaw obesity, to demand exercise from all Americans, to prohibit junk food, to limit alcohol and caffeine consumption, and so on and so forth. The irony is that Waxman is, frankly, a little chubby, Kessler used to be fat (and nothing is so unhealthy as yo-yo dieting), and Reich hardly looks like the picture of health.

Compare these three with Arnold Schwarzenegger, who is as healthy as a horse and a dedicated cigar and occasional pipe smoker. Arnold is as energetic and positive as anyone you could imagine. He has an incredibly full life, and he places a priority on finding "joy" (his word) in everything he does. That includes being a good family man, a successful movie star and businessman, and an inspiration to millions of fans around the world to get off their couches and exercise, and to eat a healthy diet. And for relaxation, Arnold enjoys kicking back with a fine cigar or comfortable old pipe -- all as part of a balanced, healthy and happy life.

Personally, I place a premium on having a balanced life, and good health is obviously essential. In fact, I work out regularly myself, and I have even trained with Arnold at World Gym. You could say that I am something of a health nut, in that I eat a healthy diet, don't drink alcohol, and I go for a five-mile run at least once a week as part of my exercise program that includes a minimum of four hours of strenuous workouts each week. And despite my moderate pipe smoking, or perhaps because of the endless joy it gives me, I am in terrific physical condition. In fact, I have been featured in three different articles in fitness magazines and one book as a businessman who is the picture of health, so to speak.

Yet I'm put on the defensive and treated as a pariah because I enjoy a pipe, and the same is true for Arnold Schwarzenegger, Michael Jordan and anyone else who relaxes with an occasional pipe or cigar, regardless of how physically fit they might be. We can only hope that laws won't be passed that will make all smokers common criminals. If our prisons are overcrowded now, can you imagine what they would be like in the future if smoking were made illegal?

It is also frightening that our tax money is used to sponsor government propaganda messages against smoking -- *official hate speech from the state.* Anti-smoking billboards and other advertisements by the government (especially by the state of California) are aimed at encouraging the average citizen to loathe smoking and, by implication, smokers. Which minority group will be targeted next for persecution? Asian women? Men with blond hair? Jews? Christians? Libertarians? Immigrants? People with suntans? Your guess is as good as mine.

Here's one illustration of how absurd the hysteria against smokers really can be. Several days ago, I was standing on a street corner in Santa Monica waiting for the light to turn green. A mass transit city bus, with an anti-smoking propaganda message on the side, passed by and spewed out soot, pollution and filthy exhaust fumes. I crossed the street and entered the Tinder Box, which was founded when Calvin Coolidge was president. The aroma was magnificent! I chatted with the store's founder, Ed Kolpin, who has come to work every day since 1928. He was puffing on his pipe, looking very contented. How many other people in this country founded stores in the 1920s and still come to work every day? Ed attributes his good health and long life to the sense of peace that 75 years of relaxed and intelligent pipe smoking have given him.

I'm sure the same would be true if we had questioned Albert Einstein or Albert Schweitzer or Friedrich Hayek or Arthur Conan Doyle or Carl Sandburg or Mark Twain or Gerald Ford or Bing Crosby or Walter Cronkite or Norman Rockwell or millions of other pipe smokers who achieved greatness in their lifetimes and who lived, or are still living, to an old age.

Ed Kolpin (left) back in 1928, when he first opened his pipe shop, and today (right), after seventy-five years of exposure to secondhand smoke -- morning, noon and night. Ed will turn 95 on his next birthday.

I read a story in a 1950s-era pipe magazine about Guizot, who was identified as "the historian of France." A lady visited Guizot one evening in his home and found him absorbed in his pipe. She exclaimed, "What! You smoke, and yet have arrived at so great an age?" "Ah, madame," the venerable statesman said in reply, "if I had not smoked, I should have been dead 10 years ago."

Pipe smoking is a hobby I began in 1978, and it has given me endless hours of enjoyment. At that time, at the age of 28, I was a two-pack-a-day cigarette smoker. I could not run a mile without collapsing from wheezing, and many nights, my hacking cough woke me up. There was no way for me to be a moderate cigarette smoker. I decided that cigarettes were poison for me, but I still wanted to smoke, so I tried smoking a pipe as a substitute.

At first, I suffered tongue bite; I broke one pipe not knowing how to handle it; I was not used to smoking without inhaling; I smoked way too fast and burned the briar on several pipes -- and made a dozen other mistakes typical of the beginning pipe smoker. But that's what makes pipe smoking so unique. It is a ritual that requires patience and study.

You can't just go to a drugstore, buy the least expensive pipe you can find, and expect to enjoy the smoke. It doesn't work that way. It can require years of study and practice before one's enjoyment of a pipe reaches that point of contentment that only experienced pipe smokers know.

Let me put it this way: I was a Phi Beta Kappa graduate of Georgetown University, I studied for a master's degree at the University of Chicago, and I make my living in the field of intellectual property rights, representing writers and artists in newspaper and Internet syndication. *But when it comes to pipes, I'm strictly a beginning student.* Every time I talk with a longtime collector like John Loring of Chicago, I realize how little I know about the history of the hobby.

Christopher Morley wrote in 1916 that "pipe smoking is properly an intellectual exercise." I have read 17 books on the subject and hundreds, perhaps thousands, of magazine and newsletter articles, and I still learn something new every time I visit a knowledgeable tobacconist. I believe the best overview on the subject is provided in *The Ultimate Pipe Book* by Richard Carleton Hacker -- a fact-filled text written in an interesting and fun style.

Pipe collecting as a hobby has become such a passion for me that I own nearly 200 pipes, some dating back to the 1920s and 1930s, and I know the history of nearly all of them and the biographies of the pipe makers. There may be only a few pipe smokers left, but we are intelligent and dedicated.

If smoking has any future at all, it lies in moderate pipe smoking. I realize that excessive pipe and cigar smoking can contribute to various forms of mouth, throat or lip cancer in rare instances, but it is the excess that is the culprit. It is relatively easy, with time and practice, to be a moderate pipe smoker. However, if you cannot smoke a pipe or cigar without chain-smoking, then I would strongly recommend giving them up altogether, or following the advice given in Chapter 24.

There was an interesting longevity study conducted in Pennsylvania during the 1960s and early 1970s. According to the magazine *The Compleat Smoker*, an organization called No Other World conducted the research with the assistance of regional chapters of the American Cancer Society, American Heart Association and the Northwestern Pennsylvania Lung Association. "In the study, pipe smokers attained an average age of 78 -- two years older than their non-smoking male counterparts." In other words, the typical pipe smoker in the study lived longer than the typical non-smoker. I believe this says a great deal about secondhand smoke -- that its dangers are grossly exaggerated. It also says a great deal about the benefits of pipe smoking to reduce stress.

But data showing that pipe smokers statistically outlive non-smokers drives anti-smokers crazy because it contradicts everything they believe about all types of tobacco use. How do they explain it? For the most part, they don't. They simply lump all smokers together and condemn smoking. Period. End of story. Some militant anti-smokers appear to be motivated by morality as much as medicine. Whenever I hear a moderate pipe smoker criticized, I know we are dealing with sin, not science.

Nonetheless, pipe smoking in America today is a lost art. *The New York Times* recently referred to pipe smokers as "oddballs," even though James Reston, one of the most influential writers and editors at the Times for decades, has been a dedicated pipe smoker for most of his life.

The Times made the comment in a story about the growth of the cigar market and the sudden success of *Cigar Aficionado* magazine, which is a very interesting publication with beautiful graphics. The pipe book author Richard Carleton Hacker also wrote the best-selling *Ultimate Cigar Book*, and he says that cigar sales have soared more than 45 percent during each of the last few years, especially premium cigars. Millions of executives, professionals and young people are discovering the pleasures of cigar smoking.

They are clearly rebelling against the Puritanism of the hard-core anti-smokers. The barrage of moralistic pronouncements, combined with a legislative stampede that is flirting with Prohibition, have encouraged many non-smokers and former cigarette smokers to take up cigars. It is a phenomenon that says a great deal about individualism and rebellion. It is also a statement of freedom to enjoy oneself because, to a real cigar smoker, there are few pleasures in life that can compare with a fine cigar.

Black-tie smoker dinners are always sold out well in advance. Successful pipe shops are packed with more customers buying cigars than pipes. Certainly many famous people have lived long lives as cigar smokers. Some were never photographed without their cigars, including Winston Churchill and Groucho Marx.

Among contemporaries, there seems to be a growing number of high-profile celebrities and business leaders who relish their cigars in public, including Rush Limbaugh, Lee Iacocca and Bill Cosby. George Burns and Milton Berle have continued to enjoy fine cigars for years and years and still more years -- in fact, for a combined total approaching two centuries! One of my favorite businessmen, the insurance billionaire and full-time positive thinker W. Clement Stone, has been smoking cigars for most of his 90-plus years.

Regardless of legislation, smoking will not go away. It just won't. It's been around for hundreds of years. All types of governments have tried banning it altogether, and people just keep puffing away. Nearly a billion people from around the world smoke cigarettes daily. The *Los Angeles Times* recently observed: "Russia once whipped smokers, Turkey beheaded them and India slit their noses. The Massachusetts colony outlawed public smoking in the 1630s, and Connecticut required smokers to have permits in the 1940s. At various times between 1893 and 1921, cigarette sales were banned in North Dakota, South Dakota, Washington, Iowa, Tennessee, Arkansas, Illinois, Utah, Kansas and Minnesota."

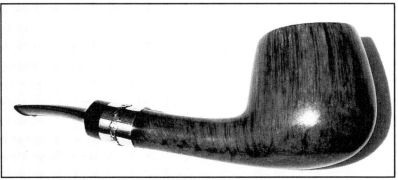

How can a cigarette compare with a beautiful pipe, such as this Savinelli Autograph 000? Savinelli is based in Milan, Italy, and their pipes are sold all over the world.

My frustration is that pipe smokers get lost in the argument because there are so few of us. And as I said, cigarette smokers generally have no enthusiasm in defending their habit, while pipe smokers feel a real passion for their pipes. Cigarette smokers want to quit. Pipe smokers are eager to learn more about their hobby. Cigarette smokers in America today are often made to feel shame and guilt while pipe smokers feel contentment and peace of mind.

So the solution is to encourage cigarette smokers to switch to a pipe. That includes women, of course. Objectively, there is absolutely no reason why women should not smoke pipes, too.

Once you start discovering the various types of briar, and the thousands of blends of exquisite tobaccos from all over the world, and the hundreds of traditional and unusual shapes, sizes and finishes for a pipe, and the possibilities for beautiful artwork carved into meerschaum and briar pipes -- a whole new world of enjoyment and independence will open up to you. It is a world that will help you relax and reduce your stress level. It is also a statement of ultimate rebellion against political correctness. To be a pipe smoker in America in 1994, you really must be an individualist.

Don't forget -- there is a direct link between freedom and the right to smoke. Cornell Professor Richard Klein has researched this issue extensively: "Like other tyrants such as Louis XIV, Napoleon, and Hitler, James I despised smoking and demonized tobacco. The relation between tyranny and the repression of the right to grow, sell, use, or smoke tobacco can be seen most clearly in the way movements of liberation, revolutions both political and cultural, have always placed those rights at the center of their political demands. The history of the struggle against tyrants has been frequently inseparable from that of the struggle on behalf of the freedom to smoke, and at no time was this more the case than during the French and American revolutions."

Make moderation a priority in your pipe smoking, and you can enjoy your hobby for many decades. You will enhance your good health and go through your days with a happy, relaxed and level-headed perspective. As the noted author and intellectual John Erskine wrote more than a half century ago, "To this day we writers rely on the pipe for patience, for good humor, and for an objective view of the universe."

That is precisely the conclusion Albert Einstein drew from his own pipe smoking. It is worth reminding those anti-smokers who are moralistic to the point of being insufferable that their most famous historical leader during the last one hundred years was none other than Adolf Hitler. At the least, that will dampen their self-righteousness. It is also worth noting the advice of the greatest scientist -- yes, *scientist* -- of the 20th century: If you want to be calm and objective in all human affairs, then by all means, become a moderate pipe smoker.

CHAPTER TWO

~~~~~

PIPE SHOPS AND PIPE MAKERS IN EUROPE

I never spent more than $15 for a pipe during my first five years of pipe smoking, but gradually I began experimenting with more expensive pipes, and by 1995, when this article was written for Pipe Friendly *magazine, I was hooked on high grade pipes hand made by individual artisans. In this article, I mentioned two individuals who were active in selling pipes but who have since died. Ole Larsen passed away in October 2002 and Jack Ehrmantraut passed away several years ago. I also began the article talking about Astley's, which has since closed its doors, although the owner of Upshall Pipes, Moty Ezrati, purchased the rights to continue the production of Astley Pipes.*

I concluded the article by wishing out loud that a really good distributor in the United States could be found for the high grade Danish pipes, and one year after this was published, my wish came true. Uptown's Smoke Shop of Nashville, Tennessee, began distributing these excellent pipes all across America, and they have been extremely successful in representing the high grade pipe makers ever since.

Bill Nunnelly, owner of Uptown's and Music City Marketing, flew to Los Angeles to meet with Jess Chonowitsch after this article appeared and Jess was starting to become known in the States. Jess and his wife, Bonnie, were visiting me in Los Angeles, and we had a series of meetings with Bill.

Bill promised to invest in promoting the Danish high grades, and he wanted a commitment that Jess and a few other outstanding pipe makers would stay loyal to Uptown's in exchange. Bill honored his word, including by producing an expensive video about the pipe makers called "The Great Danes," taking out beautiful color advertisements on their behalf in pipe magazines and hiring knowledgeable salespeople.

Bill Nunnelly

    Jess honored his word by sending Uptown's hundreds of his most beautiful pipes over the years and encouraging the other Great Dane pipe makers to do the same. They have a win/win agreement, but the ultimate winners have been the American pipe collectors who are now smoking these pipes. The highlight of those meetings, for me, was our celebration lunch at Arnold Schwarzenegger's restaurant, where Bill presented Arnold with one of Jess' pipes -- and Arnold was absolutely thrilled!

    In a follow-up letter, Arnold referred to it as "a fantastic pipe," adding, "every time I bring it out and light up, I receive so many compliments on such a unique and beautiful piece."

    I have always been impressed by the fact that Bill was one of the people responsible for raising the level of quality of pipes offered in America, yet he is virtually unknown within the pipe collecting community. Several years ago, I wrote a letter to The Pipe Smoker's Ephemeris *mentioning Bill's contribution to the hobby, and I hope that by including him in this book, and explaining the story of his involvement in the marketing of high grade pipes in the States, at least you will know a little about the man behind the scenes who has done so much to make the lives of serious pipe smokers in America more enjoyable.*

Since 1995, globalization and the Internet have also caused a revolution in the sale of high grade pipes. If you are interested in any of the pipes discussed in this book, simply Google the name of the pipe maker and you will find many places where you can buy their pipes. While many brick-and-mortar pipe shops have closed, there has been an explosion of commercial activity on the Internet for all types of pipes, ranging in price from the least expensive to the most.

Brian Godbee (left) of www.pipesmagazine.com and Brian Levine of www.smokingpipes.com are representative of the new generation of pipe enthusiasts.

* * * * *

During the summer I had business in England and Germany, and between appointments I visited some spectacular pipe shops and pipe-making workshops. Astley's in London has some of the most beautiful briar pipes I have ever seen. Its proprietor, Paul Bentley, was extremely helpful and knowledgeable. I asked him a question that I have wondered about over the years: if there is sap remaining in the briar when a pipe is made, does it eventually dry out over time and with the heat from smoking, or does it simply solidify in the wood? "It dries out," he said, "as evidenced by the fact that some pipes don't smoke well at all at first and then -- all of a sudden -- they become fantastic."

Dunhill in London was having a special pipe promotion, and I chatted with one of their pipe makers. I watched him polish some customers' pipes and marveled at his skill and care. I also bought a number of tins of their hand-blended pipe tobacco.

From there, I went to Cologne, Germany and spent several hours with Peter Heinrichs, owner of the famous "House of 10,000 Pipes." Peter was warm, friendly, charming and totally committed to the pipe business. He owns two stores, and I visited both. The first was in downtown Cologne. The first floor has displays of thousands of beautiful pipes, and the second floor offers some of the rarest high-grade collectibles I have ever seen. For instance, I looked at a half-dozen free hand pipes made by Poul Ilsted that had grain that was as tight as any I have ever seen. The bird's eye on the bottom of the bowls and on the shanks was simply not to be believed.

Hans Nielsen, left, whose pipes are known by the name "Former," with Tom Eltang. Both are excellent Danish pipe makers.

Peter said that in his opinion the two greatest pipe makers of the 20th century are Sixten Ivarsson and Bo Nordh, and he has a handful of their pipes. Neither man makes many pipes, and the demand for them has driven up their prices to astronomical levels. Some collectors, especially from Japan, have been known to pay more than $5,000 for one pipe made by Ivarsson or Nordh.

Peter also had pipes made by Ingo Garbe, Jess Chonowitsch and S. Bang that were breathtaking. In addition, there were extremely beautiful pipes by Sven Knudsen and his younger brother Teddy, Barbi, Lars Ivarsson, Nanna Ivarsson, Tonni Nielsen, Former, Tom Eltang and dozens of other master craftsmen.

Tonni Nielsen, Mette and Teddy Knudsen -- both men are also superb Danish pipe makers.

But the point is that Peter Heinrichs has hundreds of pipes that you simply won't find anywhere else. I remember once calling a well known Midwest pipe shop and asking if they had any Sixten Ivarsson pipes. The man on the phone said no, there simply are none available, and besides, he said, Ivarsson is dead. I don't think Sixten would have been too happy to hear that, considering that he is very much alive and well. He is in his mid-80s, his eyesight is failing, but he is still managing to make one or two pipes a year. The man on the phone also said, "We sold Ivarsson pipes for thousands of dollars 20 years ago. If you could find one now, I'd hate to think what it might cost." In addition to the Danish pipes, Peter Heinrichs has hundreds of gorgeous pipes from England, Germany, Italy, France and every country in the world -- except America.

This brings up a pet peeve of mine; namely, the fact that some of the best pipe makers in the world are American, and they don't get the recognition they deserve. They include Perri, Butera, Lewis, West, Cooke, Marks, Wiley, Learned, Burak, Yager, Rose, Johnson, Schulte, Roush, Davis, McNulty, and my personal favorite, Tony Rodriguez. I'm sure there are dozens of others I have forgotten to name.

Here are four great American pipe makers. (L-R) Todd Johnson, who is also a graduate student at Yale, John Eells, Jody Davis, who is also a professional musician, and Tim West.

When it was 5:00 in the afternoon, Peter drove my wife and me to his other store, located outside the city. This is a pipe store not to be believed. It has everything! Thousands and thousands of pipes, including rare pieces such as one of Joseph Stalin's pipes (a Dunhill bruyere). The amount of pipe tobacco was amazing, and there were dozens of beautiful pipe cabinets and racks.

From there, we went to Hamburg and one of the stores owned by Dan Pipe, which offers a fantastic catalog and is becoming one of the biggest mail order pipe shops in the world. I hope that next year's catalog includes English translations. They used to be called Pipe Danske (meaning Danish Pipe), but when the famous Copenhagen-based store, Pipe Dan, closed down, the owners of Pipe Danske decided to shorten the company's name to Dan Pipe. I spent several hours chatting with the store's owner, Paul Botter, and some of his customers. I also found an extremely rare Anne Julie pipe. Paul has been in the business for 25 years and has a very good relationship with Anne Julie, who is painting now. Paul and his friends were eager to hear about the American pipe market, and I encouraged them to come to one of our pipe shows.

We left Germany for Copenhagen, and I must confess that I was totally overwhelmed during the next two days. I am convinced that a handful of the world's best pipe makers live in Denmark and are virtually unknown in the United States. We think mostly of Stanwell, Larsen and Nording -- all excellent pipes. But only a few of their thousands of pipes offer the care and skill of the individual pipe makers whose work is nothing short of unbelievable.

Perhaps because we mostly see factory-made Danish pipes, there is little interest in the collector market in the U.S. Another reason might be the steep price tag for individually hand-made pieces. Understandably, many American collectors are afraid to spend large sums of money for pipes they don't know much about. That's why there is such an emphasis on old Dunhills, Charatans and Barlings. They're safe. When it comes to new high grade pipes, the vast majority of collectors seek either Dunhill or the well-known Italian brands, which are also superb products.

But I believe if Americans knew more about the individual Danish pipe makers, they would be surprised at the quality of briar (mostly Corsican) and the level of professionalism and creativity that goes into each individual piece. The result is nearly miraculous. A high grade hand-made Danish pipe will offer endless hours of pleasure and relaxation. Typically, they are shorter and lighter than other pipes, and thus are ideal for smoking when reading or working.

Getting back to Copenhagen, the first thing I did was to check the Yellow Pages for pipe shops and pipe makers. I saw the names W.O. Larsen, S. Bang, Sixten Ivarsson, and Jess Chonowitsch. I called each number. Without any difficulty, I scheduled a series of appointments.

Then I spotted the name Paul Winslow. Since I had just bought one of his pipes from Peter Heinrichs (the bird's eye is spectacular!), I decided to call him. Paul was about to leave town but wanted to get together in three days. Unfortunately, that was after I was scheduled to leave. Nonetheless, he spent about 20 minutes on the phone with me. In excellent English, he gave me directions to the various pipe stores and pipe workshops in Copenhagen.

With Peter Heinrichs in one of his two pipe stores in Cologne, Germany. Both are spectacular. Peter's e-mail address is: HeinrichsP@aol.com

My first stop was at a small pipe store called "My Own Blend." Two young men behind the counter hand-blended some great smelling tobaccos, including their version of Rattray's No. 7 Reserve. They suggested I not open the can for a few weeks to allow the blends to marry. I'll probably wait six to 12 months, and I'm sure it will taste great. It smelled wonderful at the time, and a year from now it will be awesome!

Two blocks away is the famous W.O. Larsen store, including a museum downstairs. Ole Larsen gave me a tour, and I learned a number of interesting facts of pipe history. For instance, during World War II there was a dramatic shortage of briar and tobacco. Pipe makers used other types of wood and tobacco grown from climates that were not conducive to tobacco growing.

Ole and I talked about periods when tobacco was either in short supply or subject to bans by anti-smokers. Denmark and

Germany are still healthy environments for pipe smokers. I assume that many people in those countries know how relaxing a pipe can be -- in contrast to the "fix" that cigarettes give. Even at the airport in Copenhagen -- there is a pipe shop! The first pedestrian I saw was an old man riding a bicycle with a pipe in his mouth!

When Peter Heinrichs says, "House of 10,000 Pipes," he's not kidding.

The only problem is the taxes. Personal income taxes for all workers are outrageous. The *lowest* level of taxation on personal income is 50 percent. On top of that, the national sales tax is something like 25 percent! Ole and I agreed that what we need is a country with Denmark's attitude toward pipe smoking and America's attitude toward taxes. Of course, some of us would prefer still lower taxes in the U.S., but compared with Denmark, America seems like a paradise. For instance, a tin of Larsen's delicious Old Fashioned pipe tobacco costs $15 in the States and $20 in the Larsen's own store!

Just down the street from W.O. Larsen is Sixten Ivarsson (pronounced "E-varsson"). I met with him, as well as his son Lars

-- one of the world's greatest pipe makers in his own right -- and his granddaughter Nanna, who has started making pipes herself.

Lars has a workshop out in the country, while Nanna uses the workshop that Sixten made famous. She and her grandfather sit across from each other at connecting desks so they can talk easily. Nanna had dozens of unfinished bowls on the desk. They were all gorgeous. She was open and friendly, and considering that she was trained by her talented father, Lars, and is being given suggestions regularly by her talented grandfather, Sixten, there is no question that her pipes will be among the world's best. They all use the same Corsican briar, as well. I ordered one, which we named "golf ball on a tee," because that's what it looked like. I told them the story of the American pipe shop spreading the rumor that Sixten was dead, and Sixten laughingly suggested that I tell them I have met his ghost!

One of the students of Sixten Ivarsson was Jess Chonowitsch. He is approaching 50 and, along with his now-retired father Emil, has been making pipes for three decades. Jess (pronounced "yes") Chonowitsch (pronounced "con-o-vitz") lives about 40 miles outside Copenhagen and makes 200 pipes per year. His high grade pipes are works of art, and many sell in the four figures in Switzerland, Italy, Germany and Japan. There were a handful of his earlier pieces sold years ago in the U.S., but they are nothing like the exceptional high grades that he makes today.

Some collectors consider Jess to be the No. 1 pipe maker in the world. All he cares about is making the highest quality pipes possible. We had a fantastic lunch together, and Jess analyzed many of the great pipe makers.

Like everyone else, he said Sixten Ivarsson revolutionized pipe making. He also spoke very highly of S. Bang pipes, which are made by Ulf Noltensmeier and Per Hansen, whose workshop is several miles outside of downtown Denmark. Svend Bang was a businessman and amateur pipe maker whose name appears on Per's and Ulf's pipes -- S. Bang (pronounced "S. Bong"). Per and Ulf worked for Anne Julie and Preben Holm years ago. But they have been making their own pipes for nearly three decades and are producing some of the best, if not the very best, pipes in the world.

If it sounds like I am calling everyone the best, that's because I feel like I'm choosing between Michael Jordan, Magic Johnson, Larry Byrd, and Wilt Chamberlain. They were all spectacular! Who was the best baseball player ever? Mickey Mantle, Willie Mays, Joe Di Maggio, Hank Aaron, Ty Cobb, Babe Ruth, or Ted Williams? Who was the greatest artist? Michaelangelo, da Vinci, Matisse, Monet, Rembrandt, Picasso or van Gogh? Of course, there is no right answer -- and that's how it is in trying to decide who is the world's best pipe maker. It is a matter of personal taste and opinion.

But it is obvious that collectors in Scandinavia, Germany, Japan and other countries have discovered something that most Americans know little about: many of the very best pipes in the world today are being made in the artist/workshops in Denmark and sold in some magnificent pipe stores throughout Europe. I have encouraged Jack Ehrmantraut and other distributors to offer some of these high grade collectibles. Barry Levin appreciated these pipes, and Rick Hacker and a handful of other American collectors own and savor a few of them, but these works of art are so rare in the U.S. as to be almost non-existent.

As the pipe smoking and pipe collecting renaissance gains momentum, let's hope that more of these masterpieces become available to American collectors. You won't have to move to Europe to enjoy this new level of excellence in pipe making, pipe smoking and pipe collecting.

CHAPTER THREE

~~~~~

JESS CHONOWITSCH:
CHARACTER COUNTS

At the end of the last chapter I expressed the hope that high grade, hand made pipes would become available in America, and to say they did, would be the understatement of the decade. When I attend pipe shows today, I am struck by how things have changed, where Jess Chonowitsch is a household name in the pipe collecting community, considered by many to be the best of all time. But back in 1995, when I wrote a brief essay about my first meeting with Jess and then interviewed him at length for Pipe Friendly, *he was completely unknown in the United States.*

It is quite extraordinary to go from being unknown to become one of the most sought-after pipe makers in the world in just a few years, but there are more explanations than my articles on Jess' behalf. Ahead of all others is the fact that his pipes are so good, and nearly all of his customers are repeat customers. His distributor in the United States, Uptown's, has a waiting list of special orders for Jess' pipes, and they sell out almost immediately whatever he sends them.

I am very pleased that Jess has become so successful in the United States primarily because we have become close personal friends since we first met in 1995. He is extremely honest, intelligent, straightforward, clear thinking, willing to listen to his customers, a good family man, and a remarkably skilled craftsman who has spent a lifetime committed to making the best pipes possible. It is popular these days to use the phrase, "character counts," and when it comes to Jess Chonowitsch, it is character that comes through.

* * * * *

I didn't know what to expect. My wife and I had arrived in Copenhagen for a short visit -- she to visit her Danish relatives and me to meet some master pipe makers. I looked in the Yellow Pages and saw a name that I had seen on a handful of extremely high-grade, well-made pipes: Jess Chonowitsch. I called the number and chatted with the pipe maker himself.

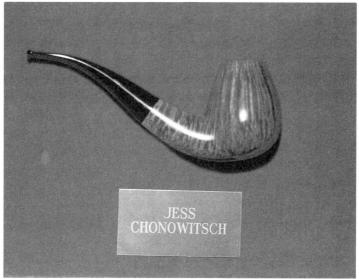

The first pipe that I bought from Jess Chonowitsch.

We had lunch together the following day. Jess showed me some of his pipes, and they were among the most beautiful I have ever seen. I bought a full bent, perfect straight grain pipe, which I have since smoked a dozen times. The pipe is perfect to smoke while reading: the wood is extremely light, and the mouthpiece is exceptionally comfortable.

I asked Jess why we can't find his pipes in the States. He said that more than a decade ago he sold a few pipes through Iwan Ries, but their interest these days is mostly in cigars. Jess said that outside of Scandinavia, his primary markets are Switzerland, Germany, Italy and Japan.

I told Jess about several possible distributors in America and asked if he would be interested in having a few of his high-grade pipes sold through them, and he said yes, he would be willing to try it as an experiment.

I should point out that during our luncheon discussion, I asked Jess dozens of questions about pipe making and was overwhelmed by his knowledge about the business. I shouldn't have been surprised, considering just a few facts from his background. For instance, he studied under and worked with some of the greatest pipe makers of this century, including Poul Rasmussen and the legendary Sixten Ivarsson.

Jess is now 48 years old and makes 200 pipes per year -- each one a masterpiece. After buying the one pipe at lunch, I have managed to acquire two others, and they are fantastic smokers. Jess Chonowitsch has brought pipe making to a new level, and I find it incredibly exciting that his pipes will be sold in the United States. I believe that their value will only increase when more American collectors realize how fantastic these pipes really are. They are simply the best in the world. As one European collector told me, "Jess is to pipes what Stradivarius is to violins."

* * * * *

On his first visit to the United States, in November 1995, Jess Chonowitsch agreed to be interviewed by me for an article that appeared in *Pipe Friendly*.

Chonowitsch makes pipes of classical shapes as well as free hands. Gordon Soladar, a pipe collector for 30 years, looked at the 36 pipes that Jess brought to America, and said, "They're mind-boggling. In fact, I wish I had a stronger description -- because mind-boggling doesn't do them justice!"

PF: How did you get started in pipe making?

JC: I was studying to become a veterinarian. During the summer break I had three months off. My plan was to work during the first two months and then have a holiday for the last month. My father is Emil Chonowitsch, and he was a tobacconist at the time. He had decided to become a pipe maker himself, and he was working for Poul Rasmussen in Copenhagen. He helped me get a job making pipes for Poul. I fell in love with the work and never went back to school.

PF: Poul Rasmussen is famous among pipe collectors in America, known as a Danish pipe maker who specialized in classical shapes. Your father, Emil, is also known for making great pipes in classical shapes. But you are known for both -- classical shapes and free hands. How did that come about?

JC: I worked for Poul Rasmussen for a year-and-a-half before he became too ill to work. He had suffered serious injuries during the war. After he died, I helped his widow, Anne Julie, make pipes for about six months. This was in 1968. Then I made pipes for W.O. Larsen and Sixten Ivarsson -- Larsen in the morning and Sixten in the afternoon. With Larsen, it was like a factory. It was a job that paid the bills. With Sixten Ivarsson, it was passion. He did not pay me with money. He paid me with advice, knowledge, insights, and critiques of my work. At first, it was very frustrating. I was considered a rising star who could turn out a factory pipe in my sleep. But then when I would show my best effort to Sixten, he would say, "That's no good." So I would use the pipe for firewood and start over. I kept trying and kept trying, and still Sixten would say, "They're not good enough. You can do better." I was discouraged but determined. I worked harder than ever. Then one day Sixten said, "Finally, you have made a pipe." Oh, the feeling of success! It was fantastic! Of course, with Sixten, we always made free hand pipes. You see -- the two great pipe makers in Denmark after the war in the late 1940s, were Poul Rasmussen with classical designs and Sixten Ivarsson, who invented free hand pipes. They were my two teachers, and I have been making both types of pipes for nearly 30 years.

Jess and me in Los Angeles on one of his many visits.

PF: How many pipes do you make per year, and how long does it take you per pipe?
JC: I make about 200 per year, and I spend about a day-and-a-half on each pipe.

PF: Where are they sold?
JC: Mostly in Switzerland, Germany, Italy and Japan. I have a few private customers in England and now suddenly, I am told that the word is out in America. I sold all 36 pipes in my first few days in the United States, and the waiting list for new pipes for Americans is growing.

PF: What kind of briar do you use?
JC: I only use Corsican briar wood. The man who provides it to me picks out only the oldest and best wood possible. For this high quality of briar wood, which is extremely expensive, he has only four customers: the Ivarssons, S. Bang, Bo Nordh and me. We pay nearly $80 for each piece of raw wood that goes into a pipe!

That's because our briar comes from areas that are very difficult to get to and is guaranteed to be the oldest and best wood possible. It is wood that grew very, very slowly. Other pipe makers and factories also use Corsican briar, or Italian briar or Grecian briar, and pay 10 cents or 50 cents or maybe $1 for each piece of raw wood. But the difference is worth it. The Corsican briar that I use is very similar to the very best old Algerian briar. But it is better. It is the best in the world.

PF: What about your mouthpieces?
JC: They are all hand-cut. I have rods of vulcanite from Germany that is hard rubber, but when I finish with a mouthpiece it is soft in the mouth. Many pipe smokers from Europe have asked me to make them new mouthpieces for their pipes because they like the feel of mine. I only do this for long-standing customers.

PF: Why do so many pipe makers today use lucite stems?
JC: They think that plastic is easier to care for and keep pretty. But any experienced pipe smoker has no problem keeping his vulcanite mouthpieces black -- shiny and pretty on the pipe.

PF: Many pipe makers today have thick and blocky stems. Why do you think that is?
JC: I suppose it is because they think that if the pipe is big, the mouthpiece must be big. But that is ridiculous. The mouthpiece should be comfortable above all else. I think some of these pipe makers must believe that their customers are elephants -- or have mouths as big as elephants!

PF: Do you have a workshop in downtown Copenhagen?
JC: No. We live in the country on a farmhouse 40 miles outside of Copenhagen. My workshop is next to the house. I like to work until late at night, where you can see the stars and it is quiet and peaceful.

Jess Chonowitsch sanding a pipe bowl in his workshop in Denmark.

PF: Have you ever considered running one of the big pipe making factories?
JC: No. Never. Of course, I have made many models for Stanwell.

PF: How does that work?
JC: I design a pipe for them, and they copy the design and then produce thousands of the pipes at the factory. Also, I have been asked to make pipes for many of the biggest brand names, but I only want to make my own pipes.

PF: We understand they are very expensive.

JC: Yes, but it depends on where they are sold. My price is always the same, but I cannot control what the middlemen and the pipe shops do. I was in Japan and saw my pipes for sale for $7,000 each.

PF: We understand that in Europe the criminals consider you the No. 1 pipe maker in the world. Can you explain?
JC: In October I made three pipes for W.O. Larsen. I delivered them on Thursday afternoon, and they called me Friday morning to say they had been stolen. Someone had smashed the window and grabbed only my pipes.

PF: Is it true that theft is extremely rare in Copenhagen and that your three pipes were displayed along with many high-grades by other pipe makers?
JC: Yes.

PF: Have you ever heard of this happening before?
JC: I'm afraid to say it, but yes, it happened once before in Switzerland several years ago. A store in Zurich displayed one of my pipes in the window and a thief broke the glass and stole the pipe.

PF: There is no question that, as regrettable as the thefts were, you were being paid a real compliment. It is only the greatest works of art that are most vulnerable to being stolen. On another subject, are all of your pipes made by hand?
JC: Yes. I do everything by hand. I use a sandpaper wheel for the free hand pipes.

PF: Is there anything special about the way you drill the air hole?
JC: I drill the hole so that the pipe smoker can draw easily. There is nothing worse than trying to smoke a pipe that feels like you're sucking on a straw through honey. The important thing is that the smoke channel is absolutely clean and is drilled so that the smoke

can pass through without any hindrance. It must never be necessary to suck too heavily.

This is certainly beautiful bird's eye on the side of a Jess Chonowitsch free hand.

PF: When you're getting ready to make a pipe, do you study the wood and then determine the shape that you will carve?
JC: No, it's quite the opposite. The first thing I do is have a shape in mind. I decide in advance what shape of pipe I want to make. Then I go through the wood to find a piece of briar that is suitable for the shape. I might find five or six pieces that are suitable, so I'll then make five or six pipes in that shape. Then I will decide on another shape for a different pipe, and I study the unfinished blocks to find pieces of briar for those pipes.

PF: Do you consider yourself an artist?
JC: I am a craftsman. I was told not so long ago that one of my pipes was displayed at the Museum of Modern Art in New York, but I regard myself as a craftsman more than an artist. In the early years I learned much from the great masters like Sixten Ivarsson, but these days I learn the most from my customers. A knowledgeable pipe smoker who tells me precisely what he wants is my best teacher. Pipe makers who ignore requests or

suggestions from their pipe-smoking customers make a big mistake, in my opinion.

PF: What do you think about collectors who buy your pipes to display them on the wall, like a painting, but who never smoke them?
JC: I am happy that they enjoy looking at them. They should also smoke them. I make pipes to be smoked, not just looked at.

PF: Tell us about your own preference in pipes. What shapes do you enjoy smoking?
JC: I prefer pipes that are light in weight and fairly compact. It is a myth to think that a long stem gives a cooler smoke. That's just not true. I keep a pipe in my mouth very often when I am working, so it must be light and not put any real pressure on my teeth or jaw.

PF: How much do you smoke?
JC: I smoke off and on all day. I light my pipe when I feel like it and then put it down for a while. Later I'll pick it back up and light it again and take a few more puffs, and then put it down again. I'm afraid I could never win one of those contests where you are given only two matches and you have to keep your pipe lit.

PF: We notice that some of your pipes have exquisite looking bamboo and ivory, both of which are difficult to obtain. Where do you get these materials?
JC: I have a very big supply of both, which I bought many years ago. For the ferrules, I also use boxwood, silver and other materials.

PF: Besides yourself, who do you think makes the best pipes today?
JC: That's a very dangerous question to answer. There are many good pipe makers, and if I start naming some, I'm sure I'll forget others. I pay more attention to my customers than I do to other pipe makers. I know what it takes to make a great pipe, and I try my hardest every time I make a pipe.

PF: The name Chonowitsch does not sound like a typical Danish name. We have been told there is an interesting story behind it.

JC: Yes -- it involves my grandfather and his desire to stay away from the Communist revolution in Russia in 1917. He was born in Russia, and he became a concert violinist. He was playing in Denmark at the time of the revolution, where he met a Danish female pianist. In fact, she accompanied him when he was playing the violin. They fell in love and were married and settled down in Denmark. I too am a musician. I play the drums. I used to play a lot more.

PF: Your father has a reputation for making outstanding pipes. Is he still making them?

JC: No, he retired a few years ago. But I agree with you that his pipes were excellent.

PF: How can a collector tell the difference between the pipes that you make and the pipes that your father made?

JC: Well, obviously if it is a brand new pipe, then I made it. As I said, my father retired several years ago. But the easiest way to tell the difference is that he always printed his name in a straight line, while I nearly always print my name in a circle. Also, my pipes have my first name ("Jess") printed on them.

PF: One European collector told us that "Jess Chonowitsch is to pipes what Stradivarius is to violins." In other words, many collectors believe that, nearly three decades after learning from Poul Rasmussen and Sixten Ivarsson, the pupil has surpassed his teachers. What do you think?

JC: I think they were both great pipe makers. Poul was very disciplined and Sixten has a brilliant imagination. As for myself, I try to do my best each day. I have made a point to work with the best briar wood and vulcanite available anywhere in the world. The same goes for any other materials I might use, such as ivory, bamboo, boxwood, elk horn, silver, gold or whatever. My customers have told me that they are very pleased. In my opinion I keep getting better each year because I try to continue learning. My pipes today are better than they were 10 years ago, and they were better then than they were 10 years before that. I am 48 years old and hope to make pipes for many, many more years. This is a good time in my life. I have been making pipes practically every day for the last 28 years, and I still feel very young.

PF: Is this your first trip to the United States?
JC: Yes. My wife Bonnie and I wanted to see your country. A pipe collector who likes my pipes invited us to visit America. We thought it would be fun.

PF: Will you custom-make pipes for Americans if they order them specially?
JC: Yes, that is no problem, as long as they understand there is a waiting list. It will take about four months.

PF: How do you and Bonnie like the United States?
JC: We like it very much. The people are quite nice. In Denmark we have heard that there are no smokers left in America, so I was surprised to find so many knowledgeable pipe collectors. We are having a wonderful time.

CHAPTER FOUR

~~~~~

THE BEST BARGAIN IMAGINABLE

Just as my own pipe-buying experience has led me to the super high grades, it has also led me to inexpensive old pipes that are great smokers. I own pipes that cost $2,000 and pipes that cost $20. Is it possible to get just as good a smoke from the less expensive old pipes? I believe the answer is yes. Maybe not all the time, but very often, as this essay points out.

So you must be thinking, if that is the case, then why would someone ever spend a lot of money on a pipe? I can think of two reasons: first, there is a beauty and personality in the high grades that is lacking in factory pipes; and secondly, the odds of getting a great smoker are enhanced immeasurably by going with the high grades. Also, there is something special about "christening" your own pipe, where you remember making the decision to buy it, lighting it for the first time -- and a hundred other memories that make your new pipe a part of your life.

Having said that, however, I cannot tell you how many fantastic smoking pipes I have that I bought for less than $50, pipes that were made many decades ago, pipes that I treasure in my collection and enjoy smoking in my rotation, as informal as that is.

* * * * *

It's hard to imagine a better bargain.

Yet I'm constantly amazed at how few collectors take advantage of it.

I am referring to the practice of buying old inexpensive pipes, having them cleaned and refinished so they look exactly as they did in that pipe shop when they were first sold in 1927 or 1935 or 1956. But they're even better now because they have been broken in, and the old briar has aged and mellowed like a fine wine. Very often, the stems on these pipes are made of rubber that is soft, resilient and incredibly comfortable in the mouth. I have hundreds of these pipes.

It all started with a filthy old free-hand bulldog, made by a Californian in the 1940s by the name of Yagerlehner. The stamping on the pipe said, "Yager Hand Made." I was given it as a gift from pipe maker John Weidemann when I purchased one of John's unique and highly desirable pipe sets -- or what he calls "smoking instruments." John's briar pipes allow you to get the true taste of the tobacco. John has been a pipe smoker, collector, and antique dealer for 50 years, and he knows as much about pipes and cigars as anyone. He is also a fantastic inventor, and part of his genius lies in the fact that he makes discoveries that challenge the conventional wisdom.

Dudleigh of Hollywood tan blast apple.

"The big secret in this business are the pipes that were made a long time ago, especially by American pipe makers, with beautiful briar that collectors never bother to look at because they don't have a name like Dunhill, Charatan or Comoy stamped on them," he said. "Yet the wood is every bit as good, if not better, than the pipes made today by those companies. It would take $300 or more to find a pipe in the 1990s with briar that is as good as many pipes from the 1930s that might cost $30 or less. The real problem is getting them cleaned. Most pipe makers like me don't specialize in cleaning pipes. Those are usually two different businesses."

So I went home with the Yager Hand Made pipe from John, almost afraid to touch it because of its filth. There was still some tobacco in the bowl. The cake was so thick that I couldn't fit my little finger into the bowl. And I wouldn't have wanted to try -- because the top of the bowl had the remnants of an old spider web. The tooth-marked mouthpiece had a thick coating of ugly, gray-yellow oxidation. Yuck!

I was determined to get it cleaned, however, so I brought it to a well known pipe store. "No problem," said the salesman.

A week later I eagerly returned to pick up the pipe. It was much improved -- reamed, waxed and buffed -- but it still looked and felt grimy. I smoked one bowl of tobacco and found it bitter and distasteful. I couldn't help but wonder about who had smoked it back in the 40s -- and what kind of diseases he might have had.

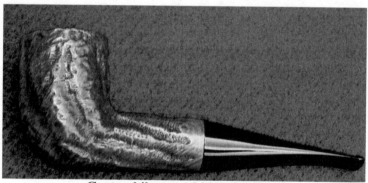
Custombilt carved blast billiard.

So I called Richard Carleton Hacker, an old friend and a knowledgeable collector who is the author of several pipe books. Rick said he completely agreed with John Weidemann about the secret value of little-known old pipes, especially old American-made pipes. In addition, he said, many of the pipes stamped with American pipe shop names were actually made in England, France and other countries. Rick gave me a name and phone number that had the effect of changing my pipe collection forever: Jim Benjamin of San Diego.

I called Jim, and he told me he has been cleaning pipes for half a century. He said many people have tried to discover and copy his secrets, but none has been successful. He said he does not do repairs. He specializes in cleaning, reconditioning and refinishing. He does the work for several pipe shops, and a number of individuals from around the world send him their pipes to be brought back to life. Jim said he charges the same flat fee per pipe for everyone, whether an individual or a store, and he guaranteed that the pipe would come back as close to brand new as possible -- inside and out.

I sent Jim my Yager Hand Made, figuring that the pipe itself hadn't cost me anything so I would lose little by paying to have it cleaned a second time.

A great smoking, light weight, JHW straight grain.

A few days later the pipe was in my mailbox, and I honestly did not recognize it. The wood was golden brown -- just as it must have looked when it was first carved. The stem literally shined. The inside of the shank and mortise were raw wood. They smelled like a brand new pipe -- with no odor whatsoever. Totally fresh.

In fact, the pipe was so brand new looking, I was afraid to smoke it at first. I showed it to two experienced pipe collectors, and they both asked variations of the same question: "Where did you get such a gorgeous pipe from 50 years ago that has never been smoked?" When I told them the story of the pipe and the cleaning, one didn't believe me; the other one said, "Yea -- it was Jim Benjamin -- I should have known."

How did the pipe smoke? Without exaggerating, it smoked (and still smokes) better -- smoother, cooler, easier draw -- than pipes that I own which retail for more than a thousand dollars.

This motivated me to do three things: 1.) Discover who Yager was and buy every Yager Hand Made pipe I could find; 2.) Buy as many other inexpensive old pipes, especially American-made, as I could find, and 3.) Send every pipe I owned, and every used pipe I bought, to Jim Benjamin for cleaning and refinishing.

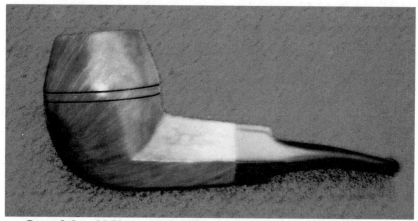

One of the old Yager Hand Made pipes made to look like new.

As I said earlier, Yager was really named Yagerlehner. He repaired pipes for the old Smoker's Den in Glendale, CA. He is long deceased, although I did manage to find two pipe makers who knew him many decades ago, and both held him in high esteem.

They are Ken Erickson and Paul Perri, and they are two of California's very best pipe makers.

As for buying more Yager Hand Made pipes, John Weidemann had 30 from Yagerlehner's private collection, and I bought them all. The old Algerian briar with a slight orange stain, which turns a kind of reddish brown with repeated smoking, provides the type of pipe smoking pleasure that almost no other pipes provide. Of course, this is after the pipes have been cleaned thoroughly and made to look brand new.

It was after my Yager experience that I discovered Bertram of Washington, D.C., Cellini, Weber, Linkman, Victor's, KB&B, Malaga, Custombilt, JHW, Dudleigh's of Hollywood, Kaywoodie, Tracy Mincer, Marxman, Ries Bros. Corp. (the predecessor to Iwan Ries), W.C. Demuth and dozens more. I'm hoping there are hundreds of others that I will find in the future.

I also discovered three of the most knowledgeable collectors in the world: Tom Colwell, John Eells, and Gordon Soladar. All three share my interest in early American pipes, and they own a combined total of something like 8,000 (!) of them.

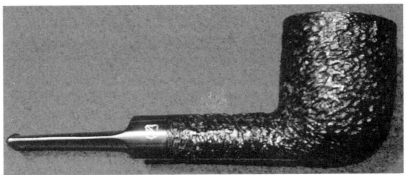

An old Sasieni second that says, "Made in England." This used pipe has been cleaned up, is as light as a feather and practically smokes itself -- it's that good. I paid $20 for it.

I don't mean to give the impression that I only buy old American pipes. In fact, I recently sent Jim the most expensive pipe I have ever bought -- a 1964 Sixten Ivarsson that was filthy beyond belief. When it came back, I showed it to an old friend who was an experienced collector. "It looks brand new," he said. "I am amazed. I've seen that pipe at shows for 10 years, yet I feel like I'm looking at it for the first time -- that's how good it looks."

I have heard collectors complain that there is little resale market for these old pipes without a trendy name or fancy nomenclature, but I say so what!

It's still the bargain of the century -- and it is only a matter of time before a growing number of experienced collectors realize this and drive up the resale price. It is a bargain because for less than $50 you can own a gorgeous pipe with beautiful old wood and a mouthpiece made from the more pliable and hard-to-find Brazilian rubber. It will look brand new after being reconditioned properly. You will complete breaking it in with your first smoke. It will be cool, fresh and relaxing, and it will last forever.

Compare that with the four or five cigars that you might buy with the same $50, and you can understand why I say that it's hard to imagine a better bargain.

CHAPTER FIVE

~~~~~

ESTATE PIPES

This chapter was written in 2001 as an article for a Dutch pipe magazine that, unfortunately, folded just before my story was published. I tried to offer arguments on both sides -- in favor of, and against, used pipes. I raise one issue that I have never once heard an American collector discuss, yet I believe is critical in evaluating a pipe; namely, how can we tell how "used" a used pipe is? In other words, if you buy an old pre-smoked pipe, how much longer does it have before it becomes useless? Is there any way to tell for sure except by cutting the pipe in half? I don't know the answer to this question, but I raise it in hopes that other collectors will address this issue in the future.

* * * * *

Most European pipe smokers would enjoy attending a pipe collector's show in America, but I suspect they would leave with two conflicting emotions: First, they would be excited about the enthusiasm and passion that American collectors feel for their pipes, and then, they would be appalled to discover that so many Americans buy (and smoke!) used pipes.

Can you imagine? How could you possibly put in your mouth, for many hours over a period of years, a pipe that a total stranger, or many strangers, had put in their mouths over however many years? How is this possible? What about contagious diseases, not to mention a sour taste?

When I posed these questions to a group of American pipe collectors, the general consensus was, "Who cares? The pipes have old wood and have already been 'broken in.' They smoke better than new pipes."

One time at a Chicago pipe show I was chatting with Niels Larsen, who runs the W.O. Larsen pipe company and store based in Copenhagen. I relayed these thoughts and asked for his opinion. Niels, who is intelligent and quick-witted, smiled, rolled his eyes and said: "You know, if you wet your pants it might feel good for a minute, but then you feel soaked, dirty and in need of a bath and a change of clothes."

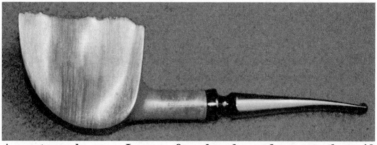

An extremely rare Larsen free hand, made more than 40 years ago, that I bought unsmoked. One of the things that makes this pipe special to me is that I am the only person who has ever smoked it.

Another European collector, Rolf Rutzen, the German author of pipe books and articles, compares smoking a used pipe to "using someone else's toothbrush."

But Richard Carleton Hacker, the prolific pipe and cigar author, whose perspective is that of an American, defends the practice of smoking used pipes, which are euphemistically known as "estate pipes," by comparing pipes to plates, glasses and silverware. We don't think twice about using the same fork in a restaurant that hundreds of other people have used, assuming, of course, that the forks have been cleaned thoroughly.

Now, the question of a thorough cleaning is a complicated one. Many collectors believe they know how to clean their pipes when, in fact, they do not. I have attended dozens of pipe shows and seen collectors buy old pipes that had been subjected to cursory ream-and-cleans but that still contained old tar and goo from past smokers. I have practically passed out watching these collectors load up one of these pipes with their own tobacco, light it and puff as if they had been smoking the pipe for 20 years.

A beautiful Peter Stokkebye pipe, which I bought pre-smoked from my friend Lowell Ellis, and eventually traded to my friend Chuck Stanion for a used Jess Chonowitsch sandblast. Trading pipes is part of the fun of the hobby, and it would be much less fun if we weren't allowed to smoke them -- if we could only trade new pipes.

While I do occasionally smoke estate pipes, I would never in a million years do that -- buy a filthy old pipe and smoke it without a thorough cleaning. But there are many opinions about how best to clean an old pipe. What is, in fact, the best way?

For me, as I have said before, the answer lies with a single individual: Jim Benjamin. Jim cleaned his first pipe when he was 16 -- in 1939 -- and he has been reconditioning pipes ever since.

If I buy an old pipe, let's say a Dunhill from the 1950s, the first thing I do is send it to Jim Benjamin, who cleans it inside and out. He also is an expert at taking a yellow or gray mouthpiece and bringing it back to the shiny black gloss that it had when it was first made.

Still, all that scrubbing is not enough to convince me that the pipe is like new. I only want to smoke tobacco through raw wood, as opposed to smoking it through a cleaned up version of someone else's carbon coatings. This means sanding the inside of the tobacco chamber so that it is just wood -- with no coating whatsoever.

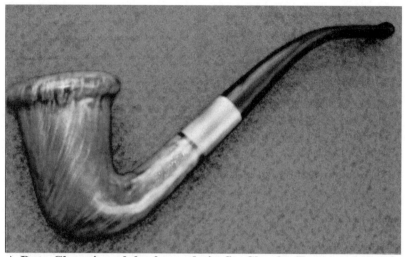

A Butz Choquin calabash, made in St. Claude, France, probably has not been smoked thousands of times as evidenced by the light color of the pipe.

Of course, if the pipe has been smoked a great deal, the wood inside the bowl is likely to be darkened or charred, but it is still raw wood. Then I ask Jim to put a 4.3 millimeter or 4.7 millimeter drill bit through the shank. Most shanks are drilled between 3.5 millimeters and 4.0 millimeters, so I am actually making a bigger smoke hole, which I prefer anyway [as discussed in Chapter 8]. Of course, sawdust comes out, so I know that the inside of the pipe is, once again, raw wood. There are a number of ways to clean the mortise, but my preference is to rely on Jim Benjamin. You can see wood that is totally clean, almost looking brand new, in the mortise area of any old pipe that he cleans up.

I realize that some American collectors of estate pipes are totally opposed to the idea of sanding and altering an old pipe. They treat them the way collectors treat antiques -- as something valued and not to be tampered with. Richard Esserman, who runs the successful New York Pipe Show, has been sharply critical of my practice of altering old pipes. "If you don't like the way a pipe was made," he says, "then don't buy it in the first place!"

My response is that I might like the way it was made, but I can only enjoy smoking it after altering the pipe to suit my taste. My guess is that about half the collectors agree with Rich on this issue, and the other half agree with me. That is just speculation, however, based on conversations with a number of pipe smokers. [In Chapter 22, I discuss this issue in greater detail.]

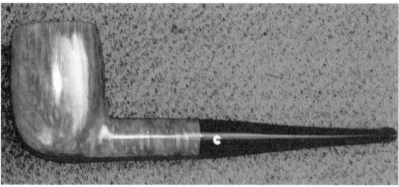

This is a Comoy blue riband straight grain that I bought from Rick Hacker. It is a very old pipe, well smoked and very well preserved.

Dr. Ulrich Wohrle of Stuttgart, Germany, is an experienced collector with hundreds of pipes who almost always prefers a new pipe to a used one. "A pipe is for me a personal thing," he said. "It becomes a part of me. I like to have new pipes. I don't always smoke a new pipe right away. Sometimes I will take it out, look it over, and then decide, 'not yet.' Then a while later I might decide, 'now this pipe will be smoked.'"

Dr. Wohrle, known as "Uli," vividly remembers selling one of his guitars 42 years ago to buy his first Dunhill. "I still smoke that pipe," he said. In addition to a large Castello collection, Uli specializes in super high grade pipes -- such as ones made by Bo

Nordh of Sweden and S. Bang and Jess Chonowitsch of Denmark, as well as Sixten and Lars Ivarsson, also of Denmark. He also recently added a very special Larsen pipe to his collection.

There is something to Uli's point about remembering when you bought a new pipe, and then associating many different memories with the many times that you enjoyed the pipe. I suppose you could do the same with an estate pipe that was cleaned up and altered, but it still would not have the same emotional significance because someone else, in effect, christened the pipe.

One other issue that needs to be addressed is the question of how long a briar pipe will last. Many American collectors answer that the pipes effectively will last forever -- because there is no way to smoke them so much that they stop functioning. But I think this is wrong.

Lars Ivarsson and Jess Chonowitsch, two of the greatest pipe makers in history, argue persuasively that the pores of the wood become clogged or totally "filled up" with repeated smoking. If you were to cut such a pipe bowl in half, they say, you would see instantly that there would be no way for the wood to "breathe." The inside of the wood would be totally darkened and charred. This makes sense, especially considering that everything else, from automobiles to clothes to buildings, eventually wears out and needs to be replaced. So the question is, when is a pipe finished?

And a related question: why don't more collectors pay attention to this issue? It is of crucial importance, yet I have never once seen it discussed. In fact, to the best of my knowledge, the question has not even been asked in a single pipe magazine or book. I can think of no other purchase where the buyer is basing his decision on outside appearances alone. If you buy a used car, you know precisely how many miles it has been driven, but when you buy a used pipe, you have no way of knowing how many times it has been smoked. That's risky, to say the least.

René Wagner, who runs a fantastic pipe store in Zurich, Switzerland, called Tabak-Lädeli, told me once that he believed it was somewhere after 1,000 to 2,000 bowls had been smoked, although he said much depends on the size of the bowl, the thickness of the wood, the quality of the briar and the quality of the tobacco that is smoked in the pipe -- among other factors.

But those numbers still sounded too low to me, so I asked René to give me a pipe that he thought was finished. He gave me a straight grain, full bent Jess Chonowitsch pipe that he had enjoyed for years -- but no longer smoked because it wasn't the same. I gave that pipe to Jim Benjamin, who cleaned it and opened it up, and who restained it to look like new. When René saw the pipe, he thought it looked beautiful. But after one or two more smokes, he was convinced that his original assessment was correct and that the pipe in fact was finished, once and for all.

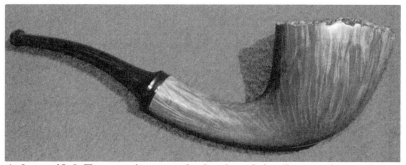

A beautiful Tsuge pipe, made by hand in Japan, is used but obviously still has many more years of smoking enjoyment left in it.

I too have owned estate pipes that smoked poorly no matter how much they were cleaned or opened. I'm sure this is because they had been smoked so much that the wood was clogged and there was no chance for the briar to breathe through its pores. The wood, which becomes very hot in these pipes, felt like metal or porcelain or some other solid substance -- but something very different from good briar wood. The test is to sand inside the tobacco chamber after taking out the cake. If the inside wood is totally dark, then in my opinion the pipe is finished.

One American collector told me that in 1941 he bought a beautiful Barling and an eight-dot Sasieni Rustic. He proceeded to smoke them between three and five times a week -- and still does to this day. Each pipe has been smoked well over 10,000 times, and he said they smoke like new. This collector added that he keeps them clean, never lets a cake build up and always keeps the draft open.

Some collectors have the pipe bowls of their estate pipes cleaned, and then they have new mouthpieces made. This way, their mouths never come in direct contact with any part of a pipe that is "used."

This 1948 gold-banded Dunhill bruyere was filthy when I bought it, but Jim Benjamin made it look, and smoke, like a new pipe.

So as you can see, there is no right or wrong answer to the question of whether it is acceptable to smoke estate pipes. But a growing number of pipe stores in America are offering them for sale, no doubt because their customers are asking for them.

"Unless you're willing to spend a lot of money on a new pipe today, you won't find the same quality of briar, vulcanite and workmanship that you find in these old pipes," according to Jim Benjamin. "Typically, they're not as expensive as newer pipes. You get great old wood, with Old World craftsmanship, so no wonder estate pipes are so popular in America. I have watched the estate market blossom over the years, growing from a small business in the 1970s to an enormous market today. I predict that it's just a matter of time before they are equally popular with pipe shops in the rest of the world."

I realize that many Americans agree with Jim Benjamin on this point, but I know that most European collectors do not. I also think that Niels Larsen makes a good point when he says that if collectors *only* bought used pipes, then where would that leave the makers of new pipes?

"Of course, we love to see our products become collectibles, being re-used, and re-sold," Niels said, but added that if no one bought new pipes, then there would be no more new pipes for sale.

This is clearly a very good point, but my impression is that the average pipe smoker wants a new pipe, not a used one. And the collector who buys estate pipes is typically passionate about all forms of pipes and is usually an excellent customer for new pipes as well. My personal recommendation -- whether you are American, European, Asian, African, or whatever -- is that you buy a minimum of 100 new pipes from your local tobacconist, over however many years it takes, before expanding your collection to include estate pipes. Then you will have a truly solid foundation for making an intelligent comparison.

If 100 pipes seem like a lot, you might consider the thoughts of Edward G. Robinson, a great actor and pipe smoker, who penned these words in the 1930s:

"Knowing the constant companionship of many pipes, it is only natural that I should be always eager to make new pipe friends, each pipe, like each man, different from all the rest. It would be strange if I were satisfied with only one pipe.

"That's why I own a hundred."

CHAPTER SIX

SIXTEN IVARSSON -- THE THOMAS EDISON OF PIPE MAKING

Sixten Ivarsson died in 2001 at the age of 91, six years after this article was written for Pipe Friendly. *His son, Lars, saw the article when it was first published and liked it, but Lars told me that I gave the impression that Sixten was losing his sight, when in fact his eyesight was fine for most people -- just not for the exacting detail required of a master pipe maker.*

There has been some talk among collectors recently about whether Sixten used the best briar or, as one writer put it, "mediocre briar." As Lars wrote in reply, "To make a blanket statement that Sixten used mediocre briar is just plain rubbish."

Sixten bought very high grade blocks of wood, but he was a product of the Great Depression -- and of World War II, when Denmark found itself an occupied country -- so he was not at all inclined toward extravagance or waste of any kind. In practical terms, this meant that he became a master at using every block of wood -- the good, the bad and the ugly. But if it started out ugly, he managed to make it beautiful. Sixten also became a master at not wasting wood, and he was able to carve four pipes out of a single block of wood that would have yielded only one pipe for the average pipe maker.

* * * * *

Sixten Ivarsson is a genius. He is the Danish pipe maker who revolutionized the business. He saw possibilities for carving briar wood in shapes and styles that no one ever thought possible.

"The now legendary Danish pipe-designer Sixten Ivarsson is considered by many as the best pipe-maker of the twentieth century," according to the book, *The Illustrated History of the Pipe*. In fact, he has even been called the greatest pipe maker of all time.

So you can imagine my excitement when I visited the master at his workshop in the middle of downtown Copenhagen. He is now in his mid-80s. He said he hardly ever makes pipes any more because his eyesight is so poor. But his granddaughter, Nanna, makes pipes at his workshop, and Sixten guides her and offers advice whenever necessary. Nanna's father is Lars Ivarsson, Sixten's son, who is almost as famous as his father for making some of the best pipes in the world.

This Sixten Ivarsson pipe, offered for sale by Iwan Ries for $3,000 in 1978, would translate to approximately $8,500 in 2003 dollars.

I met with all three Ivarssons for about an hour. Lars answered most of my questions because his English is impeccable, despite the fact that he has never been to the United States. Sixten and Nanna also speak English, and I found all three Ivarssons to be friendly, intelligent and thoughtful.

One of my first questions was to ask Sixten what shapes of pipes he personally liked to smoke. He explained that he gave up smoking around 1960 because he had developed a bad cough. I was shocked. All I could think of was Beethoven -- the genius composer who was deaf and thus could never hear his own music. Sixten Ivarsson, the pipe making genius who was responsible for sparking the revolution away from strictly classical shapes, could never enjoy smoking his own pipes!

The author with Lars and Sixten Ivarsson in Sixten's old workshop in Copenhagen, 1995.

Sixten said he made his first pipes in 1946, just after World War II. Prior to his dramatic creations, pipes were made in classical shapes only. But after he started creating free hand pipes, dozens of talented Danish pipe makers began creating their own versions of spectacular free hands. Then, the Italian and Japanese pipe makers followed suit, offering their own unique interpretations of how free hand pipes can be made. Of course, many American pipe makers have continued this tradition, and now there are literally thousands of different types of free hand designs. Even the conservative British have made some very interesting free hands, including Dunhill, Charatan and Upshall.

But it all goes back to Sixten Ivarsson. He was the first. He started the revolution. He understood the possibilities for briar better than anyone. The pipe author Richard Carleton Hacker told me at dinner one night, in his opinion, that Ivarsson was to pipe makers what Thomas Edison was to inventors. I thought that was a perfect comparison.

Not surprisingly, Sixten Ivarsson pipes are extremely rare and expensive. He spent a great deal of time carefully crafting each one. Thus, he made a relatively small number each year. He has enthusiastic fans around the world who, over the years, have bought his pipes as soon as they were made.

Several years ago, Barry Levin acquired a collection that included dozens of Ivarsson pipes. He sold them all in one phone call to a Japanese distributor. We're talking about pipes that ranged in price from $1,500 to $5,000 each!

At the time that I met with Sixten, Lars and Nanna, Lars was working on a beautiful free hand pipe that resembled a very large banker style. A German customer had ordered the pipe in advance. The cross grain was so tight that it almost looked painted on!

Lars is considered one of today's greatest pipe makers. Like his father, he is both an artist and a craftsman. He prefers to work at his house in the country, where it is quiet and peaceful.

Lars said that Sixten rides the train to work, and I told him that I found it hard to imagine such a legendary figure rubbing shoulders during rush hour with ordinary people. But it was obvious that Sixten loves pipes with a passion that rivals only his close feelings for his son and granddaughter.

CHAPTER SEVEN

~~~~~

LARS IVARSSON,
ONE IN A MILLION

Lars Ivarsson is legendary among pipe makers. He can do things with briar that no other pipe maker in the world can do. Some collectors have said that Lars is like the Muhammad Ali of pipe making ("I am the greatest!") -- I think that this is an accurate assessment. In my opinion, Lars' work is far superior to almost all other living craftsmen. If you gave Lars a block of briar, a sharp knife and some sandpaper, there is no doubt that he could produce a more beautiful pipe than any maker of the past or present. Still, I tried to put a human face on Lars in this 1996 profile that I wrote for Pipe Friendly.

In Chapter 21, I talk about the brilliant German pipe maker Karl Heinz Joura, and I remember one meeting with Joura when I was smoking a full bent Lars Ivarsson pipe and Karlo asked if he could examine it. He turned the mouthpiece around and was stunned that the fitting was exactly perfect, whether the mouthpiece was turned down or up. "You could look at a million pipes, and you won't see something made so perfectly," he said. So to call Lars one-in-a-million is not an exaggeration.

* * * * *

Pipe smokers share a secret that eludes the rest of the world. We know how much fun, how much pleasure, how much unadulterated satisfaction comes from the enjoyment of relaxing with a good pipe.

It always amazes me how few people share this secret. I remember reading in an old issue of *Pipe Lovers* magazine that one out of five American men smoked a pipe in the late 1940s. I would be surprised if that number were any higher than one out of a hundred in the 1990s.

But the pipe smokers of today include very few "drug store amateurs." The majority are connoisseurs. They have a collection of high grade pipes, and they always enjoy spending time at their local tobacconist. I asked a distributor of many different brands of pipes to name the pipes that are in greatest demand at the highest price levels. He replied:

"If you're talking about over $1,000 for a single smoking pipe -- as opposed to a cased set or pipes with a lot of gold or special commemorative value -- then you're talking about an extremely rare Dunhill, a super high grade Charatan, or a pipe made by one of the master Danish or Swedish pipe makers. Those include Jess Chonowitsch, Ivarsson, Bo Nordh and S. Bang. I can sell any of those pipes *immediately*, at prices you wouldn't believe. My problem is finding them. There just aren't that many, and those pipe makers make very few each year. They all have big waiting lists for their pipes in Germany, Switzerland, Japan and dozens of other countries."

The distributor told the story about the time that the late (and great) Barry Levin got hold of several dozen Ivarsson pipes in an estate sale. He made one phone call to Japan and sold the entire lot for $50,000. He also told the story about how one individual acquired 30 Jess Chonowitsch pipes during the past year and sold every one of them at an average price in excess of $1,000 per pipe.

Ivarsson pipes were available in the United States in the 1960s and 70s through Iwan Ries and Co. in Chicago. Once or twice each year Stan Levi, the store's owner, visited Sixten and Lars Ivarsson in Copenhagen and bought a handful of pipes that he sold in America. It was not unusual for these pipes to be priced in the $2,500 range. By today's dollars, that would be between $5,000 and $7,500 per pipe!

I met the 90-year-old Stan at the Chicago pipe show last spring, and I asked him why his store no longer sold Ivarsson pipes. He said the Japanese started offering even higher prices and he just couldn't compete.

"They would pay Sixten and Lars Ivarsson the same amount that I would charge my customers," he said.

Since then, Ivarsson pipes have simply not been available to American collectors. Of course, there is always the occasional Ivarsson pipe that might pop up at a pipe show or a garage sale, but finding them has been like looking for a needle in a haystack. Two American collectors have owned several dozen over the years: Rob Cooper, who lives in the Philadelphia area, and Ron Colter, who lives in the Washington, D.C. area. There may be others as well, but they are all the exception.

Ivarsson pipes have been largely unknown to American collectors. For example, there is hardly a mention of Ivarsson in Richard Carleton Hacker's otherwise excellent work, *The Ultimate Pipe Book*. There is not a single mention of Ivarsson in *The Pipe Smoker's Ephemeris: Book I*, which covers the subject of pipes from the years 1964 - 79. Also -- neither book gives credit to Jess Chonowitsch, considered by many collectors to be the greatest pipe maker in the world today.

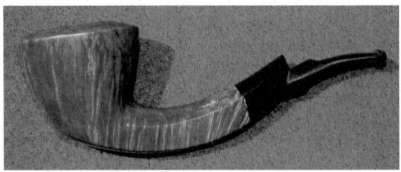

A 1976 Sixten Ivarsson gem of a pipe.

But in Europe, the story is totally different. *The Illustrated History of the Pipe*, which was written by Alexis Liebaert and

Alain Maya of France, gives the Ivarssons the credit they deserve. Sixten is called the greatest pipe maker of the 20th century. And as good as Sixten was, many collectors believe that the only pipe makers to equal or even surpass his skill are Jess Chonowitsch, Bo Nordh and Sixten's son, Lars. Other collectors believe the S. Bang pipes are the best in the world. My own opinion is that all four are fantastic, and calling one better than another is highly subjective. Who was the best composer -- Mozart, Beethoven or Bach? Of course, the answer is intensely personal. But what is not open to debate is that these three composers -- just like the four pipe makers -- were among the greatest of all time in their respective fields.

Lars makes about 70 pipes per year, and he sells them for between $1,000 and $2,000 each -- some for a little less and a few for a lot more. He brought four pipes to Los Angeles in July for the West Coast Pipe and Cigar Expo. It was Lars' first visit to the United States, and he was pleased with the results. All four pipes were sold within two hours from the time the doors were open to the public. Marty Pulvers told Lars that he can sell his pipes any time he wants to make some for him. Lars explained that he is already trying to fulfill the back orders from Japan and Europe but that he is excited to see interest in his pipes in America.

Lars is 51, and he started making pipes 40 years ago. As a child, he liked to hang around his father's workshop. "Once I turned 12, my allowance was cut off," he said. "I had to earn the money I got by helping with the pipes."

Lars remembers when Bo Nordh, an engineering student from Sweden, first visited Sixten and Lars in Copenhagen to study their pipe making techniques. They are still good friends today. He also remembers when Jess Chonowitsch worked in the Ivarsson workshop. The pipes are stamped with a circle that reads, "An Ivarsson Product." Many also include the year and the number made that year. For instance, 24/1970 stands for the 24th pipe made in 1970. Lars' pipes have an "L" stamped on them, while Sixten's have a sunshine.

Lars said that besides Sixten, he and Jess were the only pipe makers allowed to make pipes that were stamped "An Ivarsson Product." He remembers being in his 20s when the three pipe makers -- Sixten, Lars and Jess -- would work all day making pipes at the workshop in downtown Copenhagen. They had a storefront window, and many of the locals would wave or stop by for a chat.

The Japanese were extremely interested in the Dane's high grade pipes. They wanted to buy as many as they could, and they wanted to learn how to make them. Lars has visited Japan many times, and he and Jess have spent months at a time working with the very best Japanese pipe makers, teaching them their techniques. Lars says that Tsuge's high grade pipes are among the best in the world. "They not only mastered the techniques, but they captured the spirit as well," he said.

I first met Lars in Copenhagen in August 1995. He told me that he had never been to the United States, even though he had traveled all over the world many times. His English was easy to understand. "I had to learn English early in order to negotiate on behalf of my father," he said.

So I invited Lars to stay at my house in Los Angeles if he ever decided to visit America. You can imagine my excitement, then, 11 months later when I met Lars at L.A.'s airport. He had traveled nearly 24 hours and was eager for a pipe, but otherwise in good shape.

During the next five days, we had plenty of time to talk pipes, and I learned enough to fill an encyclopedia. I met Lars at the airport on Tuesday evening, and on Friday night of the same week, we met Bonnie and Jess Chonowitsch. On Wednesday and Thursday, Lars was extremely helpful in setting up my buffing wheel, showing me how to stain pipes, and showing me how to open mouthpieces that are clogged -- which are most of them! This includes straightening out bent mouthpieces, opening them up, and bending them back into shape. On Thursday Lars, Dayton Matlick, editor and publisher of *Pipes and tobaccos*, and I visited Jim Benjamin in San Diego. Jim is an expert at restoring old pipes, and he thoroughly cleaned the inside of one of Lars' pipes. I noticed that Lars traveled with only three pipes. He made all three solely for his own smoking. I asked him if I could buy one of the three and he said yes, provided I could wait until just before he left for Copenhagen on the following Monday. The pipe is stamped, "An Ivarsson Product," and it also includes the word "own," signifying that it is (or was) his own pipe.

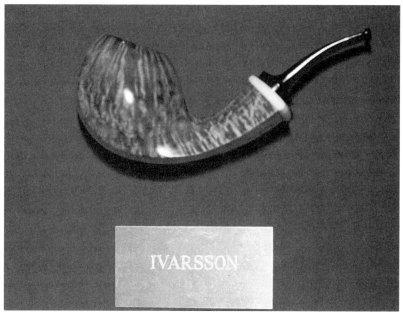

A Lars Ivarsson pipe -- as close to perfection as possible.

When we were in Jim Benjamin's workshop, I asked Lars if he would mind smoothing out the plateau top of a large free hand pipe that had been made by another pipe maker. It was amazing to watch him work, first with a sanding wheel and then with one of his handmade knives. Jim Benjamin said he'd be afraid to work with a knife. He was speaking for Dayton and me as well. But Lars took the knife to his beard, cupped his hand under his beard, and shaved off a handful of whiskers. "As long as the knife is sharp," he said, "there will be no problem."

I asked him about the age of briar, and Lars said there is a lot of misinformation on the subject. He said that most of the time he can tell the age of the briar by looking at a pipe. The range seems to be anywhere from five years to -- at the outside -- 50 years. He said the myth of hundred-year-old briar is just that -- a myth. He said that some of the wood he works with has been stored since the 1950s, but he said that's the exception. Most of the briarwood that he uses has been stored for between one and five years. As long as it is good briar, and thoroughly dry, it does not have to be so old to have good smoking qualities. In fact, Lars said, if the briarwood is too old it becomes difficult to work with. "Picture how a totally dried out cork crumbles easily in your hand," he said.

(L-R) Dayton Matlick, publisher of *Pipes and tobaccos*, me and Lars Ivarsson in Los Angeles, 1996.

But I asked about the books and anecdotes that speak of briar that is century old or even 200 or 300 years old?

"That's silly," he said. "It's not real. Even if you find a pipe made a hundred years ago, even though the briarwood is a century old, it won't smoke any better or worse than briarwood that is 25 years old. If you have high quality briarwood that is thoroughly dry, then it doesn't even matter if it's only 10 years old. Finding the quality wood is another story. That's the expensive part. It doesn't matter if it comes from Algeria or Corsica or Italy or Greece or wherever -- as long as it's good. It's the old story of the horse. It doesn't matter what color the horse is, as long as it rides well.

Lars carves knives as well as pipes, as featured in this 1997 photograph that appeared on the cover of *Pipes and tobaccos*.

"I have been buying briar from Corsica from the same man who supplies Jess, Bo Nordh and S. Bang. Unfortunately, he recently passed away so we are in the process of finding another distributor. But we don't anticipate a problem. As long as there are people supplying the highest grade briar, and a few of us pipe makers willing to buy it, then there will be a solution.

"We also use the highest quality vulcanite, which we buy from Germany. All of our mouthpieces are hand-cut. As important as the materials are, however, the way the pipe is made is most important. A good pipe is 90 percent physics, 5 percent materials and 5 percent magic."

The "magic" that Lars referred to is a reflection of the pipe maker's passion, artistry and intuitive feel for how a particular pipe should be made. A great pipe is one that draws smoothly and stays lit easily and does not require a lot of tinkering, poking, tamping, relighting and all those other things that seem par for the course for run-of-the-mill pipes.

I want to add that I think Lars' percentages might be slightly lopsided. I say this because he invests so much money in the raw materials. He has never considered using any type of plastic, lucite or acrylic mouthpiece. He insists that the vulcanite be pure rubber, without any additives or metals whatsoever. He pays $50 for each block of Corsican briar that he uses, and he always rejects the blocks that have even the slightest defects. After factoring in the rejected wood, Lars pays more than $80 for each block that he uses.

Lars offered insights into how briar colors after repeated smoking. I told him my favorite was briar that turned a dark reddish-brown over time. He said that wood only turns red because of an initial stain of red by the pipe maker. The wood itself darkens into brown or a grayish brown color, but if the pipe were given an early stain that included some red in it, the pipe will look plum-colored over time. Without that red stain, however, it won't.

There is "magic" in this Sixten Ivarsson pipe, made in 1964 and used as a model for many Stanwell pipes.

As for sandblasts, Lars brought a spectacular ring-grain to the Los Angeles show. He had just made the pipe. He does all his own sandblasting at home in a furnace he built just for that purpose.

Lars has always preferred to live and work in the country. In fact, he and his wife recently purchased a new home on the sea that is 100 kilometers from downtown Copenhagen. He says the house needs a lot of work, which he will do himself. He plans to set up his pipe making workshop adjacent to the house. "I'm just a country boy," he likes to say.

During the West Coast Pipe and Cigar Expo, Lars and Jess answered questions at the banquet. Several times they were asked about oil-curing techniques for preparing briar. Lars said he uses a little oil on the bowl after the pipe is made, but that's it. As for drying briarwood, Lars said his secret technique is nothing more sophisticated than the calendar.

Back at my house I showed Lars and Jess several of the pipes in my collection that looked beautiful but did not smoke well. In each case, they examined the pipe in the same way that you might expect Sherlock Holmes to examine an important piece of evidence. First they turned it this way, then that way -- with the mouthpiece and then without the mouthpiece. They never hesitated to blow through the pipe to listen to how the air flow sounded. "We need to avoid having the mouthpiece sound like a clarinet," Lars said at one point. In each case, they showed me the flaw. The mistakes included air holes that went below or above the bottom of the bowl; insufficient wood left at the bottom of the bowl; off-center drilling of the air hole; an oval mortise on the shank with a round tenon on the mouthpiece; excessive vulcanite on the mouthpiece; excessive vulcanite that needed to be cleaned out of the inside of the mouthpiece; pin-sized tenons; pin-sized air holes; plastic mouthpieces that were made for gorillas, not humans; and clunky designs that were not hand-sanded and lacked aesthetic appeal. In case you're interested, these pipes included a Charatan Supreme, a Ser Jacopo Gem line, an Ingo Garbe free hand and several high grade Dunhills!

One of the examples included a full bent pipe that was constructed so that no matter how open the mouthpiece and shank were, the pipe smoker would have to fight and tug to get any smoke. This was because the mouthpiece went straight down at the tenon while the air hole was nearly horizontal. "The structure of this pipe, which is common, is guaranteed to frustrate the smoker," Jess said. Lars added: "You would never see this on a well made pipe. Never. I'll bet you could look at a thousand S. Bang pipes and you'd never see this mistake. Not once. This is the type of basic technique, what you might call the fundamentals, that I keep stressing with Nanna."

Nanna and Sixten Ivarsson
in Sixten's old workshop
in Copenhagen.

Nanna is Lars' youngest of two daughters and the one person he regards as his logical successor in the future. She is 22 and already an experienced pipe maker. Nanna was recently accepted at a design school that rejected 488 of the 500 students who applied. She will continue making pipes under her father's guidance while studying design. She told me that she wants to use her study of design to create new shapes for pipes.

Lars has a terrific sense of humor, and each time we would find a technical error in the pipe he would say "Oops!" When I laughed, he explained, "this is when the pipe maker really doesn't know what he is doing and then suddenly he says, 'Oops!'" Either that — or Lars spots the mistake — and his most frequent comment is "Oops! "

It is remarkable how many designs are considered commonplace today but were revolutionary at the time that Sixten or Lars or Jess introduced them. For instance, I mentioned to Lars that the egg is one of my favorite shapes. I asked if the Ivarssons had anything to do with it. "Yes," he replied. "My father created it."

At Tivoli Gardens in Copenhagen, back row, from left to right, Jess and Bonnie Chonowitsch; Lars and Annette Ivarsson; Lars' daughters, Camilla and Nanna; my son, Jack, and me. Front row: my daughter, Sara, and my wife, Carole.

During the 40 years in which he has made pipes, Lars has stamped a fish on 35 of them, and Jess has stamped a bird on approximately the same number. The fish and the bird are reserved for those pipes that are as close to perfect in every respect possible. One of the pipes Lars sold in Los Angeles was a fish pipe. It was a free hand with a long shank. The bird's eye on both sides, and the horizontal straight grain on the front and back sides, was not to be believed, especially since the tight -- incredibly tight -- bird's eye extended the entire length of the shank.

I know some collectors will be turned off by the notion of spending $1,000 for a single pipe. But I would recommend that, if you can find one, then beg, borrow or steal (from yourself) in order to acquire one. The experience is like no other, and the pipes only get better with repeated smoking. The same goes for pipes made by Jess Chonowitsch, Bo Nordh or S. Bang. Let's say that you have 50 pipes that cost an average of $100 each, for a total investment of $5,000. I think you'd be better off selling 10 of those pipes and buying one Ivarsson, Jess, Bo Nordh or high grade S. Bang pipe. You'd still have 41 pipes, and without a doubt the high grade Danish would be the one most often smoked. In fact, you'd probably sell off another 10 and you'd have 30 plus one Jess and one Ivarsson pipe, or something similar.

When we were at the outdoor banquet dinner of the West Coast Pipe and Cigar Expo, I was smoking a Sixten Ivarsson pipe made in 1970. Shortly before dinner was served, I put the pipe down on the table and excused myself. I walked 50 or so yards to get to the lobby, asked directions to the men's room, went to the bathroom and washed my hands, then found the telephones and made two quick phone calls. I walked the 50 yards back to the table and sat down at my place. I was gone at least five minutes and perhaps as many as 10. I picked up the Ivarsson pipe I had been smoking, put it in my mouth and puffed. Unbelievably, it was still lit! I showed this to Lars and Jess, and Lars made a joke that it was a good way to waste tobacco. In truth, hardly any tobacco had burned -- just enough to allow the pipe to smolder. I told him this was incredible. I had never seen anything like it. Still not wanting to take any credit, they both said the outdoor breeze contributed to the pipe staying lit. No doubt, I said, but not for five to 10 minutes. Determined, I asked once more, "How can you explain this?"

Lars looked serious at first and then smiled as he answered, "I guess it stayed lit because of that final 5 percent -- what Sixten

calls magic. It's the magic of really knowing how to make a pipe --
what you would call a pipe that is 'one-in-a-million'."

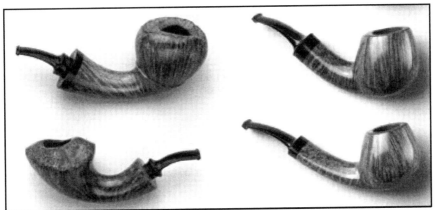

Exquisite shapes and grain on four Lars Ivarsson pipes.

CHAPTER EIGHT

~~~~~

YOUR PIPES SHOULD
HAVE AN EASY DRAW

My modest goal in this 1997 article for Pipes and tobaccos *was to offer my personal opinion that most pipes are not drilled properly. I have become more emphatic on the subject since then, and if you asked me my goal today, it would be to cause a revolution in pipe making. This article reflects the fact that I used to regard this as a matter of personal taste, but I am now convinced that ALL pipes will smoke better if they are opened to the dimensions outlined in this chapter. Just remember to keep the tobacco well tamped.*

Since this article appeared, hundreds of pipe smokers have sent their pipes to Jim Benjamin for opening, with the result being that, at the time of his death in 2007, Jim had a room full of testimonials about how their pipes are suddenly great smokers as a result of the enlarged open draft holes.

Ken Campbell wrote a brilliant essay for The Pipe Collector *newsletter in 2002 called "Airflow: The Key to Smoking Pleasure." After that, dozens of collectors wrote expressing their satisfaction with their modified (and improved) pipes. Of course, no matter how passionately some of us feel about this subject, in the end we have to concede that it is a matter of personal preference.*

* * * * *

Right in the middle of a very busy day at work I received a phone call from a reporter at Bloomberg News Service. He said he was writing a story, like *USA Today*, *The Wall Street Journal* and the *Chicago Tribune*, about the sudden resurgence of pipe smoking. The reporter asked if I thought that yuppies were jumping on a pipe-smoking bandwagon.

"Not likely," I said. "Pipes are very different from other types of smoking. You can't collect cigarettes or cigars, but you can, and thousands of us do, collect pipes. I would say that cigarettes are like television, cigars are like the movies and pipes are like reading a book. They require knowledge."

In fact, I would say that every pipe collector and pipe smoker has his own philosophy of pipes, whether he knows it or not. There are certain ideas and assumptions that he has formed that constitute his core belief system when it comes to pipes. What is so strange is how different we all are. I say this because I find myself at odds with the prevailing beliefs, held as sacred by most pipe smokers.

Perhaps the most dramatic difference is my conviction that 999 out of every thousand pipes need to be modified slightly to be enjoyed fully. Their smoke holes through the shank and mouthpiece are too narrow for my taste. Whenever I buy a pipe, new or used, I open it up before I do anything else.

Let me get technical just for a second: The air hole in most shanks is between 3.5 and 4 millimeters, but I prefer between 4.3 and 4.7 millimeters, or between 11/64" and 3/16." The same applies to having an open mouthpiece. I almost always drill a bigger air hole through the tenon, and then I use a file to go through the lip end to open up the mouthpiece. I don't consider the pipe smokable until I can slide an extra fluffy pipe cleaner through the tenon and have it come out the other end, where the lip is, with almost no resistance.

If you don't believe me, try it. When you have a pipe drilled like I just described, you'll be amazed at how easily it smokes and how easy it is to keep lit. There is no better feeling than to be enjoying a pipe, put it down for a full minute or two, and then pick it back up and puff gently as the tobacco is still smoldering. I believe this is what Alfred Dunhill meant when he called it "the gentle art of smoking." I rarely have to use more than two matches to keep a pipe lit for 45 minutes or an hour or an hour and a half, depending on the size of the bowl, and I do this without even trying. When the air hole is open properly, your pipe will stay lit.

I once asked Jess Chonowitsch and Lars Ivarsson, two of my favorite pipe makers, why they don't open all their pipes the way that I like them. I pointed out that when I bought a pipe from Lars that he had made for his own smoking enjoyment, it seemed to be a little more open in the lip area of the mouthpiece than the pipes that he made for his customers. I asked Lars and Jess, "If it's good enough for you -- why don't you make it that way for your customers?"

Jess replied that if he used a file or a drill to open up the lip area the way that I like -- so an extra fluffy cleaner slides through without resistance -- he would have to remove vulcanite from inside the mouthpiece. This would make the material, from top to bottom, extremely thin and easy to bite through. He said it is no problem for me because I almost never keep a pipe clenched between my teeth [except when I was posing for photographs for this book!]. He also said that experienced pipe smokers, like he and Lars are, know precisely how much pressure they can apply when holding a pipe between their teeth. That is why they have no problem opening the lip area of their own pipes. But Jess said that if they opened the lip area for all the pipes they made for sale, it would lead to problems. "Too many amateur smokers would chomp down on the end and bite through the mouthpiece," he said, "and then they'd tell their local tobacconist, 'This pipe's no good!'"

Lars said that the pipe I had bought from him has a military push-pull bit with a metal tenon, just like the metal sleeves inside bamboo shanks, and metal stays open. This is in contrast to briar, which has the effect of closing a little with each smoke because the tars and oils accumulate inside the wood in the shank. So a metal sleeve at 4 millimeters probably has the equivalent opening, in effect, of somewhere between 4.1 and 4.3 millimeters of wood that has been well smoked.

A Jess Chonowitsch bamboo pipe, with a metal tube inside the bamboo shank -- so no cake will build in the shank.

Jess said that the size of the air hole was the single biggest source of controversy between two of Denmark's greatest pipe makers: Poul Rasmussen and Sixten Ivarsson. Poul favored 3.5 millimeters, and Sixten was considered revolutionary because he expanded the airhole to 4 millimeters. But Sixten was not alone in this. Some of the best pipe makers from the 1920s, 30s, 40s and 50s, usually in England -- Dunhill, Charatan, Barling, Comoy and Sasieni -- drilled their air holes much wider than is common today. Many of these pipes were drilled to accommodate filters, which most smokers discarded, with the result being a wide open air hole. I believe this is one of the reasons there is such a strong demand for these older pipes. They smoke like a dream. Of course, each pipe maker was different, and not all old pipes are drilled properly by any means.

Another issue that is related to having an easy draft involves the bend of the mouthpiece. It was only after seeing about a thousand examples that it finally occurred to me that the bend on Jess' full-bent pipes was less round -- much less bent -- than the bend on Petersons or Italian pipes or almost any other pipes. I asked Jess if he avoids bending them so sharply to insure that the smoke hole stays open and the draw is smooth and easy. "Absolutely," he said. "That's an important difference between my pipes and the factory pipes like you find at Dunhill or Stanwell or the others."

If you're still skeptical about what I'm advocating, let me tell you the story of a dealer who I had given dozens of my pipes to sell. He told me that he kept one to smoke himself -- a black sandblasted prince with the name "Dorsett Knotty" stamped on it. I had opened that pipe to just the way I like it. My friend called me one day, not knowing that I had opened it, and asked where he could find more Dorsett Knotty pipes. "It's the best smoker I've ever had," he said. "I went to the post office this morning and was smoking the pipe in my car. I left the pipe, still burning, in the car's ashtray when I went into the post office. I came out three or four minutes later and, incredibly, I could still puff on it and it was still smoldering. I was going to sell it for $20 or $30 but no way, I'm keeping it. It's become my favorite smoker." I explained that it was the opening that made the pipe so good. The dealer then sent me six of his pipes, and I opened them all for him, and he has become a convert.

I sold Ed Lehman an ODA Dunhill bruyere full bent. Ed generally stays away from bent pipes, but he noticed that the bend on this one was more like a Jess pipe than a Dunhill. I had straightened it out just slightly. I forgot to tell Ed that I had opened it up for an easier draw. He called me one day to tell me about the pipe. "I can't believe how well it smokes. I can put it down for minutes at a time, then pick it up and puff, then put it back down. It hardly ever goes out!" Since then, I have stamped my initials, "R.S.N.," on some of my pipes that have been opened up either by me or by Jim Benjamin or Tony Rodriguez, a Los Angeles-based pipe maker. I did this so that if you buy a pipe from my collection, you will know that it has been opened.

I wish I could take credit for having made this discovery on my own, but it was made by working with two pipe experts -- my two gurus -- who helped show me the way: Jim Benjamin and Jess

Chonowitsch. Jess' contribution was in stressing the importance of an open airflow, even though we do not agree on what the precise measurements should be. Jess believes 4.0 to 4.3 millimeters is plenty, but I prefer 4.3 to 4.7 millimeters. Some of the difference has to do with the way we smoke our pipes. Jess lets his pipe go out all the time and then re-lights it, while I prefer to keep mine barely smoldering the whole time.

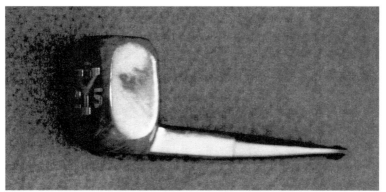
The Sasieni panel with YS25

Jim's contribution came after I sent him a 4-dot Sasieni that I had bought from Tom Colwell that has a silver stamp that says, "Y S 25." Tom thought it was a graduation pipe from "Yale, Summer of 1925." Obviously, it was a very old pipe, and it had an easy draw. I had sent it to Jim Benjamin to be cleaned up. He made it look like brand new, which is how he always makes old pipes look. I typically ask Jim, "Can you make it look like it looked in the store window when it was first offered for sale -- in this case in 1925?" He said that would be no problem, and he was true to his word. I told Jim that I couldn't believe how well it smoked, and I asked if he had any theories about why. He studied the pipe for a while and then said, "I suspect it's all in the air hole. That pipe was made by Joel Sasieni, and he knew how to make pipes. He had an opening for a smooth draft." I asked Jim if he had ever opened any of his own pipes, and he replied "yes -- nearly all of the newer ones. Many of the older ones were opened just fine."

Jim said he used 5/32" or 4.0 millimeters as his opening figure, but I measured that Sasieni pipe and called Jim on the phone. "It's open much wider than that," I said. "Let's experiment. If you're willing, I'll send you a few more pipes for opening -- only this time use 11/64" or 4.3 millimeters." In other words, I wanted to see if bigger would be better. When the pipes came back, they were dramatically better! So I knew we were on to something.

Several years later I was visiting Jim and smoking a full bent Jess Chonowitsch pipe that was beautiful but still did not seem as open as I would have liked. Jim measured it and said the opening was 11/64", so I asked him what was the next size up. He said 3/16", or 4.7 millimeters, which seemed enormous at the time. Feeling brave, or crazy, I said, "Let's try it!" And the results were phenomenal. The draw on that pipe became absolutely perfect. Consequently, I have opened the majority of my pipes to that size.

As for the mouthpiece, many different pipe makers have asked me what dimensions I like, and I have that down as well: 3.5 millimeters through the tenon as far as the drill bit will go, with the lip end opened to 2 millimeters. If these numbers bore you, just remember the pipe cleaner test: *An extra fluffy cleaner going through the tenon end should slide through the mouthpiece and come out the lip end with virtually no resistance.* If your mouthpiece passes that test, and your shank is open to at least 4.3 millimeters, you will get the best possible smoke from your pipe, in my opinion.

I once asked Jim Benjamin if having such an easy draw could cause tongue bite. "No," he said. "It's just the opposite. You get tongue bite from tugging and tugging on a pipe with a narrow smoke hole. Picture trying to suck molasses through a straw! The best way to enjoy a pipe is to take a puff or two and then put it down for 30 or 60 seconds, then take another puff or two -- you can't believe how relaxing and enjoyable your pipe smoking will be! Just remember -- let your pipe smolder and puff gently. It's important to use a tamper to keep the tobacco well packed, especially on the sides, to avoid tongue bite. Otherwise, the hot smoke will rush down the sides of the bowl, leading to tongue bite, so don't just tamp the tobacco in the center, but tamp evenly all the way around the bowl."

If you'd like to see first-hand what I'm talking about, then send one of your pipes to Jim Benjamin or any other respected pipe expert and ask him to open it up as I have described. I know it sounds heretical to change nearly every pipe I own, but I also know that it works for me.

And since I am telling you what I like, I want to stress that *all* of the high grade pipes that I discuss in this book, with the possible exception of pipes by Tony Rodriguez and the occasional Castello, need to be opened in order for me to enjoy smoking them. Let me put it another way -- I don't consider a pipe made by Jess Chonowitsch, S. Bang, Bo Nordh or Lars Ivarsson to be smokable until it is opened inside to the dimensions outlined in this chapter. That's how strongly I feel about the issue.

When I say, I don't consider them "smokable," what I really mean is that they do not smoke anywhere near as well as they do once they are opened the way that I like. Picture eating a steak in an elegant restaurant, where everything is perfect -- the salads, side dishes, wine, everything -- except your steak is either uncooked or extremely well done, and your preference is medium rare. I like the uncooked version because the steak can still be saved by cooking it to medium rare. But if the steak were totally burnt, there is not much you can do to save it. In the same way, if a pipe is too tight, it is very easy to open it, but if it is too open, how can it be closed? There is no way, unless you use artificial fillers in the shank or make a very tight new mouthpiece, neither of which is satisfactory.

I always cringe when a pipe smoker tells me that he followed my advice and bought a high grade pipe but was not impressed by its smoking qualities. Of course, this has only happened a few times, and I am 100 percent positive the problem is with the opening of the pipe. In those cases where the pipe smoker has followed my advice and sent their high grade pipes to

Jim Benjamin for opening, they have called me afterward to thank me, saying that now they understand why I was so enthusiastic about Nordh, Ivarsson and the other high grades. *Now* the pipe smokes better than any they have ever tried. Mark Shropshire once wrote about having a Lars Ivarsson pipe that did not smoke well at first but was terrific after it was opened up.

The collectors who have had this experience have asked me why the pipe makers don't follow my advice. I always tell them the same thing, "You'll have to ask the pipe makers themselves." I have told them a million times, and they open the pipes for me that I buy from them. But as a general rule, they refuse to change from the way they were taught when they were first learning to make pipes.

From left to right, Per Hansen, Chuck Stanion, editor of *Pipes and tobaccos*, and Ulf Noltensmeier. Per and Ulf make the S. Bang pipes, which are among my all-time favorites -- once they are opened the way I like.

I remember when Rolf Rutzen in Germany complained to me about a full bent S. Bang pipe that he had, saying, "I don't know what's wrong -- it just doesn't smoke well." Rolf sent me the pipe, and I forwarded it to Jim Benjamin, who opened the mouthpiece so an extra fluffy cleaner could slide through, tenon end first, without any resistance, and he opened the shank to 3/16". After getting his pipe back, Rolf called me, ecstatic, almost shouting, "I can't believe it's the same pipe! Now I can get a cleaner through, no problem, and the pipe stays lit -- it's just so much better! Why in the world don't the pipe makers do this?" I told Rolf I didn't know -- he would have to ask them.

Let me give you another example that occurred in 2003. I visited René and Rachel Wagner at Tabak-Lädeli in Zurich, Switzerland, and I bought a small (group 2) straight grain Jess Chonowitsch apple -- an absolutely gorgeous looking pipe. I paid a great deal of money for the pipe and planned to smoke it, without modifying it in any way, during the next 10 days while I was in Europe. After three or four bowls, I found myself tugging and tugging to keep it lit, and I began to associate tongue bite with that pipe, so I stopped smoking it until I arrived home in Los Angeles. I spent 15 minutes opening the mouthpiece, and one minute opening the shank to 3/16", and now the pipe is an absolute gem! It is a fantastic smoker. But without those modifications, I would have sold it or traded it as an extremely dissatisfied customer.

Some collectors have said that I am responsible for promoting the Danish high grade pipes and driving up their prices. I do not believe that is true, though obviously my enthusiastic articles about their pipes have helped generate interest in the pipes. But I want to emphasize that I only like these pipes after they have been modified. As I told collector Ken Campbell for his article on the open airflow, "I would rather smoke a no-name pipe opened the way that I like than an S. Bang pipe that has not been opened. But my first choice would be an S. Bang pipe opened the way that I like."

As you can tell, I am quite frustrated by my favorite pipe makers when it comes to this subject, yet my complaint with the opening of their pipes in no way diminishes my admiration for them in all other respects. They typically have beautiful shapes, the best briar in the world, the softest and purest vulcanite possible, exquisite grain, captured precisely as it was meant to be captured, and dead-center drilling all the way through the pipe.

From left to right, Kent Rasmussen, Kurt Balleby and Poul Ilsted, all outstanding Danish pipe makers. Once their pipes are opened as outlined in this chapter, they are fantastic smokers, in my opinion.

In other words, they do everything right except what I consider the most important step for ensuring a good smoke -- their air holes are too tight. However, I am willing to acknowledge that we are talking about matters of personal taste and opinion, and it is very easy to have a pipe opened up. As I mentioned earlier, imagine if the problem were in reverse -- if the pipes were too open to begin with. Then we would have a potentially insurmountable problem, because it is easy to make an opening bigger but nearly impossible to make it smaller.

The main point is to experiment to find what works best for you. Remember, pipe smoking is like reading a book. It requires effort and knowledge, and its rewards are enormous. I do not claim to be an expert. There are collectors who have forgotten more about pipes than I have learned. I am not saying that the open air hole is a carved-in-stone, right-or-wrong principle for everyone. I just know that for me, it has enhanced my enjoyment of pipes immeasurably. I am hoping that by writing this article I can persuade some of the better pipe makers to experiment a little and open up their drafts. In the end, though, it's all a matter of personal taste.

One of the things I like most about pipes is that I keep learning. I know more today than I did last year, and I knew more then than I did the year before. I find that exciting, anticipating that 10 or 20 or 30 years from now I'll know way more about pipes than I do today. We keep learning, and that always gives us something to look forward to. Can you imagine saying the same about cigarettes or cigars? Never.

Pipes are magical in their own way, and nothing is so fantastic as to learn how to maximize their enjoyment. This learning process is really an adventure that lasts a lifetime. What could be more fun, or more rewarding?

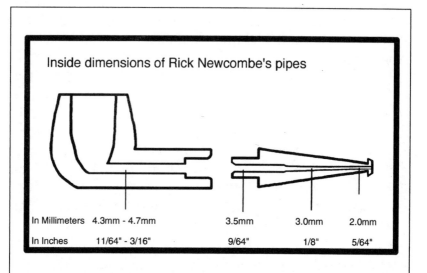

Inside dimensions of Rick Newcombe's pipes

| In Millimeters | 4.3mm - 4.7mm | 3.5mm | 3.0mm | 2.0mm |
| In Inches | 11/64" - 3/16" | 9/64" | 1/8" | 5/64" |

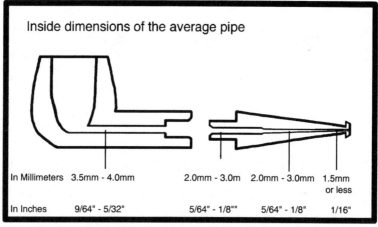

Inside dimensions of the average pipe

| In Millimeters | 3.5mm - 4.0mm | 2.0mm - 3.0m | 2.0mm - 3.0mm | 1.5mm or less |
| In Inches | 9/64" - 5/32" | 5/64" - 1/8"" | 5/64" - 1/8" | 1/16" |

Note: The conversions from millimeters to inches are approximate but not 100 percent
precise. They are as close as possible using standard drill bits.

CHAPTER NINE

S. BANG -- ULF AND PER,
TWO OF THE GREATEST EVER

This article first appeared in The Pipe Smoker's Ephemeris *in 1995, when only a handful of S. Bang pipes were available in the United States. Since my first meeting with Ulf and Per on that rainy morning in Copenhagen, I have been back to the S. Bang workshop a half dozen times or more and gotten to know Ulf and Per very well. We have had a number of lunches and dinners together in Denmark and in America over the years.*

To me, both pipe makers are interchangeable, which is extremely unusual and a real tribute to their enormous skill. I remember once thinking that I liked Per's pipes the best, including an all-time favorite apple. I told Per about that apple, and he said, "It sure looks beautiful, and I know Ulf will be pleased to hear how much you like his pipe..."

My personal goal is to own as many S. Bang pipes as possible. After they are opened the way that I like -- and in my opinion, they do need to be opened -- I believe they are among the very best pipes in the world.

* * * * *

Once in a while you get lucky. I found a filthy old Danish free hand pipe that looked like it had been smoked thousands of times. The outside of the wood was so dark you could hardly see the grain. But when I held it outside under sunlight, I realized that it was a perfect straight grain. I could barely make out the name: S. Bang, Copenhagen. I had heard good things, but very little, about S. Bang pipes. I decided to pay the $30 that the seller was asking. Little did I know that I had bought a pipe that would sell for $1,000 or more in Europe or Japan.

I immediately sent the pipe to Jim Benjamin in San Diego to have it brought back to life. No one can compare to Jim Benjamin when it comes to taking dirty old pipes and making them sparkle like new -- inside and out.

When I received the pipe back from Jim, the S. Bang nomenclature was easy to read and the straight grain was tight beyond belief. The mouthpiece, which I later learned was hand-cut from the most expensive vulcanite available, was extremely comfortable. The pipe smoked like a dream. It instantly became one of my favorites, and the longer I've had it, the more I like it. No wonder it had been smoked thousands of times!

That was several years ago, and every so often I look for more S. Bang pipes in the United Sates, but they are very tough to find. I once asked my friend Ed Lehman what he knew about S. Bang pipes. He said only that he had heard good things and that he once saw some for sale at a Montreal pipe shop -- starting at $1,200 per pipe!

Now ... fast forward to August 1995, when I had the opportunity to visit Copenhagen. I found S. Bang in the Yellow Pages and called for an appointment, not really knowing what to expect. The man on the other end of the line said yes, they would be happy to meet an American collector. The next morning I hailed a taxi and rode through a thunderstorm several miles outside of downtown Copenhagen. I saw the sign on the door of the workshop: S. Bang, Copenhagen.

I knocked on the door and was greeted by a tall man with a friendly smile. "My name is Per Hansen," he said, as we shook hands. His clothes reflected his profession: they were covered with briar dust. There were machines and tools everywhere, as well as boxes and boxes of ebauchons. In a corner, I saw bundles of long black rods -- the expensive and comfortable German vulcanite that is hand-cut for all S. Bang pipes.

Per walked me into an adjoining room that was a business office, and seated behind the desk was Ulf Noltensmeier -- the man I had spoken with on the telephone. Ulf's clothes reflected that he too had been busy making pipes before my arrival.

They said it was so unusual to have an American visitor, and they were very interested in the status of the high-grade pipe collector/smoker market in the United States. They brewed a fresh pot of coffee, and we all settled back to a stimulating conversation as we enjoyed our morning pipes while the rain continued to pound away outside.

Per Hansen, Rick Newcombe and Ulf Noltensmeier at the old S. Bang workshop in Copenhagen in the mid-1990s.

Many people in Europe have been told that smoking is against the law in America. They assumed that was the case. I told them that the anti-smokers were noisy, but that smoking will never be banned in the States. One of our biggest problems is the overcrowded prisons, and with 50 million smokers in America, if the government tried to ban smoking there would never be enough prisons -- or money to pay for the prisons -- if we had to put in jail everyone who lit up.

I did say, however, that there is encouraging news in the fact that cigarette consumption is declining and in many cases being replaced by the much healthier hobbies of moderate cigar and pipe smoking. Clearly, the ritual of smoking a pipe slowly, savoring the taste and not inhaling, is incredibly relaxing. It definitely lowers *my* blood pressure. If done moderately, I believe it is beneficial to good health.

Ulf and Per said they couldn't agree more and welcomed the news about renewed enthusiasm in America for high-grade pipes. I asked them if Svend Bang was a master pipe maker. They said Svend was a good businessman but strictly an amateur pipe maker. He never put the label of S. Bang on his own pipes because they were not good enough. He hired Per and Ulf to make the S. Bang pipes. In 1984, Svend Bang retired, and Per and Ulf took complete charge of the business, continuing to make some of the best -- if not the very best -- pipes in the world.

Per Hansen at work on a new pipe.

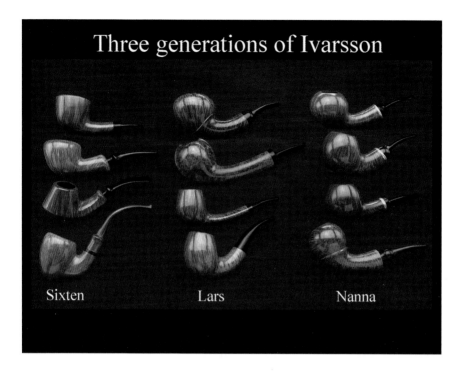

Three generations of Ivarsson

Sixten   Lars   Nanna

The photographs above, and nearly all the photos on the pages that follow, were taken in the studio of Los Angeles photographer Robert Gardner, whose award-winning work has appeared thousands of times in national magazines, newspapers and books. Bob's wife, Gail, is an expert at Photoshop, and she is the one who added water for the cover photograph. We spent a total of four days in the studio, followed by endless hours of touch-up. "They are like little jewels," Gail said. "I had no idea pipes could be so beautiful."

In preparation for these photo sessions, I spent many months cleaning and polishing the pipes to make them look as shiny and new as possible. My personal favorites are classically shaped pipes that are handmade and reflect the artisan's unique interpretation. Notice how you will see in the following pages many pipes in the apple/pot/billiard shape, yet each one is slightly different, and that difference creates a special experience.

These two pipes were made by Nanna Ivarsson, who grew up making pipes and is considered one of the best in the world today. The pipe in the top photo was made in 2007, and the pipe in the bottom photo was made in 1993, when Nanna was working alongside her famous grandfather, Sixten Ivarsson.

Lars Ivarsson has spent a lifetime creating one masterpiece after another, including these two works of art. The smooth pipe on top is giant-sized, what could be called a "mini-magnum," which is remarkable considering how beautiful the grain is. The black sandblast in the bottom photo was made from a very old and slow-growing briar burl, which is why the ring grain is extraordinarily tight.

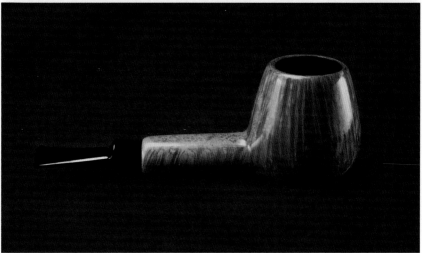

Jess Chonowitsch can capture straight grain as well as any pipe maker who has ever lived. The museum piece in the top photo includes a ring of ivory. The apple/pot/billiard in the bottom photo is nothing more than wood and rubber -- turned into an artist's masterpiece. I can't look at that photo without wanting to hold the pipe. As Frederic Chopin said about great art, "simplicity is the final achievement."

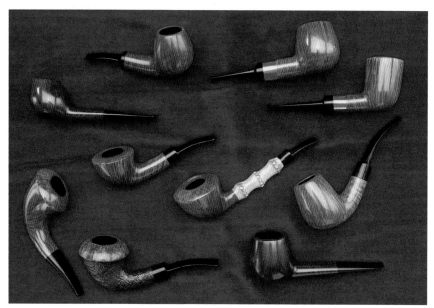

Jess Chonowitsch makes a wide variety of shapes but with the discipline of a master whose goal is to create beautiful pipes that are great smokers.

Gorgeous S. Bang pipes with a tomato on top and an apple below.

Group shots of S. Bang pipes show many similar shapes but with just enough variations to enable each pipe to create a unique experience. The artistry, beauty and craftsmanship are unequalled.

The wonderful pipes on these two pages include the following brands, in no particular order: Dunhill, Charatan, Castello, Peter Hedegaard, Tom Eltang, Tony Rodriguez, Tim West, Porsche, Gert Holbek, Paolo Becker, Poul Winslow, Ser Jacopo, Il Ceppo, Jorn

Micke, Paul Perri, John Eells, Trever Talbert, Rich Lewis, James Upshall, Peterson, Karel Krska, Brebbia, GBD, Astley's, Ashton, Davidoff and Bertram Safferling.

Relaxing in my den with Scooby after a morning workout. I opened the pipe rack behind me to select a pipe for that evening.

Arnold Schwarzenegger is a world-famous cigar smoker who also enjoys an occasional pipe. He created quite a stir when he visited Peter Heinrich's House of 10,000 Pipes in Cologne, Germany, at my recommendation. In the bottom photo, we see gorgeous pipes made by Rainer Barbi in the far left column from top to bottom, with two beautiful pipes in the center by Wolfgang Becker and three stunning pipes by Karl Heinz Joura in the far right column.

An overflowing pipe rack - - those bottom shelves are supposed to be for tins of tobacco, not more pipes!

The top photo could be labeled "Made in America," with pipes (from left to right) made by Jody Davis, Todd Johnson and Jeff Gracik. They are all part of a new generation of high-grade pipe makers that is emerging in North America. The bottom pipes feature three beauties by artisan Jeff Gracik -- a relative of Andy Warhol -- whose J. Alan pipes are gaining international recognition.

Bo Nordh once jokingly asked me whether I was gay because I kept telling him how much I liked his ball-shaped pipes, such as the three in the top photo. Obviously, I was not alone, because this was starting to become a signature shape for him later in life. The bottom photo shows a truly elegant freehand.

It is quite extraordinary to see so many Bo Nordh pipes in one place, and it is obvious that I much prefer Bo's interpretation of classical shapes to his sculptural pieces.

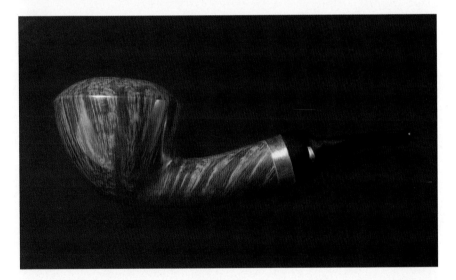

The top photo shows what is believed to be the last pipe Bo Nordh ever made, and the bottom photo shows the last pipe Sixten Ivarsson made. Bo's pipe is dated 2006, and he finished it just before the Chicago Pipe Show in May. He died in July, a few months later. The Sixten Ivarsson pipe is dated 1995, and Lars believes it was his last.

I asked about their backgrounds and current work habits. Per said he started making S. Bang pipes in 1970, after having made pipes for the late Preben Holm. A year later, Ulf joined Per at Bang, after having made pipes for Anne Julie for the prior 15 months. Before that, Ulf had worked for Preben Holm, where he first met Per. Ulf said he asked Preben if they could do something about the noise at the workshop and Preben, basically a kid at the time, said no, if you don't like it, you can leave. So he did!

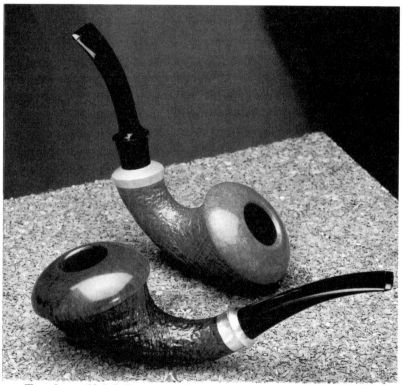

Two beautiful S. Bang sandblasted pipes with smooth tops.

Ulf and Per have spent the last 30-plus years making pipes full time. They have reached a level of pipe making that Preben Holm never dreamed of, and they don't delegate their workload. All S. Bang pipes are made either by Ulf or Per, and each stage of production is done by hand. I watched Per hold a classical shaped bowl, which might be described as an ODA brandy glass, to a drill with the expertise that only comes to talented craftsmen after years and years of practice. They said they are making more pipes in classical shapes because there is a huge demand in Germany. I saw some finished products that were gorgeous! They were some of the prettiest pipes I have ever seen -- ever.

When Ulf and Per make free form pipes, they use what looks like a grinding wheel of sand paper. Whether classical or free hand, *all* of the S. Bang mouthpieces are hand-cut. As an article in a Danish pipe magazine once stated, "Whether this makes a pipe better is arguable, but the awareness of feeling a hand-made mouthbite clasped between one's teeth has a mystical appeal to the true pipe connoisseur."

S. Bang pipes are made with the finest briar available, and it is thoroughly dry before the pipes are made. I asked Per and Ulf if there were any way possible to make their pipes available to the American market. They said they were willing to try on a highly selective basis.

To me, Per and Ulf offer the best of all worlds when it comes to pipe making. They have studied the techniques of the great masters of the 20th century, especially Sixten Ivarsson. Yet they have developed their own unique style. They are totally dedicated to making pipes, as they have been for the past three decades. They haven't tried to start their own line of cigars; their only passion is pipes. Each day, they spend their time making some of the best briar pipes ever made in human history.

Whether you invest hundreds of dollars, or thousands of dollars, for a pipe that says "S. Bang, Copenhagen," you will receive enjoyment far beyond anything you have experienced before. It's no wonder that so many collectors overseas consider them the best pipes in the world today.

~~~~~

CHAPTER TEN

BREAKING IN A NEW PIPE

The most controversial part of this article, which appeared in Pipes *and* tobaccos *in 1998, concerned how many bowls are required to break in a new pipe. There is no right or wrong answer, and obviously some bowls break in quickly while others take a long time. But I still believe that after 50 or 100 pipe bowls, assuming your pipe is kept open and clean, as outlined in Chapters 8 and 11, your pipe will smoke better than those first few bowls.*

Bo Nordh called me after this article appeared to say that he did not mean to imply that it takes 50 bowls for a pipe to be a good smoker. "My pipes are good smokers from the very first bowl," he said. "But they get even better as they are broken in over time."

* * * * *

Did you ever put on a pair of brand new jeans that felt tight, stiff and scratchy? Compare that to wearing a pair of old comfortable jeans that you've worn a hundred times before, that have been washed dozens of times, and that fit you perfectly. They are the essence of comfort and relaxation. Isn't it the same with shoes? How many times have you bought a new pair of leather shoes that felt stiff and uncomfortable at first, sometimes even giving you a blister? Again, compare that with slipping on an old pair of shoes that you've worn a thousand times and that have become contoured to your feet. The leather is so soft that your feet feel like they are wrapped in silk. In fact, we use the expression that it "fits him like an old shoe" when we want to describe something that is familiar and comfortable.

What is the difference between the starched jeans and the well-worn jeans, or between the stiff shoes and the comfortable old shoes? Obviously, the ones that we like most are the jeans and shoes that have been "broken in." They fit us; they suit our personality; it's almost as if they're a part of us. Well I believe the same applies to pipes, and I can assure you that I am not alone. I discussed the issue of breaking in pipes, including various techniques for facilitating the process, with dozens of experienced pipe smokers, and I was struck by how important this issue is to all of them. I also was struck by the number of highly creative suggestions they had for making it easier to enjoy your new pipes just as quickly as possible.

While breaking in a pipe is a concept we hear about frequently, as if it had only one meaning, the truth is that it means different things to different collectors. It is a more complicated subject than most pipe smokers realize, but it is worth studying the issue, and mastering the system that works best for you, because the only way to reach the highest level of pipe smoking enjoyment, relaxation and total satisfaction is to smoke a pipe that has been broken in completely. It's just like those soft jeans and comfortable old shoes.

Obviously, the techniques for the beginning pipe smoker apply to everyone, including the most experienced collector. When you have a new pipe, the key is to smoke slowly. Some pipe experts recommend filling the bowl half way and smoking all the way to the bottom, or until all the tobacco has turned to ash. They say that with each bowl you should gradually fill the pipe with just a little more tobacco, so that you won't be smoking a complete pipe bowl, from top to bottom, until the fifth or sixth time that you smoke the pipe.

Other pipe experts disagree entirely and recommend loading the pipe to the top on the very first bowl. I remember once buying a pipe from Bill Fader of Fader's Tobacconist in Baltimore, and he asked me what kind of tobacco I liked. I said English/Oriental, and he loaded the pipe to the top of the bowl with his blend called Istanbul. A number of years later I visited the workshop of S. Bang in Copenhagen, Denmark, and one of the two pipe makers, Per Hansen, watched me load up a new pipe he had just made for me. I filled it about two-thirds of the way to the top. "Why don't you fill it all the way?" he asked. "You know it's a myth that you should start half-way and work your way up. That only applies to very cheap wood that might crack. With a good pipe, you should start with a bowlful of tobacco."

An S. Bang pipe that has been broken in and now smokes like a dream.

One of the most experienced American pipe makers is Paul Perri, who has been making pipes for more than 60 (!) years. Paul was friends with another great American pipe maker, Sydney Ram, who had an interesting theory about new pipes. "We used to call him Sydney 'God-Bless-America' Ram," Paul said. "That's because Sydney recommended taking a new pipe and dipping it into a glass of water long enough to say 'God Bless America.' Then he would dry it off with a towel and run a pipe cleaner through it. Sydney believed that a quick dip in the water would prevent the wood from cracking."

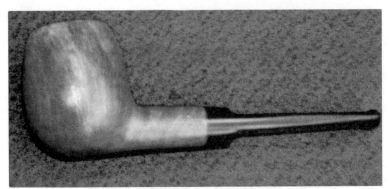

A pipe by Sydney P. Ram, which I dipped in water while saying the words, "God Bless America," and then dried off with a towel and pipe cleaner. It smokes great!

Personally, I tried this once, and it was on a pipe made by Sydney Ram. The pipe was unsmoked and it had been made 50 years earlier. The water did not appear to cause any damage, and the pipe smoked fine. Still, I think the best way to avoid problems at the beginning is to smoke a new pipe extremely slowly. If you are a hot smoker and find this too difficult to do, then during the break-in period you might want to keep two pipes lit at the same time: one of your regular, broken-in pipes that you can smoke, and the new one, that you just want to keep barely smoldering with an occasional puff. Randy Wiley, one of America's best contemporary pipe makers, says it is extremely important that the tobacco burns uniformly. "You want to keep it well lit in the center," he said. "What you want to avoid is having an intensely heated area on one side or the other."

Many people like to put a light coating of honey inside the bowl, while others use water or saliva, and of course many pipe makers use a carbon coating. My personal favorites are Jess Chonowitsch's and Jim Cooke's. Jim developed the secret formula for his coating with the late Barry Levin. There are plenty of other good ones. Of course, there are many pipe experts who want raw wood only.

Gary Humphrey, a passionate pipe collector from Anchorage, Alaska, has a unique system for breaking in pipes. "I mostly smoke pipes with giant bowls, and when I get a new pipe I'll smoke it every day for seven days in a row," he said. "At that point, I figure it's about as broken in as it will ever be."

Gary Humphrey, left, with collector Rob Cooper, who specializes in pipes by W.O. Larsen.

Richard Esserman, an experienced collector who is one of the organizers of the New York Pipe Show, has a similar attitude. "I'm an impatient guy," he said. "None of my pipes take over 10 bowls to break in." Rich has developed a very specific procedure for treating new pipes. First, he applies a small amount of water to the inside of the bowl -- just a light coating. He lets it dry and then repeats the procedure. He likes to do this two or three times to let the water soak in and then evaporate. Then, he applies just a little bit of honey to coat the inside of the bowl before he puts in his tobacco. "The first bowl that I smoke is irrelevant," he said. "It's mostly to make sure that the pipe doesn't crack. With each new bowlful of tobacco, the pipe keeps getting better."

Basil Sullivan, the renowned Charatan collector who for years organized the annual Indiana Briar Friars meeting, speaks for many pipe smokers when he says, "I just hate to break in new pipes. I much prefer to buy estate pipes because someone else already did the hard work of breaking in the pipe -- and I do mean hard work!" On the opposite end of the spectrum is Shane Pappas, a successful tobacconist who sold the Briar Rose pipe shop in

Carson, CA, last year. Shane takes an extremely controversial position on this issue. "For me, the best smoke on any pipe is the first bowl. It only gets worse with each successive smoke," he said, as I looked at him in disbelief. "Yes, I'm talking about briar pipes," Shane said, reading my mind, because I was about to suggest that he might be referring to corncobs and clay pipes, but surely not briar. Without question, my experience is that the vast majority of collectors agree with Basil. In fact, I do not know a single pipe smoker who shares Shane's opinion on this matter, but if you do, please let me know of your experience.

Andy Herbruck of Del Mar, CA, who has bought and sold thousands of pipes over the years, has a very interesting technique for breaking in a new pipe. "I'll light it, take a few puffs, tamp down the tobacco, and then let the pipe sit overnight," he said. "The following day I'll do the same thing all over again. It might take me five or six days to smoke a single bowl. I'll repeat this process five or six times. I believe it is very important to smoke the same type of tobacco in the pipe. I've been a collector for 25 years, and I just discovered this system by accident. My new pipes just seem to smoke better if they're broken in this way. I think what's happening is that you're warming it up and then letting it dry out, and you may be getting the moisture out."

It would seem that there is no right or wrong way to break in a pipe. As tobacconist John Cox of W. Curtis Draper in Washington, D.C., once told me: "If you put five pipe smokers in a room, you'll get five different opinions." [I have subsequently visited Cox, who is known as "Duke," to tell him that I believe his statement is the most profound sentiment expressed in this entire book.]

But there are a couple of points that nearly all pipe makers agree on. For instance, most people agree that you should use the same tobacco in a pipe to avoid creating conflicting tastes. Otherwise, it would be like drinking tea out of the same cup from which you just drank coffee and before you had a chance to wash the cup. Another area where everyone agrees is that if you allow the briarwood to become too hot, it will crack. That's what is called an absolute. All collectors, with a dozen different theories each on how best to break in a pipe, understand that new pipes should be smoked slowly -- repeat slowly -- and the tobacco should burn evenly down the center of the bowl.

(L-R) High grade collector Joe Lankford, with Corinna Vogt and Hans Joachim Frank, who can be reached at frank_rheinbach@hotmail.com. Joachim has created a revolutionary technique for filling, and breaking in, your new pipe.

While researching this topic, I came across a copy of *Pipe Lovers* magazine from nearly half a century ago, and it is obvious that nothing has changed on this subject in the past 50 years, nor will it change in the next 50. The September 1949 issue of the magazine offered this advice: "Most burn-outs are attributed to improperly breaking in the pipe. It is important to make sure only the best of care is given a new pipe during its breaking-in period. The temperature of the burning tobacco must be kept low enough to keep the bowl from scorching and yet at the same time help form the first layer of cake."

As for when a pipe should be considered broken in, we're back to five-different-pipe-smokers-with-five-different-opinions. In other words, there is no single answer. What you might consider to be broken in, I might consider to be mostly unsmoked. Bo Nordh of Sweden, who is recognized as one of the best pipe makers of all time, once told me that a pipe might need to be smoked as many as 50 times before it is thoroughly broken in. Personally, I agree with Bo. That is exactly what my experience has been. But then there's Rich Esserman, who couldn't disagree more. "If I had to wait 50 bowls, I wouldn't own any pipes," he said. Bob Hamlin, president of the Pipe Collector's Club of America, has sold thousands of pipes over the years and is very knowledgeable on the subject. "I doubt if there is a consensus," he said, "but if I had to pick a number out of the air that I've heard most, I'd say about 20 bowls before a pipe is really broken in. Of course, there is no single magic number, and each pipe is different."

On that issue -- that each pipe is different -- I'm sure there is universal agreement. Some pipes break in more easily than others. Jean Luc Silbereis, a pipe collector who lives in Paris, France and loves Lars Ivarsson's pipes, said: "It's not a matter of a number. It takes the time that it takes. It can happen or never happen. Some never break in -- others are fantastic after five or six smokes." Jim Benjamin of San Diego, an expert at cleaning up old pipes to look like new and to smoke better than ever, said there are mysteries about briar that we will never understand. "I've got a Barling that didn't smoke well for 32 years, then all of a sudden it just blossomed," he said. "Now it's one of my favorites."

As you can see, there are no hard and fast rules -- other than to smoke your new pipes slowly so they don't overheat the wood. Beyond that, I'd suggest trying some of these different systems and experimenting with your own techniques. But keep in mind that pipe smoking is an enjoyable hobby and should never become a complicated chore. As Randy Wiley said, "The system that works best is the one that requires the least amount of hassle."

In the end, regardless of which techniques they use, all pipe smokers know that it is worth the effort to break in their new pipes carefully. Few things in life are as comfortable or give as much pleasure and satisfaction as a pipe that has been thoroughly broken in, cleaned, allowed to air out and dry, and then smoked again -- over and over. The beauty is that with each successive bowl, the briar just keeps getting better and better. Imagine what it would be like if every pipe you reached for had the same comfort level as fitting you like an old shoe or a pair of soft jeans. That is what it is like for most experienced pipe smokers, and it is why they view their collections as an endless source of enjoyment.

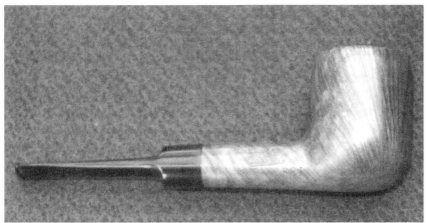

A well-smoked Bertram pipe made many decades ago. It looks as if it can be smoked for many more.

Here is an unusual new pipe by Italian artisan Alberto Bonfiglioli, and it will last a lifetime if it is broken in slowly.

CHAPTER ELEVEN

KEEPING THE INSIDE
OF YOUR PIPE CLEAN

This is a how-to article I wrote for Pipes and tobaccos *in 1997. I still believe that a clean pipe makes all the difference. One minor point that I need to clarify, which several readers called me on, concerns my statement that it is best not to separate the bowl and shank from the mouthpiece too often. Those readers smoked pipes with military push-pull bits, where the only way you can get a pipe cleaner through is to separate the two. This proves the old maxim that for every rule there is at least one exception.*

* * * * *

Bing Crosby once said that the secret to a clean pipe is to smoke slowly. That's so true. I have test-cleaned pipes that I had smoked just the way pipes were designed: puffing slowly and rhythmically. I have cleaned other pipes that I had smoked hot: puffing and puffing, for instance, watching a very close basketball game. The pipes that I smoked slowly hardly needed any cleaning at all, while the pipes that I smoked hot were totally filthy inside.

A clean pipe makes all the difference in the world. I'm talking about the inside of a pipe -- not the outside. Even if you spend a lot of time with your local tobacconist examining different pipes before carefully selecting one, or if you sample a number of different tobaccos to test which ones you like best -- all your efforts will be undermined if you allow your pipe to become dirty.

On the other hand, they will be enhanced immeasurably if your pipe is kept clean.

A surprising number of experienced pipe smokers do *not* know how to keep their pipes clean. The problem is that they don't know what they are missing. I speak from experience. I had smoked pipes for nearly 20 years before I learned how to clean them thoroughly. Once I realized the difference, a whole new world of taste and pleasure opened up to me. Before that, however, what I thought was a clean pipe, because I used a lot of pipe cleaners, really had a lot of built-up cake that affected the smoke. But I didn't know the difference because I hadn't learned to clean them.

My teacher was Jim Benjamin, who has specialized in cleaning and restoring old pipes for more than half a century. Whenever I buy an "estate" (euphemism for "used") pipe, I send it to Jim to be cleaned thoroughly inside and out. I wouldn't consider trying it myself.

I'm always amazed at the number of pipe collectors who think they know how to clean their pipes, when they really don't. To me, what Jim Benjamin or other similar professionals do is every bit as technical and sophisticated as making a new mouthpiece or other forms of pipe repair. Yet collectors who wouldn't know where to begin in making a new mouthpiece don't hesitate to claim that they know how to clean and restore their old pipes. They don't. I know this because I have studied a number of these so-called "clean" pipes and been astounded at how filthy they were inside. I also know it because I have bought some of these pipes, which looked beautiful outside, and practically gagged while trying to smoke them. But after I sent them to Benjamin, they were returned totally clean and fresh tasting. The pipes that Jim sent back appeared to be bone dry, raw wood -- but wood that had already been broken in by repeated smoking before I had bought the pipe. Whenever I get a pipe back like that, I can really taste the tobacco.

What I am presenting here, then, is a system for keeping your new pipes clean from the day you first buy them, and a system that will work for estate pipes, but only after they have been cleaned professionally by someone with the knowledge and skill of Jim Benjamin.

My friend and mentor, Jim Benjamin.

You need a handful of supplies, and you can find nearly all of them at your local tobacconist. Let's start with pipe cleaners. I use three types: bristled -- my preference is Long's; thin and soft, such as the yellow-packaged Dill's; and extra fluffy. If you want to use the tapered cleaners as a way to combine the thins and extra fluffy, that's fine. Other materials you'll need include Q-Tips, alcohol or pipe sweetener, paper towels and the little brushes that your tobacconist sells for around $1 each. You'll also need a pipe tool with a poker, spoon and tamper, which also costs about $1. Those are the only materials you will need to keep your pipes clean and tasting fresh at all times.

The American pipe maker Mike Butera says that he uses as many as eight pipe cleaners during each bowl that he smokes. That sounds like a lot, but it is not unusual, and it is probably because the air hole is too tight.

After the tobacco has turned to gray or white ash, when I am finished, I use an old technique that Tim West, another American pipe maker, once taught me. I use the poker, or the straight piece of metal on the pipe tool, to make sure the ash at the bottom of the bowl is fluffy and loose so there isn't a dottle stuck to the bottom. I then hold a paper towel, or the palm of my hand, over the top of the bowl and shake the bowl up and down to let the ash gently accumulate on the sides of the bowl. Then I dump out the remaining ash. After that, I run another pipe cleaner through the pipe, and then blow gently through the stem. I try not to separate the mouthpiece from the pipe for as long as possible -- between five and ten bowls. Jim Cooke, an accomplished pipe repairman and pipe maker, strongly cautions against separating the mouthpiece from the pipe, and I'm sure Jim would say that every five to ten bowls is still too often to be pulling them apart. But Jim's criticism is mainly aimed at those smokers who separate the mouthpiece from the shank after *every* smoke.

I agree with Jim Cooke that constantly pulling apart the mouthpiece will ultimately damage your pipe. It puts pressure on the wood in the shank, and on the tenon. But at the same time, I agree with Jim Benjamin that you need to separate them occasionally to clean up what he calls the "oil change" that is accumulating in the mortise area of the pipe. "If pipes weren't designed to be separated, then why did Alfred Dunhill put a white dot on the mouthpiece?" Benjamin asks rhetorically. "He did it so that pipe smokers will know which side is up when they put the mouthpiece back after having separated it from the pipe."

So let's say you have smoked your new pipe ten times. On the tenth bowl you start to notice a slight change in the taste of the tobacco. It tastes heavier, or just a little bitter. To me, it tastes like black coffee that has sat in the pot all day. Once the tobacco in your new pipe tastes that way, and it's typically between the fifth and tenth bowl, it's time for a serious cleaning.

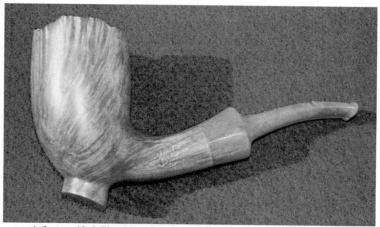

A beautiful Jim Cooke pipe kept clean over the years.

I'll spend about a half hour a week cleaning six pipes, or an average of five minutes each. I sit at a table with the following materials spread out: Six paper towels piled on top of one another; a wide-mouth jar filled with alcohol such as rum, vodka or whiskey -- or pipe sweetener, if it has a high alcohol content; Q-Tips; pipe cleaners; a pipe tool, and one of those pipe-cleaning brushes that you can find at most tobacconists.

I start by separating the mouthpiece from the shank. I dip the tenon in the jar filled with alcohol, then use a paper towel to dry it off. I then dip an entire bristled cleaner in the alcohol and run it through the mouthpiece, starting at the tenon end. The next step is to use the brush to clean the inside of the mouthpiece. Dip the brush in the alcohol, then run it through the mouthpiece, starting at the tenon hole. After scrubbing back and forth, five or six times, pull out the brush and dry off the bristles, which will be brown or black, on the paper towels. Dip the brush back into the alcohol and then run it through the mouthpiece again. Do this as many times as necessary -- until the brush is as clean coming out of the mouthpiece as it was going in. Then use an extra fluffy cleaner to dry out the inside of the mouthpiece. Blow through the lip end to get rid of any pipe cleaner fuzz.

Now you're ready to clean the pipe itself. I start with the mortise area, using a Q-Tip to wipe away any tars or other accumulated gunk. You can dip the Q-Tip in alcohol before using it to clean the mortise area. Jess Chonowitsch warns that if too much alcohol seeps into the wood, it will prevent the natural oils from coming to the surface. This has not been my experience, but it is one more example of the fact that there are few rules when it comes to enjoying your pipes, and you should experiment to find what works best for you. After using the Q-Tips, the mortise will be noticeably cleaner, which you should be able to see with the naked eye by looking at it under a light.

Next, you are ready to clean the shank. Barry Levin once told me that the key to a clean pipe is to have a clean shank. I agree. Dip the brush in alcohol and start scrubbing inside the shank, just like you did inside the mouthpiece. Use the paper towels to dry off the brush, dip it back into the alcohol, then run it back and forth in the shank. I do this procedure five or six times. Because I smoke heavy latakia blends, my brush looks pitch black after its first time through the pipe. I dip the brush in alcohol again, then scrub inside the shank some more, then dry off the brush. After five or six of these of these dip-scrub-and-dry procedures, the brush starts coming out noticeably cleaner than when I started. I'll then use an extra fluffy cleaner to dry out the inside of the shank, and then blow through the shank end once or twice.

For the bowl itself, I do very little. I like only the smallest amount of cake -- somewhere between the thickness of a sheet of paper and a dime. If I notice flakes of ash are starting to accumulate in an uneven pattern, I'll fold a bristled cleaner and rub it along the inside of the bowl to even out the cake. This is a very gentle process. I rarely use a reamer other than a gentle scraper, such as the "British Buttner." If a pipe needs a serious reaming, I send it to a professional. This is one more example where many pipe smokers think it's no big deal to ream a pipe, but in reality it explains why so many estate pipes have uneven cakes, which can easily cause the briarwood to crack.

I leave the mouthpiece separated from the shank for about five minutes to make sure the alcohol in the mortise area has dried. Then I put the pipe back together. If the tenon squeaks even slightly, I'll rub a little beeswax or soap on it and then gently connect the mouthpiece with the shank.

Then I let the pipe rest and totally dry out -- at least for 24 hours and sometimes for two or three days. The next time I smoke it, I can taste the tobacco just as if I were smoking it in a brand new clay pipe -- which is precisely what most expert blenders use to test new tobacco mixtures.

So give this system a try and let me know what you think. But remember, this program only applies to your new pipes and to your professionally cleaned estate pipes. It is not to be used to clean those estate pipes in the first place. You need a professional for that because it is so much more complicated. In fact, even using my system, I still recommend having your pipes cleaned professionally every few years. There are several reasons for this. One is that the Q-Tips will never clean out the cake that builds up in the mortise. Another is that, while the brushes are good for cleaning the shank, they won't prevent the natural build-up of a cake that has the effect of closing the smoke hole. The real

Danish pipe expert Rex Poggenpohl, left, and Chuck Levi, owner of Iwan Ries & Co. of Chicago, which is one of the finest pipe and tobacco stores in America. Chuck is the current president of RTDA. Both men know the importance of a clean pipe.

professional will be able to remove the build-up of tars in the shank.

My system of cleaning only takes about five minutes for every five to ten bowls of tobacco, which is hardly a lot. Yet that five minute investment will give you hundreds of hours of pure pleasure, where you enjoy every pipe bowl because you are able to experience the true taste of the tobacco just as it was meant to be tasted.

CHAPTER TWELVE

~~~~~

BO NORDH: IN A LEAGUE OF HIS OWN

Since this article was written for Pipe Friendly *in 1997, Bo Nordh has encountered a series of health problems, including suffering a stroke and the loss of one leg, yet through it all, Bo continues to make pipes, though not as many as before. Because of their scarcity, the prices of Bo's pipes have gone beyond stratospheric, e.g., I was told that a Japanese collector recently paid $16,000 for a Bo Nordh ballerina pipe. Even to me, the ultimate lover of high grades, that seems high -- but if you compare it to the prices that are paid for great works of art, which Bo's pipes are, it is a relatively modest sum.*

* * * * *

Bo Nordh is the consummate pipe maker. He has been making pipes for nearly all of his adult life, and now at age 57, is at the top of his game. His pipes are probably the most expensive in the world, yet the demand for them far exceeds their supply. The pipes that Bo is working on today were ordered months ago. Here is another way to look at it: on August 15, I met with Bo and ordered a pipe -- picture a full-bent pipe with a rounded bowl something like a soccer ball -- and he promised that I would have it before Christmas. But that is one of the keys to his success: Bo never rushes the process of pipe making.

I first met Bo in August 1996. His good friend Jess Chonowitsch arranged the meeting at my request. Before then, the name "Bo Nordh" was both an image and a legend to me. I remembered nearly 20 years ago seeing his unbelievably beautiful pipes in Iwan Ries' catalogs, priced at $5,000 each by today's dollars. I remembered chatting years ago with an experienced German collector who told me that he smoked hundreds of different pipes but that he buys Bo Nordh pipes only to put them on display in his den. "They are too beautiful to smoke," he said, expressing a sentiment that I have never understood. I remembered reading an article in *The Pipe Smoker's Ephemeris* about Bo Nordh that was reprinted from the Swedish magazine *Rökringar*. The article was written by Jan Andersson, and he pointed out the incredible fact that the first pipe Bo ever made is on display at a museum in Germany! I also remembered chatting with two collectors who have specialized in high grade pipes from Denmark and Sweden -- Rob Cooper and Ron Colter -- when I told them that my favorite pipes were those made by Jess Chonowitsch, the Ivarssons and S. Bang. They replied: "But you don't know Bo Nordh. He is the best in the world!" Finally, I remembered the one Bo Nordh pipe that I owned -- a hand-turned billiard with a seamless horn ferrule. It smoked like a dream, and when Gordon Soladar, who owns thousands of pipes, saw it, he literally did a double-take. "The bird's eye is so spectacular that it looks three dimensional," he said.

So you can imagine how excited I was when Jess said that a meeting would be no problem. We boarded a Hovercraft, also known as a "flying boat," in Copenhagen and set off for the city of Malmö, Sweden. We arrived in less than an hour, and Bo showed up in his Volvo station wagon, which is specially equipped to allow him to drive using only his hands. Bo's legs were paralyzed in a motorcycle accident when he was 19. "Before that, motorcycles were my passion," he later explained to me when I was asking about his early interests in life. Bo has mastered the wheelchair and is amazingly agile and competent at getting around. "It is important to be active in sport," he said. "I am in better shape today than I was years ago because I swim three times a week. That keeps me fit, and it keeps my muscles toned."

Jess, Bo and I spent several hours in Malmö talking about pipes. I learned an enormous amount by asking questions and paying very careful attention to the answers. I felt like I was sitting with Leonardo da Vinci and Michelangelo asking questions about art. I bought several more Bo Nordh pipes at that meeting -- and cannot tell you how pleased I am with them.

So now it is one year later, in August 1997. I am back in Malmö, and Bo meets me at the Central Station, which is located in the middle of the city. We stop for breakfast at an outdoor cafe and share a bond that only pipe smokers know -- the relaxed contentment of puffing slowly after a hearty meal. We then drive to Bo's beautiful house in the country, where he shows me his workshop. Bo's English is quite good -- he understands everything that I say and is able to answer slowly but clearly. "We get American television and movies," he said. "So it has become easy for me to understand English." I try to master a single phrase in Swedish, "Triv lijt att se er," which means, "It's nice to see you." Bo's wife, Birgit, greets us at the door and welcomes me to Sweden.

In the workshop, Bo shows me two finished pipes that I had ordered by phone several months earlier: an apple and a canadian. It is difficult to describe how beautiful they look in their highly polished state. I then notice that he has five semi-finished pipe bowls hanging on a rack. Four of them are just bowls without mouthpieces and the fifth one has a short vulcanite rod in it, waiting for Bo to shape it into a finished mouthpiece. I asked about these bowls, and Bo explained, "after I have made the pipe, but before I make the mouthpiece, I let them dry out, in many cases for several months, so that when I make the mouthpieces, it will fit perfectly. If you rush the process, you will have problems with the fit of the mouthpiece later. Briarwood expands and contracts. It absorbs water and releases water. Each piece is different and has a life of its own. It's just like with people -- there are Scandinavians and Americans and Chinese and Africans -- and we are not all exactly alike. You have to know how to treat each briar bowl individually. That takes a lot of time."

My mind flashed to a typical factory that grinds out thousands of pipes each year. What they do and what Bo Nordh does is like the difference between a poster of a Rembrandt painting versus an original Rembrandt.

I am reminded of the time that Jess Chonowitsch spent two weeks in Greece, mostly on his hands and knees searching through thousands of blocks of briarwood. He found about 100 pieces that looked up to his standards. But after working with only one or two, he decided they were not good enough so he traded the Grecian plateau briar to a large factory for eight nearly flawless blocks of the very best Corsican briar. Talk about an extraordinary commitment to excellence! Two weeks of searching to find eight blocks of wood! And that's only one of the reasons why Jess Chonowitsch and Bo Nordh are considered among the best ever.

Jess Chonowtisch (left) and Bo Nordh. "I felt like I was sitting with Leonardo da Vinci and Michelangelo."

I notice an unfinished turned bowl on Bo's desk and ask him about it. "I shaped that pipe four years ago," he said. "But I'm not satisfied with the shape. I just let it sit there because I know that one of these days it will come to me how to change it so that I will be satisfied. For now, I just leave it there."

Bo uses extremely expensive briar from Corsica -- the same briar used by Jess, the Ivarssons and S. Bang. They all use the same pure vulcanite as well, which they buy in rods from Germany. In addition, Bo has a big supply of very beautiful bamboo, horn, boxwood and other materials that he uses to make pipes.

For his own smoking enjoyment, Bo has about 20 old pipes in something like a shoe box. They are obviously well smoked, and some are pretty badly banged up. "I've dropped a few on the ground," he said. "I've even run over some of them with the car!" I asked if he did this to test their durability. "No, these were just accidents," he said. "As long as they still smoke well, I'll hang on to them. I'm pretty lazy when it comes to making pipes for myself."

Bo said there are mysteries of pipe making that he still doesn't understand. "For instance, I can make two pipes of the same shape, using what appear to be identical materials, and one of them will smoke better than the other. We just don't know what happens to the briarwood as it grows. Obviously, the more hardships the wood survives while growing in the wild, the better the burl. But I can remember when Sixten Ivarsson made two similar pipes from the same piece of briarwood for one customer -- he called the pipes 'twins' -- and the customer later said that one of the pipes smoked so much better than the other. Now the mechanical processes for making both pipes were identical. So why didn't they smoke the same? I have to believe that part of the burl withstood more hardship from nature, while the other part of the burl was shielded and had it easier. The part that had it easier did not smoke as well." [This issue is discussed in greater detail in Chapter 22.]

Bo's reference to Sixten Ivarsson was typical, since Sixten and his son, Lars, were extremely helpful to Bo Nordh when he was getting started. It was Bo's wife, Birgit, who bought him his first unshaped blocks of briarwood and encouraged him to try making pipes. He was naturally very skillful with his hands, and he loved smoking pipes.

"In the early days, I was calling Sixten and Lars five or six times a week with questions about pipe making," he said. "They were always generous with their time, and they were very helpful with their answers." It has been reported that when Sixten first met Bo, and saw his work, he was extremely impressed by his natural abilities as a pipe maker. This is saying a lot, because Sixten Ivarsson has been called the greatest pipe maker of the 20th century, and it is well known that he was not easily impressed. Bo said that his earlier conversations were mostly with Sixten, as he learned the basics. Gradually, however, he spent most of his time on the telephone with Lars, discussing pipe shapes. "Lars is extremely creative, and I was always stimulated with new ideas after our conversations," he said.

Bo said that Sixten called him one day to tell him that a Japanese pipe collector was asking for his pipes. Sixten arranged for the collector to visit Bo at his farm house. Bo said he was panicked because he only had two pipes in his workshop to show the man. So he went around Sweden to all the pipe stores where he had left pipes to be sold on consignment and managed to retrieve a total of 23 of his finished pipes.

"I displayed them on a table outside," Bo said. "The Japanese man said very little. He picked one off the table, held it up to the sunlight, and then set it aside. He did this with another one, then another, and so on until there were only two left. I assumed he was going to buy those two. Instead, he bought 21 of the pipes and left those two! Now remember, at this time in my life I had just spent the past year looking for a job. I could not find work anywhere, and in the meanwhile I had fallen in love with pipe making. Once he bought 21 pipes, I made the decision then and there to become a full-time pipe maker. It was an easy decision at that point. I knew I could make a living at it."

Later, Lars Ivarsson was in Japan and saw Bo's pipes for sale at astronomical prices. "I would sell a pipe to a buyer for $600, and they would sell it in the store for $3,000." Despite the high prices, they were demanding more pipes than Bo could possibly make. The same was true in Germany, Switzerland and other European countries. At that point, Bo started raising his own prices, and now his pipes sell for thousands of dollars -- probably more than any other pipe maker's. As for the estate market, it is almost impossible to find a Bo Nordh pipe. The only one that I know of was a briar calabash that came on the market in Italy last year. The owner of the pipe had died, and his widow sold it for nearly $3,000.

The mouthpieces on Bo Nordh's pipes are extremely comfortable. They are thin, yet have plenty of material so there is no risk of biting through. Bo files the edges of each side of the mouthpiece at the lip area. This was the first thing I noticed when I smoked one of his pipes. I told Bo that I had never seen this before and that I found it more relaxing than any other mouthpiece on any pipe that I had smoked. Was there a secret principle of physics involved? "Not that I know of," he said. "I make them that way because that's the way I like them for myself."

All of the mouthpieces on Bo Nordh pipes are hand cut, and the very expensive vulcanite that he uses is reminiscent of many Dunhill mouthpieces from the 1920s. It is amazing how shiny and black they look when polished. The inside of the mouthpieces of his pipes are always open so there is an easy draw of smoke. If you slide an extra fluffy cleaner through the tenon and out the lip area, it should go through with virtually no resistance. I have rarely had a problem getting an easy draw of smoke from one of his pipes. [When I do, I open them as outlined in Chapter 8.]

The blocks of briar in Bo's workshop are all super high-grade from Corsica and are numbered according to the year in which he acquired it. For instance, I saw a 96, a 92 and an 89, representing 1996, 1992 and 1989. Some of the wood has been stored in his workshop for more than 20 years. "Most of the briarwood that I am using in 1997 was bought before 1992," he said. "I prefer to let the wood dry out for at least 4 or 5 years, and usually longer."

On the day that I visited Bo, the temperature was unusually hot, well over 90 degrees, as Scandinavia was experiencing a totally unprecedented heat wave. We went outside to a garden area and sat around an outdoor table that was shaded by trees. There was a gentle breeze that cooled us down considerably, and there was the smell of freshly harvested corn in the air. "My neighbor cut all the corn in his field yesterday," Bo said, as I looked out at acres and acres of beautiful farmland. It was the perfect setting to just sit back, relax, sip a cool drink and puff slowly and contentedly on our pipes. After about an hour, Birgit joined us. She too smokes Bo Nordh pipes.

Bo said he gets most excited when creating a new shape for a pipe. "That's the most fun part," he said. "That's what really turns me on. The rest of the pipe is work, or more mechanical work. Being creative is what I like best. But the problem is that there are just so many shapes that are possible. There are times when I start thinking that all the really good shapes have already been created."

Bo works in spurts on as many as 25 pipes at a time, frequently until 4:00 in the morning. "There are days when I am getting up just when Bo is going to sleep," Birgit says. Those 25 pipes typically take an entire year of craftsmanship to complete. Every detail imaginable is taken care of, and the completed pipes are in a league of their own. Bo said that at times he loses much of the skin off his thumb -- caused by the constant rubbing and sanding of the wood. "This usually happens when I make a snail," he said, referring to one of his favorite shapes. I have never seen a Bo Nordh snail pipe priced at less than $5,000. "If the outside of my thumb starts to bleed, then I'll wear white gloves as I work," he said. "I guess I'm like those salesmen at Dunhill who wear white gloves when they handle pipes!"

I then asked him in a serious way his opinion of other pipe makers. Bo replied, "I never smoke anyone else's pipes. I only smoke my own, so I don't really have an opinion. Of course, I like Sixten's and Lars' pipes, and I like Jess' pipes, but other than that, I don't have an opinion." I asked if he likes the S. Bang pipes, and he said yes, they are nice looking. "I've met Ulf and Per [the two S. Bang pipe makers] at pipe shows, and I like them very much."

I asked Bo if that is typical, if he talks frequently with other pipe makers, and he said no. "I don't think there is anything I can learn," he said, sounding confident but not conceited, as if he were merely stating a fact. "I do see Jess Chonowitsch more than the others. He has introduced me to pipe collectors like you, and I always enjoy seeing Jess," he said.

By early evening the weather had cooled off and we moved to a different garden where Birgit had set the table for dinner. She had prepared Janson's Temptation, a popular Swedish dish of potatoes and ground up anchovies, onions, and cream -- served like a casserole. It was delicious. We also had fresh blueberries and cream for dessert while Bo told me the story of a recent rock concert in the area featuring Chuck Berry, Little Richard and Jerry Lee Lewis. He said he had a great time, particularly because he likes all kinds of music so much. We listened to rhythm and blues, then jazz, then rock-and-roll oldies and then Johann Sebastian Bach.

When we returned to his workshop after dinner, Bo showed me how he drills full bent pipes differently from other pipe makers. He had cut a full bent pipe in half so that I could see the inside of the air hole. It was amazing, though difficult to describe. At the sharpest point in the bend of the pipe, Bo opens up the air hole a little more than the 4.0 diameter. "That's what insures that the smoke passes easily," he said, not realizing that he was preaching to the choir. [Several years later, when I showed Bo the diagram of how open I like my pipes, which is reprinted in Chapter 8, he laughed and said it reminded him of a Marx Brothers movie when Harpo is smoking out of his hand, using his thumb as the mouthpiece. Jokes notwithstanding, however, Bo follows my specifications if I special order one of his pipes, i.e., he has no philosophical objections to it. He said that if it is what I want, then he has no problem making it that way for me.]

Bo keeps photographs of every pipe that he makes, and there is a large poster on one wall showing some of his most beautiful pipes. One of them he calls a ballerina because it comes to a flat point at the bottom of the bowl, and when the pipe is displayed with the point down, it looks very much like a ballerina standing on her toes. The bird's eye on the front and back is so tight, so dense, so absolutely flawless that it is simply hard to believe. The pipe, which has also been called an "apostrophe," has perfect straight grain on each side. "I only made three of those pipes," he said. "One went to Germany, one to Japan and the third to the United States."

Bo smokes straight Virginia tobacco, and as he loaded one of his favorite old pipes, he talked about breaking in briar. "It takes longer than most people think," he said. "To get a pipe to the point where it is really comfortable, where it smokes so easily and feels so friendly to the pipe smoker, it takes about three cans of tobacco." He said this as he held up a 100 gram tin. I asked him to estimate how many bowls that might represent, obviously in rough terms. He did some mental calculations and then said, "About 50 bowls." He added: "I know that sounds like a lot, and there are smokers who think a pipe is broken in after only a few bowls. But to get a pipe to the point of true comfort, you might need to smoke it 50 times. Of course, some pipes can be broken in faster than other pipes." As Bo said this, I couldn't help but think of the American collector's interest in estate pipes. When we buy an old Barling or Dunhill, say from the 1950s, it is obviously well broken in, and that is certainly one of the main reasons for their attraction.

As we continued smoking and chatting, Birgit joined us and sewed the leather sleeves for the two pipes that I had bought. Bo discussed dozens of pipe-making issues. For instance, he has an unusual process for staining and finishing pipes, which he discovered through years of experimentation. The result is that he avoids varnish, the pores of his briar are open, yet alcohol won't take off the finish. The details of how he accomplishes this are one of the only things that he asked be kept a trade secret.

It is difficult to describe how helpful, open and intelligent Bo Nordh is. In fact, his hospitality was such that I was concerned about not over-staying my welcome. But Bo is an "evening person," and as the day wore on, he became increasingly enthusiastic when discussing all aspects of making pipes. The time was flying, and as the clock approached midnight, we headed back to the hotel.

The Bo Nordh ballerina pipe.

There was a full moon as we drove through the otherwise pitch black Swedish countryside. It is a half hour drive from Bo's farmhouse to Malmö, which is the third largest city in Sweden. He put in a tape of Bach's cello concertos. "I find this music very relaxing." he said. "My mind is always racing, and I need to relax in order to be creative. I love to create shapes for pipes. Even if it is a classical shape, like your apple, I carved that bowl by hand and rounded it in a different way from any other apple pipe ever made."

Bo asked me what I knew about Uptown's Smoke Shop in Nashville, Tennessee. He said that Uptown's representatives were coming to visit him next month in hopes of being able to pick up where Iwan Ries left off 15 years ago by becoming the exclusive retailer to offer Bo Nordh pipes for sale in the United States. I told him that Uptown's has an excellent reputation and that their salesmen have a genuine love of high grade pipes. "When they visit you, they will think they have gone to pipe heaven," I said, speaking from experience.

Bo Nordh at home, with photos of some of his masterpieces.

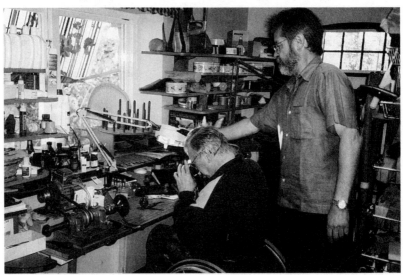

Bo Nordh and Jess Chonowitsch in Bo's workshop at his house near Malmö, Sweden.

Two photos of the same Bo Nordh pipe. I simply cannot imagine
how the grain could be any better.

CHAPTER THIRTEEN

AN ANSWER TO
MR. ROBERT SCHRIRE

This article was written in 2003 in response to a profile of Bo Nordh that had appeared in a newsletter called The Pipe Collector. *Since then, Robert Schrire and I have communicated by e-mail and telephone several times, and we are looking forward to getting together soon. This is one of the primary benefits of pipe collecting -- making friends from all over the world.*

* * * * *

I knew something was up ... Shortly after the December issue of *The Pipe Collector* was published, three different collectors telephoned me, including Fred Janusek, from his home in Green Bay, Wisconsin. There was a distinct hint of panic in his voice.

"This is serious, Rick," Fred said. "A Bo Nordh collector from South Africa has written that Bo's pipes have fills, and if that's the case, Bo's in big trouble as far as the American market is concerned. He would be making 'seconds', and selling them as 'firsts.'" Another collector I heard from, quoted the article as saying that Sixten Ivarsson used "mediocre briar." Still another collector called to say that the author complained that Bo's pipes do not sell well on the Internet.

All of these calls came in before my issue of *The Pipe Collector* had even arrived, so I contacted America's leading Bo Nordh collector, Mark Shropshire, to see what he knew. He had read the article, and was annoyed with the author's prediction that the current high prices for super high grade pipes would not last.

At this point, I still didn't have a copy of the article to look at, so Fred e-mailed it to me, and I was finally able to read some of it, but -- due to computer problems -- not all of it. This is when I decided to telephone Bo, and see if I could find out what was going on.

Wisconsin collectors Fred Heim, left, and Fred Janusek. While concerned when he called me on the phone, Fred Janusek was relieved to hear Bo say that his pipes have "flaws" and not "fills." There is no such thing as a flawless pipe.

Bo said that his friend, Robert Schrire, who lives in Cape Town, South Africa, and has been a collector of his pipes for many years, had told him that he was writing an article about Bo Nordh pipes.

"He is a very intelligent man, a college professor, and I consider him a good friend," said Bo.

"Bo," I blurted out, "with friends like this, who needs enemies?" Remember, I hadn't yet read the entire article.

I mentioned all of this to another collector, Rob Cooper, and asked him if he knew Robert Schrire.

"Yes, I know that he is very interested in Sixten Ivarsson pipes," Rob said.

Now I was scratching my head in wonder; this is a joke, right? I mean, why would a highly intelligent, dedicated collector of pipes by Bo Nordh and Sixten Ivarsson, write that Bo's pipes have fills; that Sixten used mediocre briar; that there is no strong market on the Internet for these pipes; and that we can expect prices to collapse in the future?

Bill Unger, left, and John Tolle of *The Pipe Collector*, based in Columbus, Ohio. They love a good debate in their newsletter!

Still not having read the article in its entirety, and being a hard-headed businessman, I became more than a little suspicious. I started wondering if maybe the author concluded the article by offering ten cents on the dollar for pipes by Bo Nordh and Sixten Ivarsson. After all, what better way to drive down the prices of these highly desirable pipes (enabling one to buy them easily, at very favorable prices) than to spread erroneous information, and make bleak predictions about their future values?

And then, finally, my issue of *The Pipe Collector* arrived in the mail, and I was able to read the article, Bo Nordh: The Wizard of Briar, from beginning to end.

Happily, rather than being disappointed, I was enormously impressed by Mr. Schrire's eloquent tribute to Bo. I agreed with ninety percent of what he wrote, and found his essay to be accurate, informative, interesting, and very supportive of Bo Nordh. I instantly liked Mr. Schrire, and sympathized with his passion for finding the very best pipes in the world.

The other ten percent of the article -- the negative parts that were relayed to me by phone before I could read the essay for myself -- stand in need of correction, or perhaps merely clarification. Personally, it is my belief that many of the problems can be traced to simple gaps in communication. For example, Bo Nordh pipes do *not* have putty fills. However, according to Bo, all pipes have some minor flaws, including his own. But then, a "flaw" to Bo could very well be a bowl that begins as a perfect straight grain, and then spreads into flame grain at the top. The problem here is the difference between the words "fill" and "flaw." Bo speaks of flaws, not fills; Mr. Schrire appears to use the words interchangeably. As Bo said, "When I need a filling, I go to the dentist."

If one had the knowledge, the experience, and the keen eye of a Bo Nordh, a Lars Ivarsson, or a Jess Chonowitsch, one could write an entire volume on the subject of "flaws" in pipes -- including those made by the Ivarssons, Nordh, Chonowitsch, Bang, Dunhill, Charatan, Castello, etc.

The notion that Sixten Ivarsson pipes, "reflect superlative workmanship on mediocre briar," as Mr. Schrire wrote, is not quite accurate. Over six decades, Sixten has made thousands of pipes. These include the high grade pipes made for pipe shops, and individual customers around the world, the pipes made for Pipe Dan, and for Stanwell, and a handful of inexpensive pipes with many flaws, including fills, made for what Lars calls "friends of the workshop." Lars has an exceptionally good memory, and if you want to know more about the briar that Sixten used, the pipe stores that bought his pipes, and the variation in prices, then by all means speak to Lars directly.

Mr. Schrire writes that Bo "was fortunate in having an agent who provided him with the cream of the crop" in terms of the best briar in the world. This is true, but it is also true that Sixten had the same agent. His name was Per Hermann, and he secured the very best Corsican briar for Bo Nordh, for Sixten and Lars Ivarsson, and for Jess Chonowitsch, and S. Bang, until his death in the middle of the past decade.

Dr. George Amrom, left, a high grade collector from Philadelphia, and Per Bilhall of Gothenburg, Sweden, who specializes in selling high grade pipes on the Internet (www.scandpipes.com).

The bottom line is that the vast majority of Sixten Ivarsson pipes were made with the best briar in the world, although some Sixten pipes, especially those made for his "friends of the workshop," and sold very cheaply, were made with only average materials. Mr. Schrire's third objectionable point is that there is only a limited market for high grade pipes on the Internet. "The market is already thin, as is confirmed by the relatively low prices attained by Nordh, Bang, and Ivarsson pipes on eBay, when they can even be sold at all," he writes.

Surely not? Every time I have bid for a high grade pipe on eBay, I've had to drop out because the prices climbed too high. I don't claim to be a computer wiz, but please, Mr. Schrire, telephone me, or send me an e-mail, whenever you see Bo Nordh pipes on eBay that nobody wants, and the owner is concerned about whether "they can even be sold at all." I have yet to see anything that is even close to the situation you describe.

As for predicting future prices, who knows? Mr. Schrire may be right in saying that they will decline, and then again, he may be wrong. We do know for certain that prices have climbed sharply in recent years, and I vividly remember five years ago, when many people were predicting that the high prices would soon collapse. It never happened—in fact, they've just kept right on climbing. But since neither of us knows for certain where the market is headed, why offer pessimistic predictions for the future? Such gloomy prophecies can unintentionally imperil the livelihood of these pipe makers.

When it comes to Jess Chonowitsch, Bo Nordh, S. Bang and Lars Ivarsson, the reality is that they are at the peak of their careers, and the pipes they make today will be incredibly valuable, and difficult to find, ten or twenty years from now. Because I firmly believe these to be the facts, my own, personal prediction is that the prices will continue to rise.

It is no accident that all of them have been making pipes for thirty-five to forty years, and have been considered among the best makers in the world, almost from the time that they started work. Nearly all of their customers are repeat customers, and some have been buying their pipes for decades. Every few years or so, there have been rumors that their prices will soon fall. In most cases, pipe sellers who are unable to acquire and keep any inventory of these high grade pipes spread these rumors to justify their lack of stock. The rumors always die down eventually, and they have yet to put a damper on the popularity of these great pipes.

Meeting with Bo at a restaurant in Malmö, Sweden.

One of the reasons that the prices of these pipes keep climbing, is that it is becoming increasingly difficult to find the very best briar. Mr. Schrire is correct in pointing out that Bo may use only one block of briar out of an entire bag, and then discard the remaining wood. When Bo, Lars, Jess, Ulf and Per stop making pipes, it will become nearly impossible to find their high grades, and if you think they are expensive today, wait until they are no longer available. In my opinion, they will then quickly appreciate from very expensive pipes, to the category of works of art, safely out of reach of all but a handful of collectors.

There is just one final point in the Bo Nordh essay that requires some clarification, and that concerns the noted maker, Jess Chonowitsch. The author gives the equivocal impression that it would be a relatively simple matter to assemble a collection of Jess' pipes. "Indeed," he writes, "one European retailer is presently selling about 40 of his pipes." This is quite correct, but Mr. Schrire failed to mention that the "one European retailer" in question is the only one in all of Europe who is in a position to do this. His name is René Wagner, and his shop is Tabak-Lädeli, of Zurich, Switzerland. René and Jess have been close personal friends for many years (Jess was best man at René's wedding), and René has the exclusive license to sell Jess Chonowitsch pipes in Europe. René once told me that his goal is to have one hundred Jess Chonowitsch pipes in his shop at all times, but the demand is so great, and the supply so limited, that it is difficult for him to keep even half of that amount, at any one time.

René Wagner in front of his store, Tabak-Lädeli, in Zurich, Switzerland (www.wagner-tabak-laedeli.com).

Many, many European pipe shops desperately want Jess Chonowitsch pipes but cannot get them. Whenever I speak with Peter Heinrichs in Cologne, he always asks, "When can you get me some Jess Chonowitsch pipes?" The same is true of the owners of Ostermann Pipes in Vienna, and also in America, where Iwan Ries, Gus' Smoke Shop, Liberty Tobacco, and many others have asked me numerous times if I can get them some pipes by Jess Chonowitsch, and I have always had to say no. Uptown's, his distributor in the United States, is lucky to have an inventory of three or four at any one time. When they get a dozen, they sell a dozen.

Since up to this point I have focused primarily on those areas where Mr. Schrire and I differ, I should now like to review the remaining ninety percent of his essay, which I found to be absolutely terrific. We are obviously in complete agreement, as to who our personal favorites are in the world of pipes. As he writes, "the top carvers [are] Nordh, Lars Ivarsson, Chonowitsch, and Bang." I also admire the fact that Mr. Schrire visits Bo Nordh, asks questions, and is genuinely interested in learning more about the very best pipes he can find, and acquiring them.

Mr. Schrire has a gentle approach and truly understands what makes Bo Nordh pipes so special. He obviously holds Bo in great esteem, and overall, his essay is a very touching tribute. I was particularly impressed by his description of what makes the Bo Nordh calabash so extraordinary. In fact, his description of Bo's calabash was as breathtaking and unusual as the pipe is:

"Bo's attention to detail is remarkable. Take his calabash pipe, which is the most labour intensive of all his shapes. Bo works with briar for the basic structure, vulcanite for the mouthpiece, and briar and either ivory or boxwood for the cup -- four separate components. When the pipe is assembled, Bo must anticipate the influence of weather, temperature and humidity and design the pipe so that all four elements fit together properly for many years. In addition, he has designed a ridge within the bowl to ensure that, when the pipe is placed on its side, the liquids do not spill into the cup. Remarkable!"

I'd like to conclude by commenting on the fact that the pipe world really is becoming a smaller place. I found the international background to this discussion to be almost intoxicating. Picture this: A man in Cape Town, South Africa travels to Malmö, Sweden, writes an essay for a publication in Columbus, Ohio, that gets the goat of a collector in Green Bay, Wisconsin, who then tells a collector in Los Angeles, California, who makes calls to Sweden and Demark to verify certain information, and then writes a response that is certain to spark a debate that will travel once again around the world. That is fantastic!

Lively debates like this are so much fun for me. They are one of the main reasons I am so passionate about pipe collecting, and I can't wait to meet Mr. Robert Schrire in person. I know we will get along and have much more in common than is reflected in this letter. In the meantime, if any of you want to sell your pipes made by Sixten Ivarsson, or Bo Nordh, please remember that I'm the one to call. For anyone in the States, a call to Los Angeles costs a lot less than a call to Cape Town!

CHAPTER FOURTEEN

COLORING YOUR MEERSCHAUM PIPE EASILY

This is a short article I wrote for Pipes and tobaccos *in 2003. I own four meerschaum pipes, and I rarely smoke them any more primarily because I prefer the taste of tobacco in a briar pipe. But every so often, meerschaum pipes provide a nice change of pace. Over the years, I have smoked many meerschaums, and it was not until recently that I figured out how to color my meerschaum bowls.*

* * * * *

After struggling unsuccessfully for 20 years to color meerschaum pipes, I have finally figured out how to do it.

There is a three-step process, and I absolutely guarantee that you will be able to turn your white meerschaum bowls into a golden brown color, like an evenly roasted marshmallow, or, if you prefer something darker, into a reddish black color similar to a bing cherry.

Let's look at each step, one at a time.

STEP 1: Smoke the pipe. Some people prefer meerschaum to briar while other pipe smokers use meerschaum for a change of pace. Either way, the whole point is to enjoy smoking your meerschaum pipes.

STEP 2: Blow smoke on your pipe. Remember when you bought your first meerschaum and your tobacconist told you the bowl would gradually turn brown as you smoked it? What he failed to mention was that it might take 30 years of daily smoking for the pipe to color deeply.

In *The Ultimate Pipe Video*, Rick Hacker drops his meerschaum pipe into a wide-mouthed jar, blows smoke into the jar, and then tightens the lid. That's really all there is to Step 2, although I would recommend placing a small pipe stand inside the jar or figuring out some other way to prevent the meerschaum from directly touching the jar.

One way would be to place a paper towel on the bottom of the jar, and then put the pipe bowl on the paper towel. You can rotate the bowl to a different position each day, using a clean paper towel each day, so that one day you are blowing smoke to the pipe's left side, another day to the right side, then to the bottom, front and top on successive days -- so the pipe will color evenly.

Believe it or not, this meerschaum pipe was white when I first started smoking it many years ago.

Tony Rodriguez, my pipe maker friend, bought an ordinary plastic jar and drilled some wooden pegs into the side and in the jar's bottom -- so that a meerschaum bowl can be rotated on a regular basis.

The inside of the jar will turn very dark over time, but this is easily cleaned out with SOS or even with a wet cloth.

STEP 3: Melt beeswax into the meerschaum. We have Beth Sermet of SMS Meerschaum to thank for this step. Beth uses a powerful hair dryer, but I prefer a hot air gun because it is much faster.

Place clear beeswax in a container such as an empty tobacco tin, then blast hot air from the gun or hair dryer to melt the beeswax until it is mostly liquid.

Dip a Q-Tip into the melted wax and rub it on the meerschaum bowl. Do this again and again until the entire bowl is covered in beeswax, using as many Q-Tips as necessary. You might have to re-melt the wax several times because it hardens quickly.

Your pipe will look like it is coated in vanilla frosting after the melted wax hardens. Don't worry if some of the cotton from the Q-Tips spreads onto the pipe.

Then, hold the pipe by the mouthpiece over a waste basket and blast the bowl with your hot air gun, watching the wax drip off the bowl. Wipe off the bowl with a clean paper towel.

You will be amazed at how brown the bowl turns as the melted wax drips off. Unfortunately, the bowl will lighten in color after it cools off. But that's all right -- because you are seeing what your pipe will look like in the future.

All of these steps have been common knowledge for years. My only contribution was to use all three in combination -- using Step 1 or Step 2 every day and Step 3 once a month.

This system is all natural, and it works every time.

CHAPTER FIFTEEN

~~~~~

PAUL PERRI: QUIET DIGNITY

The American pipe maker Paul Perri is a true gentleman whose pipes are reasonably priced but not so easy to find, so if you're lucky enough to come across one, I strongly recommend that you try it. Pipe Friendly *published a special edition that was largely a tribute to Paul in 2001, and this chapter was my contribution.*

* * * * *

Paul Perri and his wife, Margaret, are two of the nicest, most decent people you could ever meet. I remember first running into them about a decade ago, when they were sitting behind several tables filled with Paul's beautiful pipes at a Los Angeles hotel convention hall during a West Coast Pipe Expo. Marty Pulvers was buying a dozen or so for Sherlock's Haven, his tobacco store in San Francisco.

"So you like these pipes?" I asked.

"You bet," Marty said. "I consider Paul one of the best American pipe makers, and my customers do too. You can only get his pipes at these shows, and whatever I buy here, I sell to my customers almost immediately."

Over the years, Paul never did change his policy for selling his pipes. He limited his offerings to West Coast pipe shows. He also limited his production to something like 200 pipes per year. Consequently, very few collectors own his pipes, and many have never even heard the name Paul Perri. Too bad -- because his pipes are superb. He has many creative designs, and the pipes smoke exceptionally well.

After that first meeting, I spent many hours talking with Paul and Margaret in the 1990s during the meetings of the Los Angeles pipe club. I was always impressed by Paul's quiet dignity. At that time he was in his late 70s. Perhaps because of his generation, or because of his personality, Paul always wore a coat and tie to our meetings. He would arrive early, lay out about 20 pipes that he had made during the previous month, sell every one of them, and then regale us with tales about his past. He is soft-spoken and a naturally quiet man, so we had to coax the stories out of him.

Paul's grandfather and father were both pipe makers, and they used briar from their ancestral home in Calabria, Italy. "Calabrian briar is the toughest and, in my opinion, the best briar there is for pipe making," Paul said many times. He said that he made his first pipe when he was 12, growing up in New York City.

During the Great Depression of the 1930s, Paul helped his father set up cigar and candy stores in New York. Paul's father, who was also a pipe maker, loved his pipes so much that he insisted before his death that his entire collection of 1,500 pipes be buried with him. "My father felt strongly that things taken from nature should be returned to nature," Paul said. "Since briar comes from the earth, he wanted it returned to the earth."

When Paul and Margaret moved to Los Angeles and opened their pipe store, Paul imported enough briar from Italy and Greece to supply dozens of well known American pipe makers as well as for his own pipe making. As Paul's pipes became known among West Coast pipe smokers, their sales continued to climb without any advertisements or distribution. Their popularity is solely the result of word-of-mouth recommendations from satisfied customers. One of the most enthusiastic is Gordon Soladar, a Los Angeles attorney who has collected several thousand pipes during the past four decades. What is particularly noteworthy about Gordon's opinion is that he is a truly knowledgeable collector with Dunhill DRs, Charatan Supremes, Ser Jacopo gemlines, and hundreds of other super high grade pipes. Gordon also worked for a pipe maker when he was in law school -- Jack Henry Weinberger, another outstanding American pipe maker who used "JHW" as the brand name on his pipes.

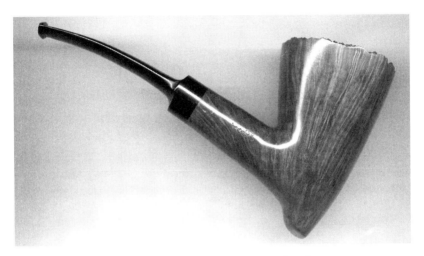

Two beautiful Perri straight grain pipes.

"I like many different pipes," Gordon said. "But my all-time favorites are Paul Perri pipes. Those are the ones I smoke the most. They are the best."

That's high praise from an expert collector. But it is not unusual. I know many other knowledgeable collectors who have made similar comments, including Joel Farr, the editor and publisher of *Pipe Friendly*.

As for my own experience, I have about 20 Paul Perri pipes, and I enjoy them all. There are four that I smoke most frequently because they are just right: light in weight, comfortable and nicely designed. One of them is a perfect straight grain that my wife gave me for Christmas several years ago after calling Paul to order it. Another is a beautiful pipe that Lars Ivarsson, at my request, modified slightly. Lars is the famous Danish pipe maker who is one of the best of all time. The original pipe had a plateau top and I wanted to see it rounded. Using nothing more that a sharp knife, Lars rounded most of the top but deliberately left just a slight amount of rough area. The pipe looks beautiful and smokes incredibly easily. It also has a huge bowl capacity yet hardly weighs anything at all.

In case you're wondering why Lars would do that, you should know that he emphatically did not want to change Paul's pipe but was persuaded to do so by Dayton Matlick, Jim Benjamin and me. We were all in Jim's famous pipe-cleaning workshop and Dayton was gathering information about Lars and Jim for future stories in *Pipes and tobaccos* magazine. After Lars rounded the top, Tony Rodriguez made a new mouthpiece and re-stained the pipe a bruyere type of color. I subsequently showed the pipe to Paul Perri, and he thought it was beautiful. He said he had no objections to my having the pipe modified -- as long as I enjoyed it!

Paul's attitude was refreshing. It was also consistent with my own philosophy. I believe strongly that your pipes should fit you and not vice versa. If you like most of the features of a pipe, but you want to modify it, by all means do so. At one of our L.A. pipe meetings, I remember once asking Paul if he could thin out a few mouthpieces on pipes that I had bought from him, and he suggested finding someone else to do it or having new mouthpieces made. Please don't misunderstand -- he was not in any way rude nor did he give me the brush off. His tone was more, "Rick, I do everything by hand and therefore have only a limited amount of time for making pipes each month. I'd much rather make you a new pipe than make you a new mouthpiece. You're better off getting someone else to make you a new mouthpiece."

Paul Perri (left) seated next to Brian McNulty of Anima Pipes. Both are excellent American pipe makers.

Paul and I also had a number of conversations as to how open a pipe should be. Paul had a chart showing what each of the major pipe factories did, and if my memory is correct, I believe the openings varied with the length of the shank. I told him that I prefer at least 4.3 millimeters, or 11/64 inches, for all of my pipes, and we agreed to disagree on the subject. When I told him that I opened the smoke hole on all of his pipes that I own, he said that was fine, as long as I enjoyed them.

In addition to his free style and classical pipes, Paul Perri is known for making pipes that are totally unusual. I have a Perri canadian that is almost nine inches long -- a seven inch bowl and shank (all one piece of wood) plus a two inch vulcanite mouthpiece. I also own a Perri pipe that is the size of a large grapefruit. Gary Humphrey from Alaska has offered me a lot of money for that pipe, since Gary likes enormous pipes, but I'm just not ready to sell it.

Paul's pipes sell at moderate prices -- between $100 and $400, with the majority being in the $150 range. Paul has slowed down in his pipe making in recent years, though he still produces some beautiful pipes. He and Margaret have "retired" in Hawaii, so if you want to buy a Perri pipe, I'd recommend getting what you can now because it is becoming increasingly difficult to find them.

To me, one of the things that enhances enjoying a pipe is to know the pipe maker and his philosophy, work habits, attitudes and general approach to our hobby. This is one of the reasons I like Jess Chonowitsch pipes so much -- because Jess is so knowledgeable about pipe making. Spend five minutes listening to him and you realize there isn't anyone who knows more about making pipes than Jess. In the same way, Paul Perri is extremely knowledgeable about pipes, how they are made, the history of pipe making, and how each collector has different needs and desires. Paul's knowledge of pipe history, and his quiet dignity, come through loud and clear in personal conversations, just as his unique pipe making skills, and vast experience -- 70 years of pipe making -- come through loud and clear whenever you smoke a pipe made by Paul Perri.

CHAPTER SIXTEEN

~~~~~

PETERSON PIPES

While my emphasis has been on individually hand-made pipes, I have a soft spot for Peterson pipes mainly because they were my favorites for a number of years when I first began smoking a pipe. I found it fascinating to spend a day at the Peterson factory in 1998.

A few years after this article was published in Pipe Friendly, *Tom Palmer visited Gus's Smoke Shop in suburban Los Angeles and conducted an informal seminar. During a short break, Tom and I were standing on the sidewalk outside the store, chatting and soaking up the sun and fresh air, when a young man approached us to say, "Petersons are the best pipes in the world! I won't smoke anything else!" With that, he lifted one of his pant legs to show that he had had the Peterson logo tattooed on his calf! Now that's what I call dedication to a pipe brand.*

* * * * *

Tom Palmer was an accountant who worked as a corporate executive for years but always yearned to own his own business. Now he does. Six years ago, Tom bought the Peterson pipe company in Ireland, and it is hardly surprising that he has never been happier and that Peterson pipes are going stronger than ever.

I visited Tom this summer at his office outside Dublin, in Sallynoggin, and toured the Peterson factory. "Come back next year, and tell the American pipe smokers to come visit us then," he said. "We will have a complete museum open at that time.

Whenever an enthusiastic collector tours the factory, he always feels closer to the pipe." As for the museum, it promises to be fascinating. A relative of Charles Peterson, who invented the unique "system pipes," has donated to the company all kinds of historical treasures, including Peterson's personal pipes, passport, birth certificate and other personal effects.

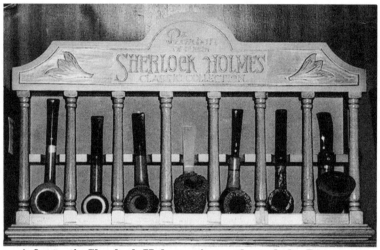

A fantastic Sherlock Holmes pipe rack made by Peterson.

When I arrived at the Peterson building, the glass doors in front were locked. I peered through and saw no one, so I rang the bell. Tom's assistant, Angela Fortune, greeted me warmly and showed me to a waiting room filled with Peterson pipe memorabilia. Tom arrived in a minute or so and we passed several executive offices before entering his, which was spacious, friendly and smelled of pipe and cigar smoke -- aromas that I'll always love. In fact, if I might diverge just for a second, I am like many other pipe smokers in that we very often judge pipe stores by their aromas. I'm serious. I love dropping by the Tinder Box in Santa Monica because nearly everyone behind the counter will be smoking a pipe or cigar. When I bought my first pipe, at Fader's Tobacconist in Baltimore in the 1970s, I remember clearly that everyone in the store was smoking a pipe. Nowadays, too many pipe stores have the feel of clothing stores or gift shops where we're reluctant to light up for fear of offending the sales clerks.

At any rate, Tom has some beautiful Peterson pipes and cigars in his office, and he obviously enjoys smoking them. The aroma was from one of Peterson's superb pipe tobaccos, and as I said, it smelled fantastic. Tom introduced me to Joe Kenny, Peterson's factory manager. Joe and I walked past the business offices to a door that led to a large, busy, and productive pipe factory -- just what you'd expect! Peterson has a total of 48 employees, and a good number of them were there -- grading bowls, fitting mouthpieces, staining the wood, hand-cutting silver bands, and polishing the finished pipes, among other things. Each employee has an area of specialty and spends his time on that area.

For instance, Tony Whelan is the Bowl Department Manager. He has been with Peterson since 1952, so you can imagine how knowledgeable he is when it comes to evaluating the grain on a pipe bowl. Tony said that Peterson uses briar from the coast of Morocco, which is of course next to Algeria. I mention Algeria because many collectors place a premium on Algerian briar. "We've seen some of the most beautiful pieces in recent times," he said. "Our pipes in 1998 and for 1999 are just absolutely superb. It's really been a very good year for Peterson in terms of the quality of briar."

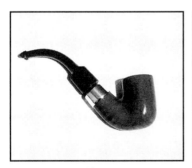 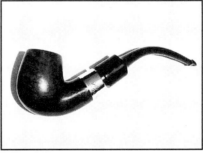

Two beautiful old Peterson system pipes. The hallmark on the silver bands shows the pipe on the left was made in the 1930s, and the one on the right in the 1920s.

It is understandable if you thought I made a mistake with the 1952 date, but it's true. Tony has been with Peterson for 47 years, and his career pattern is typical of the longevity and loyalty of the employees. "I've been here 22 years, and I'm the baby in the place," Joe Kenny said.

Peterson pipes are stamped "Made in the Republic of Ireland." Occasionally, you might find an older Peterson with the stamp, "Made in Ireland." Tony explained that those pipes were made prior to 1949. "Ireland changed its status from a free state and became a Republic in 1949, and that's the year we started using the stamp, 'Made in the Republic of Ireland.'" he said. "It's also the year we stopped using the 'Made in Ireland' stamp. If you find a pipe with the latter stamp, then you know for sure that it was made prior to 1949." [Since our conversation, Peterson has come out with a line of commemorative pipes, which are made now but have the old "Made in Ireland" stamp.]

David Blake is the silversmith in the factory, and he fits each band, cap and silver and gold spigot by hand. Peterson is known for its exceptionally beautiful silver and gold bands.

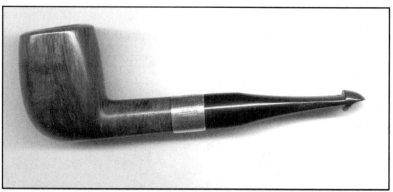

A silver-banded Peterson "Made in Ireland" in the 1920s.

When Tom bought the Peterson company, he not only acquired the factory but also the Peterson pipe store, which is located in downtown Dublin. The store is on Grafton Street and is very close to the world famous Trinity College. If you visit

Dublin, I strongly recommend that you drop by the store. You'll see a fantastic assortment of Peterson pipes with a wide range of prices and designs.

That's one of the advantages of Peterson pipes. You can get a real bargain for a small amount of money, or you can spend a lot of money and buy an absolute masterpiece that is among the very best pipes in the world today. The company's owner, Tom Palmer, is totally committed to Peterson's continued success. "We have a wonderful tradition and an incredibly rich history behind us," he said. "We have many long-time employees who are extremely competent and committed to their jobs, to making great pipes, and the future looks very bright indeed. If you were to visit tobacconists in Eastern Europe, you'd be amazed at their sophistication and popularity. Also, the sudden boom in pipe collecting in America is quite unexpected and very exciting. We see a tremendous future ahead. Our goal is to continue making the highest quality Peterson pipes, which clearly are among the best smoking pipes, and most beautiful pipes, in the world."

CHAPTER SEVENTEEN

~~~~~

TOO MANY PIPES? NEVER!

This chapter, which appeared as an article in 1998 in Pipe Friendly, *comments on the fact that at the time there were four pipe publications coming out simultaneously. Regrettably, two of those magazines --* Pipe Friendly *and* Pipesmoke, *have since ceased publication.*

I wrote this essay primarily in response to an editorial that Alan Schwartz had written for Pipesmoke *criticizing my advocacy of the very expensive high grade pipes. The irony is that, since then, Alan and I have become good friends. The same is true of Rich Esserman, who is also mentioned in this chapter, and of Jim Cooke, another one of my critics years ago. I'll say it again: one of the beauties of this hobby is that we can disagree strongly on certain issues and still remain good friends.*

As for limiting my pipe purchases, I am not sure how many new pipes I have bought since I wrote this article, or how many more I will buy in the future, but if I had to guess, I'd say it is a safe bet that you can count me as a member of the "Around 200 Club."

* * * * *

Do you own enough pipes? Of course not. In fact, most pipe collectors are like the late J. Paul Getty, who was once asked, "How much money is enough?" and who answered: "Just a little bit more." It doesn't matter if a collector owns 20 pipes or 2,000 pipes. He always wants to try a new shape, or a pipe with a different grain pattern, or a pipe from a particular era, or a pipe from a new tobacconist. Alas, any one of a hundred different reasons for adding to his collection will suffice.

When I first discussed this article with Joel Farr, editor and publisher of *Pipe Friendly*, I proposed talking about the disadvantage of having too many pipes. I said that if you have too many, you run the risk of never getting to know any of them. Joel agreed wholeheartedly, but he couldn't stop laughing. He said that many times he had vowed to quit buying pipes, but then some temptation would come along and his resolve would wither away. He was speaking for the majority of pipe collectors. Nearly all of us have had that same experience.

We really are talking about a serious issue, for if you have too many pipes, it is difficult to get to know each one. And it is amazing that each pipe has a personality of its own. By "personality," I mean that our reaction to the unique aspects of each pipe is highly personal.

Now I realize that I've gotten into trouble lately with pipe experts because I have expressed my highly personal opinions about my pipes, and I certainly didn't mean to offend. Anyone who smokes a pipe in this era of Prohibition is my friend and ally.

But I do find it a little disconcerting that every time I pick up a new pipe publication, I find myself under attack. For instance, in *Pipes and tobaccos*, pipemakers Jim Cooke and Ed Burak disagreed with my opinion about how open a pipe should be. Fair enough. We have an honest disagreement, and they can enjoy their pipes their way while I enjoy mine my way. But the fact that I insist that each pipe I smoke be opened to a precise millimeter argues against having too many pipes. It takes a lot of time and effort to get a pipe just right for me, and once it is exactly the way I like it, then I want to enjoy it over and over.

Just when I thought that controversy had passed, I picked up the latest issue of *The Pipe Smoker's Ephemeris* and discovered that I was involved in a new disagreement. This one was with Rich Esserman, whom I like and respect as a knowledgeable collector. It seems that Rich was appalled by the fact that I would buy an expensive pipe, such as an Upshall XX or Savinelli Autograph 000, and then persuade Jess Chonowitsch to re-drill the pipes and make new mouthpieces. Or I might buy a Dunhill Root Briar from 1967 that has spectacular grain but a thick, clunky mouthpiece -- so of course I would ask Jim Cooke or Tony Rodriguez to make a 1937-type of super comfortable, thin and somewhat more narrow mouthpiece. I have always been more impressed by how a pipe looks and smokes than I have been by the name or brand on the pipe, which I discuss in greater detail in Chapter 22.

Rich says that my pipes are no longer manufactured; they are "remanufactured." I think Rich makes a good point on behalf of the experienced collector, and if you agree with him, you should stick to your guns and preserve your pipes without changing them. As for me, however, I really don't care if they are manufactured or remanufactured, as long as they smoke well. The goal is to have them smoke better -- to suit my taste. That's why I have them altered. The pipes that I have altered are pipes that I like the looks of, and the feel of, but pipes that just don't smoke as well as they should -- for me.

I compare it to having a suit altered. I buy my suits off the rack and then have them tailored to fit me. And that's precisely what I do with pipes. I do this because I'm a pipe smoker more than a pipe collector. I only collect them to smoke them. But if you have too many pipes, there is no way to alter each one to fit your needs and personality. It would be too time-consuming, too costly and too frustrating -- because you would be so busy smoking and altering different pipes you would never get the chance to know each one.

In that same article in the *Ephemeris*, Rich addresses the issue of the optimum number of pipes for a collector to own. "I have noticed that those who collect and *smoke* high-grades generally have fewer pipes -- 15 to 100." That would be ideal, but my impression is that many collectors are as fanatical as I am. They just keep adding and adding to their collection. I have been thinking of forming the "Around 200 Club" in honor of the dozens of collectors I know who own hundreds, and in some cases thousands, of pipes. When asked how many pipes they own, invariably they will respond, "around 200," even if the honest answer is 2,000.

As I see it, there are two problems with paring down one's collection. First, we want to buy new pipes. By "new," I am including estate as well as unsmoked pipes. Second, we don't want to let go of any of our old pipes. How many times have you sold or traded a pipe, and then months or even years later wished you could enjoy it again? I think we've all had that experience.

The only feasible solution that I have come across has been to upgrade my collection to pipes made by Jess Chonowitsch and S. Bang. After they are opened to my specifications, these pipes smoke so much better than most of the others in my collection that I am naturally drawn to them and thus don't feel quite the same withdrawal symptoms that I might otherwise feel in trading or selling one of the old pipes from my collection. But I'm suddenly on very dangerous ground here in advocating this type of upgrade. I say that because I found myself assailed in the Spring issue of *Pipesmoke*, which is the insert to *Smoke* magazine.

Now I want to applaud any publication that encourages pipe collecting and moderate pipe smoking, but this magazine's editorial director, Alan Schwartz, devoted his entire editorial to attacking me without naming me. He told a friend that he anticipated getting me riled up but also that he hoped to spark a debate in the pipe-collecting community. If you read his editorial, it is obvious that he is attacking an article that I wrote for *Pipes and tobaccos* called "The Perfect Pipe". Alan believes that I am an elitist because I like pipes that are made by Jess Chonowitsch, Bo Nordh, S. Bang and Sixten and Lars Ivarsson. Alan refers to my article as advocating "a pernicious idea." I looked up "pernicious" and my dictionary said, "highly injurious or destructive: tending to a fatal issue: deadly." All because I like certain pipes that happen to be expensive? Alan, please, come to a pipe show and join in the fun of collecting.

And while you're at it, bring some of your old pipe tobacco to give away. I say this because Alan Schwartz is the "expert" who wrote in an earlier editorial that pipe tobacco has a shelf life of two years and is totally worthless after six years. As Gordon Soladar, a very knowledgeable collector, put it during the banquet dinner at the West Coast Pipe and Cigar Expo: "If he wants to throw out his old tobacco, tell him to throw it out my way!"

The essence of Alan Schwartz's complaint was that he believed I was saying that "if you don't have it, you don't count." For the record: I was not saying that. I don't believe that. I have never believed that. I can't stand people who put on airs like that.

Alan and Joan Schwartz -- we can disagree and still be good friends.

In fact, the more that I think about it, the more I realize that Alan and I are in agreement. We both abhor pretension in pipe collecting. I'll never forget an experience that I had in the late 1970s at the Dunhill store in Beverly Hills. I was asking the salesman questions about Dunhill pipes, and he was extremely snooty. In those days, you could smoke anywhere in the store without having to enter a private smoking lounge. As we talked, I pulled out my pipe and started to light it. The salesman looked aghast. "It that a Peterson?!" he asked, with incredulity in his voice. "Yes," I replied. "They're my favorite," which was true at the time. "Well if you're into Peterson, you really don't belong at Dunhill," he said. I agreed -- and didn't go back to that store for more than a decade.

But that unpleasant experience was extremely unusual, and I have been to many Dunhill stores over the years and consistently been impressed by their high level of customer service. Normally, people in the pipe business are friendly, knowledgeable and, most important, non-dogmatic. I collect and smoke pipes because they give me an unlimited source of satisfaction. I am enthusiastic about the hobby. I love to meet fellow pipe smokers and couldn't care less if they smoke $15 pipes or $1,500 pipes. In fact, I smoke both myself.

But that doesn't mean that they are of equal quality. I get excited about Bo Nordh pipes because they smoke so well and are so beautiful -- and for no other reasons.

Of course, there are exceptions. I have a $40 pipe that smokes better than one of my Bo Nordh pipes. But that is a fluke. Statistically, nearly all of Bo Nordh's pipes are fantastic smokers, but you might have to go through a thousand of the $40 pipes to find one as good as the one that I have.

Contrary to the portrait painted in *Pipesmoke*, I do not have a Piaget watch, or a Rolls Royce, or a Mont Blanc pen. In fact, I am hand-writing this article with a Paper Mate felt-tipped pen. I don't own those other luxury products because any extra savings that I have go toward the purchase of pipes -- not cigars or watches or cars or fountain pens.

If Alan and I were standing in a pipe shop having a conversation, here is what I would say: of course, you can get a good night's sleep at a Motel 6, but your odds of being more comfortable are enhanced immeasurably if you stay at the Ritz. You can get a tasty, filling meal at a fast food restaurant, but you are more likely to enjoy the experience if you dine at a 5-star restaurant.

Still … many more people prefer rap music to Beethoven. They prefer tabloid television to Shakespeare. We are talking about matters of taste and personal opinion, and what I offer in my pipe articles is nothing more (or less) than my personal opinion. I am not saying that I am right and you are wrong. It's not a question of right or wrong. It's a question of which pipe makers I like best. Period.

How's this for a straight grain on a Jess Chonowitsch billiard?

Having said this much, however, I want to stress what I view as the positive contributions that Alan Schwartz and *Pipesmoke* magazine are making to the hobby. The same is true for Dayton Matlick and Chuck Stanion at *Pipes and tobaccos*, Joel Farr at *Pipe Friendly* and the legendary Tom Dunn at the *Ephemeris*. It's remarkable that we have so many interesting publications coming out at the same time, and it is no doubt an historic first. As enthusiasts of the hobby, we really are fortunate to see the results of so many dedicated individuals, and as I said, I certainly include Alan Schwartz in that group. He may have created a straw man in his editorial who was easy to knock down, but I admire his spunk in wanting to spark a debate over some of these issues.

I also want to point out that, in addition to the high grade Danish pipes that I mentioned, there are plenty of other pipes that I absolutely love. I once wrote an article called "The Best Bargain Imaginable" [see Chapter 4] about old pipes that can be purchased for less than $50 each, and then sent to Jim Benjamin for a thorough cleaning, and that come back like new. Many have old

Algerian briar, soft-rubber mouthpieces, and were made by expert craftsmen from another era. While it is difficult to find that kind of workmanship today, you still can find it if you look hard enough.

In America alone, there are some terrific pipe makers who don't require that you mortgage your house to get an enjoyable smoke. They include Sam Learned, Rich Lewis, Tim West, Mark Tinsky, Paul Bonaquisti, Brian McNulty, Steve Anderson, John Eells, Trever Talbert, Larry Roush, Ed Jurkiewicz, Jody Davis, and dozens of others.

At this point, I could start praising pipe brands that I like as well, including Dunhill, Charatan, Upshall, Comoy, Sasieni, Barling, Ashton, Peterson, Ser Jacopo, Castello, and on and on. But that's the problem. How do we keep our collections small so that we can savor each individual pipe that we own, yet continue to experiment with different pipe makers? The truth is, I don't have the faintest idea. And I have been singularly unsuccessful in my determination to pare down my collection.

The only real consolation is to consider what I would spend the money on if I weren't buying pipes. J.M. Barrie, in his brilliant book, *My Lady Nicotine*, sarcastically chronicles a few of the gems in home furnishings he was able to acquire after his wife made him quit smoking:

"Once a man marries, his eyes are opened to many things that he was quite unaware of previously, among them being the delight of adding an article of furniture to the drawing-room every month and having a bedroom in pink and gold, the door of which is always kept locked. If men would only consider that every cigar they smoke would buy part of a new piano stool in terra-cotta plush, and that for every pound tin of tobacco purchased away goes a vase for growing dead geraniums in, they would surely hesitate."

Yes, of course they would.

How can you have too many pipes?

Too many pipes? Never!

CHAPTER EIGHTEEN

~~~~~

BERTRAM: THE NATION'S PIPE MAKER

This article appeared in The Pipe Smoker's Ephemeris *in 2002. Subsequently, several different collectors have called me to say they have picked up some Bertram pipes as a result of the story, and they seemed to be pleased. They really can offer a good bargain.*

* * * * *

There is a wonderful irony in the fact that some of the best pipe shops in America are located in Washington, D.C. and its surrounding areas. They are all in close proximity to the legislative chambers and bureaucratic office buildings in the nation's capital where politicians are climbing on top of each other to see who can sound the most hostile toward anything to do with tobacco, except, of course, for spending the tax revenue that it generates.

The city also has a rich tradition of terrific pipe stores dating back to more than a century ago. One of the most interesting was Bertram's, which was open from the 1870s until the late 1960s, when the store was gutted during the riots and fires following the assassination of Dr. Martin Luther King Jr.

But during the nearly 100 years of its existence, Bertram was known around the world primarily because of the outstanding pipes that were stamped "Bertram Washington, D.C." The company became known as "The Nation's Pipe Maker."

PIPES BY SYDNEY
ARE THE CHOICE OF
THE DISCRIMINATING
SMOKER

BERTRAM "Master Craftsman"

The patronage of Presidents, Ambassadors, Senators, Congressmen, famous writers, musicians, artists, actors . . . attest to the preeminence of BERTRAM'S craftsmanship. To his unique shop in Washington, D. C., come notables from the four corners of the earth . . . and men less prominent in the world's affairs, but all kindred spirits in their search for the Perfect Pipe Smoke.

In addition to turning pipes, BERTRAM maintains a completely equipped factory repair department. No matter how badly your pipe, cigar or cigarette holder is broken, if you will send us the pieces we will gladly quote you the price of its repair by return mail.

BERTRAM assures complete satisfaction on all repairs. Remember, no pipe is beyond repair.

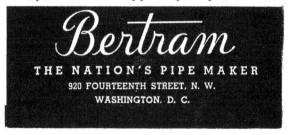

Bertram

THE NATION'S PIPE MAKER
920 FOURTEENTH STREET, N. W.
WASHINGTON, D. C.

This is a reprint from the 1930s Bertram brochure that was given to each customer who bought a Bertram pipe.

Many of these pipes can be found today in the estate section of pipe stores and on collectors' tables at pipe shows from coast to coast. Most are offered at bargain basement prices, ranging from $10 to $50. This has always struck me as peculiar because so many of the Bertram pipes are so outstanding.

One large straight grain billiard that I own, which I bought from the pipe author Richard Carleton Hacker for $40, is one of my all-time favorite smokers. I like it so much that I would not take a thousand dollars for that pipe. But not all Bertrams are great, and you might have to experiment with a few to find one that suits your taste.

There were three generations of Bertrams who made these extraordinary pipes. It all started in 1874 when the original Mr. Bertram, who was a pipe maker in Leipzig, Germany, came to America and settled in Washington, where he opened his pipe store and workshop. His son, Sydney Bertram, also became an accomplished pipe maker, and eventually Bertram pipes were sought after by senators, congressmen, judges, ambassadors and world leaders.

Joseph Stalin had his ambassador buy pipes and tobaccos from Bertram's. President Franklin Roosevelt's celebrated cigarette holders were designed by Sydney Bertram. Generals MacArthur and Patton were among the military brass who were customers, and many other celebrities, including Red Skelton and Edward G. Robinson, smoked Bertram pipes and tobaccos.

Back in the 1930s and 40s, Sydney Bertram, the son of the founder, gave his customers a two-page brochure with each pipe they bought that included instructions on how to care for a pipe. It is fascinating to read, and it provides insights into why pipes hold so much interest for so many of us in the 21st century. One reason is that the advice given in the brochure 70 years ago still applies today.

In other words, while the world is changing around us at light speed, there are still a few things that remain the same.

Sydney wrote: "Remember, it is not the man who gets the most smoke who derives the greatest benefit from his pipe, but the man who smokes slowly and cooly." I have heard the same advice, almost in the same words, from pipe experts such as Jim Benjamin, who reconditions old pipes, and Rich Esserman, who offers his advice and wisdom on a regular basis in pipe journals.

Sydney Bertram also recommended keeping your carbon cake to a minimum. His concern was with the fact that carbon expands faster than briar when exposed to heat, and thus, a cake that is too thick can cause a pipe bowl to crack. "Your Bertram pipe, being completely porous, requires no 'cake' or carbon to absorb the heat and moisture," he wrote. "The walls of the pipe perform that function, allowing only the coolest and driest of smoke to reach the mouth."

While I agree with everything Sydney Bertram said about carbon cake, I prefer almost no cake for a different reason: so that I can taste the tobacco. Nothing is worse than smoking a tobacco that is tainted by the taste of tar and goo left over from previous smokes, especially if it is from a so-called "estate pipe," where the solidified tar and goo were left by someone else. Ugh!

The earliest Bertram pipes were made with Algerian briar and, according to their brochure, were neither stained nor varnished. After repeated smoking, the pipes darken into a cherry mahogany color.

Some of my favorite Bertram pipes, which were made in the 1940s, have turned exactly that color. The fact that they have turned this color leads me to believe that they put a slight amount of red, orange or mahogany stain when the pipes were first made. As Lars Ivarsson points out, briar that is totally unstained will darken and eventually turn a grayish brown; but if the pipe maker adds a bit of red or dark orange stain, it will most likely, after a period of decades, turn the cherry mahogany color that the Bertrams advertised.

The third generation of Bertram pipes was headed by Sydney Bertram's son, known by the shortened name with a different spelling, "Sid." The store in the nation's capital that Sid inherited had a series of large windows with magnificent pipe displays.

A reporter for the old *Pipe Lovers* magazine visited the store in 1949 and wrote that under the name Bertram were the words, "Craftsmanship Is Our Tradition." The reporter continued: "Directly below this is a hunting scene which is not just painted, but is actually hand-carved in glass. The scene runs almost the whole length of the front of the store, a symbol to the quality which one may expect inside."

In addition to the Bertram pipes in the display windows, the store featured dozens of other pipe brands and carvings from around the world. One was a meerschaum pipe with Napoleon on a sleigh, with beautifully carved horses. That pipe was valued at $1,200 in 1949, which translates to something like $25,000 in today's dollars, especially when considering the dramatic appreciation that expensive and rare pipes have shown since the mid-20th century.

Sid Bertram fought and was wounded in World War II, and when he returned to the store he took a particular interest in fellow veterans who also had been wounded. In 1945, Sid founded "The Bertram School for Disabled Veterans," where he taught these men to become pipe makers. His goal was to help them develop the skills so they could make a living as pipe makers, even if they had lost a limb during the war.

Unfortunately, as you might imagine, some were better than others, and many Bertram pipes made after the war were not of the same quality as the earlier ones, especially when compared with those that were hand-made by Sydney Bertram and his father who had emigrated from Germany.

The quality deteriorated even more in later years, when Bertram pipes were made at various factories. Bob Hamlin, president of the Pipe Collector's Club of America, remembers seeing Bertram pipes made in the 1960s at a factory in New York.

John Eells, a pipe maker from Richmond, VA, once owned a beautiful old Bertram pipe that was stamped, "Made in France."

John said that pipe was drilled perfectly, and the wood was beautiful. "I wish I had never sold it," he said.

Robert Peretti, a Boston pipe maker who runs the L.J. Peretti Co., which his grandfather founded, believes that the Weber Pipe Co. made many of the later Bertram pipes. "I remember visiting the Bertram store several times in the 50s and 60s," Mr. Peretti said. "It was a beautiful shop -- a real pipe shop, very well stocked, and they had an excellent repair service. Sid Bertram was about 10 years older than me, and I remember him as a very nice man."

Here are two of my Bertram straight grains – both made in the 1940s.

So when you run across a pipe that is stamped "Bertram Washington, D.C.," it is worth studying it carefully. Try to determine if it is one of the elegant hand-made pipes, with Algerian briar, that has turned a cherry mahogany color, or if it is a brownish orange pipe that looks like an old factory pipe. Either way, you will find a pipe with old wood and, very often, superb smoking qualities.

The last Bertram pipe was made in the late 1960s, so you know that your Bertram pipe is more than three decades old -- at a minimum.

For those of you who are new to pipe collecting, you should know that the Bertram situation is not unusual -- where the earlier pipes were exceptionally well made and the later pipes were clearly inferior.

That is why, for example, "pre-trans" Barlings are in greater demand than Barlings made in the 1980s. The term "pre-trans" refers to the time period before the company was sold in 1960; then there was a transition period in which a number of good Barlings were made as well, and that was followed by the period that is known for the production of post-transition Barlings. In the collector market, the big money is paid for the pre-trans Barlings.

If you look at pipe advertisements from the 1930s, you can see very little price difference between a Dunhill, Comoy or Kaywoodie. But today, old Dunhills are far more valuable than old Comoys or old Kaywoodies. The reason for this is that Comoy and Kaywoodie followed the same path as Bertram: They altered their production and sales strategies in later years to attract a mass market with less expensive pipes that had little in common with those company's earlier pipes.

Collectors don't always know if they are buying an expensive old pipe or a cheap newer one that looks old because it was smoked so much. Also, Dunhill was wise to date its pipes, so today, in 2002, you can know for sure if you are smoking a Dunhill pipe that was made in 1992, 1952 or, for that matter, 1912.

I know there are experts who can date, at least by decade, Kaywoodies and Comoys. But the only way I know of to date a Bertram is if the seller is honest and knows when the pipe was made -- especially if he bought it from the store. One of the pipes I own was sold to me by a Chicago collector, who told me that his father bought it at Bertram's in the 1940s.

There is one additional point I'd like to make so I don't leave you with the impression that old pipes are necessarily better than pipes made today. While this might be true when discussing some of the old factories, it is definitely not true when discussing individual pipe makers.

Just as I am better at my profession today than I was 10 or 20 years ago, as I'm sure you are, so too are the pipes made by individuals. Two of my personal favorites are Jess Chonowitsch and S. Bang pipes, both made in Denmark, and both considered among the best pipe brands in the world.

At the Chicago Pipe Show in 2001, an Austrian company offered a half dozen unsmoked S. Bang pipes that were made in the mid-70s. I asked Jess Chonowitsch if he would examine them to give me his opinion as to their quality. "There is nothing wrong with them," he said, "but you'd be better off buying the S. Bang pipes that were made during the last few months. The quality of workmanship is far superior today, and the briar is infinitely better. In the early days, we couldn't afford the quality of briar that we buy today."

I have talked with Tim West, Jim Cooke, Paul Bonaquisti and many other pipe makers, and they all agree that their most recent pipes are among their best.

To confuse the situation further, however, there is 60-year-old Bo Nordh who believes that the most beautiful pipe he ever made was a "ballerina" that he crafted when he was 40. [See page 126 in Chapter 12 for a photo of that pipe.] "Everything went right with that pipe, and I simply can't imagine making another pipe as beautiful as that one," he said. Still -- the pipes that Bo has made during the last decade are incredibly valuable and worth far more than the ones that he made when he was in his 20s.

Although there is no way of knowing for certain if a Bertram pipe was made by an expert craftsman in the 1930s or if it came off a factory assembly line in the 1960s, I strongly recommend that you try this brand when you find them for sale. The good ones are so good that it is worth experimenting with a few to find just the right one.

I always feel a sense of American history when I enjoy my Bertram pipes, particularly because they represent something special about this country. They reflect a tradition of excellence, dating back to the 1800s, when the nation's capital was a very different place, especially in its appreciation of pipes and tobacco. That in itself makes the search for a good Bertram pipe worth the effort.

• DUNHILL •

PROBABLY no English pipe maker is more famous in this country than Alfred Dunhill of London. A visit to the spacious Dunhill Fifth Avenue Shop in Radio City's British Empire Building is a definite "must" for every connoisseur of fine pipes when visiting New York. As a satisfying alternative, however, the GUILD invites you to inspect at your leisure the display of Dunhill and other celebrated pipes offered on this page.

Illustrated
Shell Briar
½ Actual Size

STANDARD BRUYERE—The original Dunhill pipe which has made the name Dunhill famous. The manufacturing process takes a minimum of 10 weeks—the hand-polishing alone in its various stages, occupies 10 days. Available in MAHOGANY or WALNUT finishes, in the 12 shapes shown in the Pipe Shape Chart on this page....................... **$10.00**

ROOT BRIAR—The new Root Briar is of an attractive light brown tint, and the intriguing lineation of diverse grains lends a most pleasing colour effect. With use, the Root Briar mellows to a rich, dark shade. Available in the 12 shapes shown in the Pipe Shape Chart on this page........................... **$10.00**

SHELL BRIAR—The gnarled bowl provides an unusually large radiating surface. Tough, seasoned, sapless, hard and light, the natural grain stands out boldly in relief. Available in DARK finish only, in the 12 shapes shown in the Pipe Shape Chart on this page........................... **$10.00**

• KAYWOODIE •

"DRINKLESS" KAYWOODIE pipes are currently perhaps the most widely advertised brand in the United States. Since before the Civil War the makers, Kaufmann Bros. & Bondy, Inc., have been engaged exclusively in the making of fine briars. The GUILD is proud to sponsor this splendid Kaywoodie—a pipe built to high specifications by America's largest, and one of its oldest, pipe manufacturers.

Illustrated
Drinkless Kaywoodie
½ Actual Size

KAYWOODIE DRINKLESS—The famous Drinkless pipe —you can't get a drink from it. All Kaywoodies now have the original Drinkless Attachment and Syncro-Stem fitting. Available in VIRGIN, MIAMI BROWN, DARK SUNTAN and THORN finishes in the 12 shapes shown in the Pipe Chart on this page........................ **$3.50**

KAYWOODIE CARBURETOR—With Carburetor in the bowl. "Up-draft" keeps heel dry and sweet, cools bowl, cools smoke. Mild enough for cigarette smokers. Available in VIRGIN, MIAMI BROWN, DARK, SUNTAN and THORN finishes in the 12 shapes shown in the Pipe Shape Chart on this page **$4.00**

KAYWOODIE FLAME-GRAIN—Specimen pipes, from the oldest briar on earth. Masterpieces of "flame" grain Briar. Available in the 12 shapes shown in the Pipe Shape Chart on this page **$10.00**

Advertisements that appeared in *Pipe & Pouch* magazine in 1937. As you can see, the Kaywoodie flame-grain cost the same as the Dunhill root briar.

CHAPTER NINETEEN

~~~~~

GERMANY: A GOLD MINE FOR GREAT PIPES

My trip to Germany in the summer of 2002 was so much fun, and I learned so much, that I felt compelled to write about it in detail during the long flight home from Frankfurt to Los Angeles. I was especially encouraged that Rainer Barbi agrees with me about opening his pipes more in the future. The Pipe Smoker's Ephemeris *published this article in 2003.*

* * * * *

Pipe collecting is a great hobby because there are no limits to where we can go in our quest for more knowledge. We can each define our own rules, our own interests and the areas where we want to become experts.

For many years, I have tried to become an expert on the subject of super high grade pipes hand-made by individual artisans. I believe these are the best pipes in the world in terms of their beauty and superb smoking qualities.

My quest inevitably led me to specialize in pipes made by the individuals known as "The Great Danes" -- Sixten and Lars Ivarsson, Jess Chonowitsch, S. Bang and Bo Nordh. I have written numerous articles offering my opinion that they are among the very best of all time -- provided their pipes are opened to my specifications.

There are also some outstanding German pipe makers who specialize in super high grade pipes, and I visited three of them in the summer of 2002 -- Wolfgang Becker, Karl Heinz Joura and Rainer Barbi. Their pipes are considered among the best in the world as well -- and for good reason.

I met all three men at the 2002 Chicago Pipe Show, which is one of the reasons I absolutely love the Chicago show -- because of its international character. You can start the day by having breakfast with Italians, followed by lunch with Danish or Irish or Japanese pipe makers, and then dinner with English or German pipe makers or pipe store owners or other people involved with pipes from all over the world.

In addition, many of the best American pipe makers and pipe store representatives attend that show. Frank Burla and Mike Reschke do a fantastic job year after year.

There are many great German pipe makers besides Barbi, Becker and Joura, but I only had time to meet with these three on my trip to Germany in August.

My wife, Carole, and I flew from Los Angeles to Kennedy Airport in New York, and then on to Reykjavik, Iceland, where we spent three days sightseeing, relaxing and unwinding as far away from crowds as possible. I believe there is something in the psyche of the pipe smoker that seeks peace and quiet even more than most people -- if not all the time, then at least as an occasional break from our hectic everyday routines.

Chuck Stanion once observed in *Pipes and tobaccos* that a great many pipe makers live and work in out-of-the-way places that are invariably difficult to find. He wanted to know why -- and I think it is this yearning for alone time in order to have periods of intense concentration as well as relaxed contemplation.

Along the same lines, many pipe collectors who want to be left alone have told me they dread flying these days because airport security is so strict, and they cringe at the thought of having their best pipes dumped on a table by an inspector in front of hundreds of other passengers.

So I have a few suggestions that might be helpful -- at least this is what I do:

First, I do not carry metal tins of tobacco, preferring to leave them at home or to pack them in my suitcase.

Second, I try to wear a workshirt that I bought several years ago at the New York Pipe Show because it has a drawing over the pocket of Sherlock Holmes smoking a pipe. I am grateful to the Boston Pipe Club for making these shirts. At least three times I have had to point to the picture of Holmes as a shorthand way of explaining why I have pipes in my carry-on bag. It always works. The security guard usually smiles as if to say, "Oh, I get it. That's really something...Next!" And I'm on my way.

Third, in case you don't have a Holmes shirt, why not bring a pipe magazine so that, if necessary, you can point to pictures? Also, you might find some interesting articles to read on the plane.

Finally, I put all lighters, pipe tools and anything else that might have metal in my suitcase -- not the carry-on. These are the items that triggered those three earlier inspections.

George Amrom, M.D., recommends putting all your pipes in a separate bag -- and nothing else. I have tried this a number of times recently and the bag sailed through the security x-ray machines every time without anyone feeling the need to open it. What a great suggestion!

My first meeting in Germany was with Wolfgang Becker and his wife, Gitta, in Frankfurt. They live near Dusseldorf, several hours by car from Frankfurt, and I felt very honored that they would make such a long drive to see us. Carole and I took Wolfgang and Gitta to dinner at an outdoor café that served traditional German food, where Wolfgang and I both ordered Wienerschnitzel.

I bought a short pipe with a giant bowl, which I had asked Wolfgang by e-mail to make in advance of our meeting.

Wolfgang has been a pipe maker since 1987, but it was not until the mid-90s that he abandoned his job of being a technical draftsman for an engineering firm to become a full-time pipe maker. He works in a basement workshop in his house about 10 hours a day, and he gives the impression of being absorbed in total concentration in every facet of pipe making.

Wolfgang Becker with his wife Gitta at a sidewalk café in Frankfurt, Germany.

For instance, when he told me that he wanted to improve his English, I suggested that he listen to English language tapes while making his pipes, and he immediately recoiled.

"I would lose my concentration on the pipe," he said.

Wolfgang is a perfectionist whose goal is precision to the nth degree. His role model is Lars Ivarsson.

"Lars is as close to perfect as any pipe maker can be," Wolfgang said. "His creative shapes, combined with his precise craftsmanship, put his pipes in a class by themselves."

Wolfgang recently spent a couple of days at Lars' house in Denmark, and he said he learned an enormous amount.

"Just watching Lars work was an inspiration," he said.

I asked Wolfgang if he was concerned that the shapes of his pipes too closely resembled Lars' pipe shapes, and he said he is working on developing his own style as well.

The short pipe that I bought from Wolfgang could be described as a giant billiard or apple (the bowl is bigger than an ODA), and it is a perfect straight grain with a bright reddish-orange finish. It also has a white ring of ivory at the end of the shank. At my request before our meeting, Wolfgang opened the pipe just the way that I like. The pipe has one sand pit, which is clearly visible, precisely because Wolfgang refuses to hide any flaws. He said you will never find a putty fill in one of his pipes.

We were saying goodbye after a terrific dinner.

"If the pipe has a flaw that needs to be hidden, I throw it away," he said.

Wolfgang, 50, makes about 80 pipes per year, and his distributor in the United States is Marty Pulvers. His pipes range in price from $250 to $1,000 -- for the time being. I predict that the prices will go up as his pipes become better known. He uses the best Italian briar he can find, and his mouthpieces are all hand-cut vulcanite.

Gitta and Wolfgang, who were about to celebrate their 25th wedding anniversary when we had dinner together, plan to attend the 2003 Chicago Pipe Show. Gitta's English is good, and she is very friendly, so if you plan to attend that show, by all means introduce yourself and look at the outstanding pipes made by Wolfgang Becker.

My next stop was in the German city of Bremen, where I spent the night at the house of Karl Heinz Joura. Karl, who is known as "Karlo," met me at the train station with a friend, who was there to translate -- and to have fun learning about crazy American pipe collecting!

I was surprised that they met me at the station with bicycles, and I was eternally grateful to Carole for her insistence that we travel light.

Incidentally, Carole and I had agreed to separate for two days so she could do some sightseeing on her own while I had my pipe visits, and then we were to meet up in Vienna. She tolerates my passion for pipe collecting, but the idea of forfeiting two whole days while on a European vacation was more than she could take.

We put my suitcase on the back of Karlo's bike (I have no idea how it fit) and my pipe-filled briefcase on the back of his friend's bike, and we all walked the three blocks to Karlo's house, which is enormous.

The house was built in 1910, and the walls are unbelievably thick and solid. It is right in the heart of Bremen, and in America it would be described as a big city brownstone.

While we were walking the bicycles, Karlo explained to me that a television crew was at his house filming a documentary about his life. When we arrived, the producer asked if I would agree to be interviewed for the show.

"No problem," I said, quietly wondering if I knew anyone in Hanover, Germany, where the one hour documentary will air next December or January.

"Your visit here seems remarkable considering that there are so many anti-smoking messages in America," the reporter said. "Is there sudden interest in pipe smoking?"

"Perhaps," I replied. "There certainly is interest in high grade pipes -- the ones that are considered the best in the world."

"Is Karl Heinz Joura the best in the world?" the reporter asked.

"There is no 'best' in the sense of winning the World Cup or the World Series," I said. "It's more like classical music. You can't say that Beethoven was 'better' than Bach or vice versa. You can say there have been hundreds of brilliant composers over the years and perhaps a dozen or so who stood alone above the rest. Many pipe collectors from around the world would put Karl Heinz Joura in that class."

Karl Heinz Joura in his home town of Bremen, Germany.

Karlo's personal story is fascinating. When he was a 19-year-old champion diver, training for the East German Olympic team in 1961, he defected to West Germany.

Being a great athlete, he taught physical education at schools in West Germany. He noticed that many of his fellow teachers were pipe smokers, and since he liked machines and working with his hands, he decided to try making a pipe. In a short while, his pipes were very popular, so he started selling them and realized he could devote his life to pipe making.

Karlo is a passionate man, and his passion comes out in the beautiful shapes and colors of his pipes. Many are red and reddish-orange in color, and the shapes are classical but with Karlo's unique touches. For instance, his apple shape is well rounded but slightly a-symmetrical, which reflects his dramatic artistic side.

A handful of Joura pipes in the final stages of production.

I have heard some critics complain that he does not pay as much attention to detail as some of the other great pipe makers, or that his classical shapes are not perfect, and that may be true -- and it is also what makes his pipes special. There is a flair to the design that makes the pipes totally unique, and his pipes are incredibly great smokers.

One European collector told me, "I buy Bo Nordh pipes to admire, but I buy Joura pipes to smoke." As for me, I buy pipes by both men -- to admire *and* to smoke.

I picked out a couple of beautiful pipes -- bent and straight -- from a group of 40 gorgeous pieces. Karlo, who makes about 200 pipes per year, would not normally have so many pipes on hand, but three factors came together to motivate him to save his supply: he wanted a good selection for the TV documentary; he was preparing to travel to Cologne the next day to deliver 20 pipes to Peter Heinrich's House of 10,000 Pipes, and he was getting ready for the annual pipe show at Dortmund, Germany.

One of the pipes that I bought was made with a 9 millimeter filter for the German market, so we went downstairs to Karlo's workshop to find an adaptor, which is a small piece of vulcanite that fits where the filter would normally go. The adaptor makes the pipe as close to normal as possible without having to make a new mouthpiece. We also opened the pipes that I bought because I found the inside of Karlo's pipes to be too restricted for my taste.

I met Karlo's two adorable children, his daughter Coco, 12, and his son Fabian, 8, and their mother, Chini, when we had a barbeque feast outside with typical German food, including sausages, pork chops, steaks and salad.

After dinner, we rode bicycles into Bremen with the children, and they gave me a sightseeing tour, including a visit to the old house in the middle of the village where the family used to live and Karlo had his workshop on the street level with large windows -- where the pedestrians passing by could see a pipe maker at work.

When we returned home and parked our bicycles in the back yard, where there must have been seven or eight, I noticed an additional half dozen or so antique bicycles alongside the hallway wall inside the house -- all collector items. Karlo pointed out one bicycle from England from the 1920s and several turn-of-the-century models.

Karlo and I stayed up late and talked about pipes, with his friend, Regina Neubert, providing excellent translating help. I smoked a quarter bent Joura pipe made from Corsican briar that I had bought from Karlo in Chicago, and he was very pleased with the way it was coloring. His pipes are stamped with a leaf for Sardinian briar and a star for Corsican briar, and he hand-cuts all mouthpieces, which are made of the finest vulcanite.

I asked Karlo what he thought of various pipe makers, and he said he has always forged his own way and does not pay much attention to the others. He said he likes some of the old Charatans from the 1960s and 70s. He also said he is impressed by Bo Nordh and Jess Chonowitsch and that he enjoyed talking with Jess at the Chicago Pipe Show.

"Chonowitsch was friendly, and his pipes are good -- very well made," he said. "As for Bo Nordh, he is the only pipe maker I have ever visited -- and that's because Bo and I are both good at making machines, and I wanted to see his machinery."

As for the Bo Nordh pipe, Karlo said he likes them but cannot fathom spending two or three months on just a few pipes.

"He is such a perfectionist -- it almost seems like too much," he said. "But the results are obviously beautiful. They belong in a museum more than a pipe rack!"

I asked Karlo what he envisioned for his future, and he became philosophical, saying that after nearly 30 years of making pipes he still feels passionately about the craft.

"I must have fun doing what I do," he said. "I love making pipes. The work is rewarding. You have to find joy in life -- you must enjoy yourself, or why bother?

"I am now 60 years old, and I plan to continue making pipes for the indefinite future. Since I have so much more experience and skill than I had in the past, I plan on making fewer pipes but more of the high grades," he said.

Karlo's pipes have only occasionally been offered in the United States, but he recently entered into an agreement with Marty Pulvers and Dave Field. He said he is putting together a grading system for his pipes at the request of Marty and Dave, who no doubt want to use it as a guideline for pricing the pipes.

We talked so late that it was after 2:00 a.m. before we called it a night. I slept deeply in one of several guest rooms before being awakened at 7:00 a.m. for breakfast of coffee, yogurt, bread, cheese and meats. Suddenly the doorbell rang and the television film crew from the previous day was at the front door, apologizing for being late. They were to accompany Karlo on the train to Cologne to film at Peter Heinrich's pipe store.

Karlo was running late as well, having gotten the time mixed up by one hour, so he jumped up, raced into the bathroom, turned on the electric razor for a few seconds, threw on a shirt, gave the kids a hug and said good-bye to all of us as he ran out the door.

For some reason, as I think back and picture him at home, Karlo reminds me of Picasso. I can see him walking around his artist's studio, which is what his pipe workshop felt like, wearing a pair of sandals and shorts, but no shirt, or maybe a t-shirt, with a cigarette or pipe hanging from his mouth, either designing creative new shapes or sanding, filing, staining and buffing his latest creation.

Karlo's pipes range widely in price, from $500 to $2,500 with the average being in the $600 to $800 range.

Incidentally, if you think I'm on the payroll of Marty Pulvers and Dave Field, I don't blame you. But I'm not. It is coincidental that the first two German pipe makers I met with are now being represented by Marty and Dave.

But it's not totally coincidental. All three of us -- Marty, Dave and I -- have devoted decades to finding the best high grade pipes in the world. In their case, their primary goal has been for good business reasons, and in my case, my primary goal has been to put together the best pipe collection I can of hand made pipes.

Also, we all three are intensely interested in learning as much about pipes as possible.

A Joura masterpiece.

After I first met Karlo at the Chicago show, and found out that he did not have a sales agent in the United States, I ran into Marty and urged him to represent Joura pipes. To his credit, Marty was already a big fan, and he followed through.

"Joura pipes are quickly gaining recognition in America," he said. "We anticipate big things in the future with these pipes."

About an hour after Karlo raced off to the train station, I went there to catch the train to Hamburg to see Rainer Barbi.

The ride from Bremen to Hamburg is about an hour, and we were due to arrive at 10:20 a.m. At about 10:00 a.m., I decided to visit the restaurant car to get a quick coffee. Just as I reached the counter, the train started slowing to a stop.

"Hamburg?!" I asked in a panic. After all, my suitcase was on a rack that was three train cars back.

"Ya -- Hamburg," the man behind the counter replied, mumbling another word that I couldn't quite make out.

"No time for coffee," I said, as I raced back to retrieve my luggage.

I got it just in time and ran to the exit door, not bothering to notice that I was the only person getting off the train. The temperature was easily 90° with plenty of August humidity. The train stopped, I stepped outside, hoisting my suitcase and carry-on bag, sweating hard, but excited that I had made it! I was so proud of myself for managing to hopscotch over the German landscape, traveling from city to city, and now I was to see the famous pipe maker Rainer Barbi!

As I walked outside, I realized that I was alone on the platform. Totally alone. And the train was already pulling out of the station.

The sign said "Hamburg/Harburg," and I suddenly remembered that was the word the man at the restaurant counter had mumbled. I looked around and felt like I was in that scene in Butch Cassidy and the Sundance Kid where Butch and Sundance get off a train in Bolivia, fully expecting some real excitement, and instead see nothing but barren countryside.

I carried my bags downstairs, which led to a train tunnel, and saw a young man walking ahead of me.

"Excuse me," I said loudly, but trying to sound polite, "do you speak English?"

"A little bit," he said.

"Is this Hamburg?" I asked

"This is Hamburg/Harburg. Did you want the central train station in Hamburg?"

"Yes," I replied.

"Well, follow me," he said. "That is where I am going, and the next train arrives in five minutes."

So…in the end I was only 10 minutes late, and Rainer and I spotted each other almost immediately.

"I was concerned that you weren't on your train," he said, adding that he was just about to leave, fretting over the fact that he had no way of reaching me.

Rainer Barbi at work in his studio outside Hamburg, Germany.

I explained what happened, we had a good laugh (sort of)…and headed for the high grade pipe store Tesch, located in downtown Hamburg. The store manager, who is the grandson of the founder, was very friendly, and I bought a 5-pack of 50 gram bags of Balkan Sobranie, which is no longer sold in the United States.

Rainer and I also visited two other pipe stores in Hamburg, all within a few blocks of each other, before heading out to the country to see the famous Dan Pipe factory.

Rainer introduced me to the two managing partners, Heiko Behrens and Holger Frickert. They were upbeat and optimistic about the pipe business, as evidenced by the fact that they excused themselves several times to meet in another room, saying, "We're in the process of buying a pipe factory in Poland right now."

Michael Apitz, who has worked for Dan Pipe for 12 years, gave us a tour of the tobacco factory. Talk about fun!

I have never seen 25-pound rectangular bricks of vanilla-cased tobacco, ready for the cutting machine, nor have I dipped my hands into a box of Cyprean Latakia that was at least four feet wide and four feet tall.

Dan Pipe makes many of its own tobacco blends, and because of their annual catalogs, which are spectacular -- almost works of art -- they have built up quite a following in the United States. Many of their products are distributed to pipe stores by CAO, and the others are available directly from Dan Pipe.

Last November there was a terrible fire that totally destroyed their factory near Hamburg known as the "Grashof." But it hardly slowed them down.

"You have to look to the future," Heiko said in response to my question about the fire.

I suggested that they have dozens of the Dan Pipe catalog sent to me in Chicago next Spring, saying that I would put them on my table and hand them out for free. Heiko said he would very much like to do that.

I picked up some Mountain Village Evening Standard tobacco, an English blend that I like, as well as a certain type of Corona lighter -- an old favorite that broke -- that I have been unable to find in the States.

This was one of my favorite covers on a Dan Pipe catalog.

Rainer and I then left for his home and pipe workshop. He lives in a spacious second floor apartment in a quiet country house about 15 miles outside Hamburg. His apartment is beautiful, filled with dozens of interesting collectible items and trinkets, including carvings, dolls, lighters, toys, paper weights, horses, and anything to do with beer, not to mention Rainer's three beloved black-and-white cats, one of whom is 22 years old!

He had about a dozen pipes ready to be shipped to his distributors, and I picked out a few beauties. We then went to his workshop, which is located in a red brick building about 50 yards from the house.

Rainer opened my new pipes with a wider draft hole in the shank and mouthpiece, at my request, and he was quite interested in the issue of how open the inside of a pipe should be.

"You might be on to something in advocating a more open draft," he said. "I have been giving this subject a great deal of thought lately because of your e-mails about it, and it occurred to me that pipes and tobaccos are very different today from the way they were 60 or 70 years ago, yet the draft hole has remained the same. We have changed everything -- but kept the air hole the same!

"In the old days, pipes were typically smaller, with smaller tobacco chambers, so the draft holes did not need to be so big. Also, the tobacco mostly came in smaller flakes, which burn easily, so there was no need for an air hole of 4.5 millimeters.

"But now, the pipe bowls are usually much larger, and the pipes are bigger as well, and most tobacco is ribbon cut, yet the old draft hole has not been modified in any way. In theory, there is no question that it should be made bigger. But that is only a theory. I will experiment with my own pipes and let you know the verdict, as I see it.

"However, I think it's great that you have analyzed the issue and you know what you like," he said. "I have a second theory as well, and that is that you are probably a wet smoker."

"Many times I am," I replied. "I have tried not to be -- using my tongue as a plug, slowing down, holding the pipe bowl in my hand -- that sort of thing, but sometimes I notice that I revert to being a wet smoker."

Rainer explained that moisture and heat cause wood to expand, so it makes sense that the briar inside the shank closes a little, making the draft hole tighter, as I am smoking my pipe. This explains why many pipe smokers need to run pipe cleaners through their pipes while they are smoking them.

Rainer, 54, has been making pipes for 30 years. He makes between 150 and 200 pipes per year, with the highest quality Italian briar and all with beautiful hand-cut mouthpieces of soft vulcanite that have the logo of RB on top.

"My first choice would have been the white dot," he said. "But that was already taken, so my initials are the next best thing."

It was in the mid-1990s that his pipes were introduced to the United States by Michael Butera. A friend of Rainer's had taken some of his pipes to Bob Gaddis, a Houston tobacconist, who in turn showed them to Mike.

Rainer and Mike corresponded by fax for several months, and an agreement was reached. Rainer sends Mike up to 100 pipes each year for sale in the United States, and they are all sold immediately. [David Field and Marty Pulvers took over the distribution of the Barbi pipes in the United States in mid-2003.]

Back in the mid-1980s, Rainer had tried to break into the American pipe market, but he was told, to his astonishment, that he had no choice but to change his name, which he absolutely refused to do.

"I was told that Barbi pipes would not sell because the headlines were filled with stories about the Nazi Klaus Barbie, who was no relation to my family. He was Italian, and my family was Hugenotts. But I had to wait 10 more years," he said. "It did not matter, though, because the demand for my pipes has always been greater than the supply. I always feel the pressure of letting people down because I don't make enough pipes to satisfy the demand."

Rainer was studying law in the early 1970s, and he would occasionally take a break by visiting pipe stores and studying the high grade pipes.

"I wanted them so much," he said. "But I was a student, and so I could not afford the expensive prices."

Rainer started making pipes on his own and won a contest held by the old Pipe Dan in Copenhagen. He still has that pipe, along with the next 30 pipes that he made, in a rack in his apartment.

There is a wide range in prices for Barbi pipes -- from $340 to $3,500.

"It is important to me to be able to offer beautiful pipes as inexpensively as possible," he said. "I identify with young people who want to buy the high grades but can't afford them."

The telephone rang two or three times when we were in the workshop, but Rainer let the answering machine pick up the calls. Once he starts working on a pipe, he becomes totally absorbed.

Rainer uses a long sanding belt that is rather unique. It saves sanding time both for the bowls and the mouthpieces, but it is extremely difficult to master.

I asked if there were other pipe makers whom he admires, and he said that he particularly likes the S. Bang pipes, which are made by two Danes, Ulf Noltensmeier and Per Hansen.

"Their pipes are very beautiful," he said, adding that he likes other pipe makers as well, including Eltang, Chonowitsch and Bo Nordh.

After spending several hours in the workshop, we went to a restaurant in the country, where we had a feast of venison, red cabbage, potatoes, brussel sprouts, and other foods that are found in traditional German restaurants.

It was a balmy night, and we ate, drank and smoked as much as we wanted. I told Rainer that America is the land of the free -- except when it comes to enjoying your pipe in a restaurant after dinner!

Rainer travels often to give many speeches each year about pipes, pipe making, briar, and other related subjects, and twice a year for 10 days at a time, he teaches a series of two-day courses in pipe making to dozens of aspiring pipe makers of all ages. His students are mostly men but there have been some women as well.

Beautiful straight grain on a Barbi pipe.

He showed me a series of slides from the school on his computer, and I could tell how much he cares about this project.

Then Rainer played a video showing him on German television last year on that country's equivalent of the show, "What's My Line?" It took about 10 minutes for the panelists to guess "pipe maker," and after they did, the TV show featured a clip of Rainer making a pipe.

Just like the night before with Karl Joura, Rainer and I talked late into the night about pipes. He feels strongly about making only the best that he can, and he intends to make pipes for as long as he can. Barbi pipes are fantastic smokers, and he has developed a worldwide following of devoted customers, including me.

We talked until after 2:00 in the morning, and since I had to get up early for my flight to Vienna, I knew it would be another night with less than five hours sleep. But I didn't care because I was having so much fun -- and learning so much.

On the way to the airport the next morning, Rainer echoed Lars Ivarsson's theory that a pipe renaissance, which we are experiencing now, brings out a lot of bad pipe makers.

"The ones who couldn't make it before, the ones who took jobs making furniture, selling in stores, painting, or whatever, now they are suddenly pipe makers again," he said. "And then there are the beginners who see a pipe sold for $1,500 and say, 'How difficult can it be to make a pipe? What a great way to make money!' But they won't last, I guarantee you."

We said good-bye, and I flew to Vienna to meet Carole and to enjoy traditional sightseeing in Austria. On the following day I couldn't resist, however, making one quick stop at Ostermann Pipes in Vienna, since it is a world famous pipe store with a fantastic website (www.pipes.at). The store is absolutely wonderful.

Mrs. Maszynski and her daughter, Eva.

I had met Eva Abi-Fadel and her parents, who own the store, at the Chicago Show (where else?), but unfortunately Eva was on vacation. However, her mother, Felizitas Maszynski, was there and offered me coffee and a choice of several hundred super high grade pipes. I succumbed to a straight grained S. Bang billiard with a tapered mouthpiece. The pipe is beautiful, and I was pleased to give some business to Ostermann's.

I am writing these words on the plane back to America, with a warm feeling inside as I look forward to enjoying my new pipes for many years to come, and feeling happy for having become friends with three outstanding German pipe makers -- each of whom has his own unique style.

Rainer Barbi with an award he received from the West Coast Pipe and Cigar Expo.

CHAPTER TWENTY

~~~~~

CASTELLO'S TRADITION
OF EXCELLENCE

Castello is considered one of the finest factory pipes in the world, so I really wanted to see what their shop looks like first hand. As you can tell by this report, I had a terrific time and was very impressed.

* * * * *

Italy is known for art, beauty, fashion, food, music, literature, architecture, design and a hundred other qualities of culture and civilization. So not surprisingly, some of the best pipes produced today are made in the small factories and workshops scattered throughout the country.

One of the most expensive Italian pipes I ever bought was a beautiful straight grain calabash made by Ser Jacopo. I paid Bob Hamlin $550 for the pipe, and it will always have a special place in my collection. It is my absolute favorite "Sherlock Holmes pipe." I want to point out that I have bought a handful of pipes, and a closetful of tobacco, from Bob Hamlin over the years, and I have never regretted a single purchase. That is definitely the sign of someone I would recommend doing business with.

There have been several books devoted exclusively to Italian pipes, including Savinelli, Brebbia, Mastro de Paja, Radice, Il Ceppo, Ardor, Amorelli, Don Carlos, and many others -- too many, in fact, to mention.

But one of the very best names, without question, is Castello. Many American collectors consider Castello the only serious rival to Dunhill when it comes to pipes made in a factory, and I know a good number who regard Castello as the best in the world.

Regardless of where you come down on this debate, I think we can all agree that Castello pipes are high quality. One of the things that appeals most to me about Castello pipes is their opening. Their air holes inside the pipes and mouthpieces are frequently very close to the dimensions I outline in Chapter 8. My only complaint is that their mouthpieces are a little thick for my taste, so I always have them thinned out -- and theirs is an acrylic that I find reasonably comfortable, though my preference is vulcanite.

On a trip to Rome I visited Marco Parascenzo at his store, Novelli. Marco is extremely knowledgeable about pipes, so it is not surprising that Castello entrusts its distribution in the United States to Marco, and he in turn entrusts Bob Hamlin of Virginia with the responsibility of getting Castello pipes to as many American collectors as possible.

Visiting the Novelli pipe store in Rome and Marco Parascenzo (right) as he was showing me some fantastic Castello pipes.

Marco has a charismatic smile and a natural friendliness about him. He travels to the United States three times each year -- for the Retail Tobacco Dealers Association's annual convention and for the annual pipe shows in Chicago and Richmond. He shook his head and laughed when I suggested that he attend a Los Angeles pipe show. Considering how weary I was feeling after flying across the ocean, I was totally sympathetic.

Marco brought out dozens of beautiful Castello pipes, including some that were made decades ago. He also opened the drawers in a shelf behind the counter, one at a time, and put them on the glass counter top. Each drawer contained about a dozen gorgeous Castellos, and he must have shown me four or five drawers. I was suddenly feeling grateful to the two fanatical American collectors, Chuck Stanion and Ed Lehman, who strongly recommended that I visit Marco on my trip to Italy.

I selected a straight grain Collection Fiammata billiard with a plateau top. It is a beautiful pipe, but I really didn't enjoy smoking it because the mouthpiece felt so thick in my mouth.

When I told Marco that I would be in Milan later in the week, he volunteered to call Franco Coppo to arrange for me to visit the Castello factory, which is located in Cantu -- a 45-minute drive from downtown Milan. When I arrived at the factory on Friday afternoon, Franco came out to the courtyard to greet me. He was smoking his pipe and appeared to be in a very good mood.

Romeo Domenico of Italy is one of the world's best suppliers of high grade briar, including to Castello's factory.

I asked if it was OK to smoke in the factory. "OK?! It is mandatory!" he laughed. So I pulled out my newly bought

Fiammata and loaded it with some old Dunhill 965. Just after I had lit the pipe, tamped the tobacco, lit it again and really got it going, I couldn't help myself. "This mouthpiece feels too thick between my teeth," I said, hoping not to offend my host.

"No problem -- we can fix that in five minutes," Franco said, leading me into the spacious factory filled with beautiful blocks of briar on the floor. "They are all around 10 years old," he said.

Franco approached one of the half-dozen artisans, explained the problem, asked me how thick I like it ("around 4 millimeters from top-to-bottom"), and stood next to me as we watched the pipe maker file and sand the mouthpiece. When it was just right for my taste, I re-lit the pipe and now consider it one of my very favorites.

Franco's father-in-law was the legendary Carlo Scotti, who was to Castello pipes what Alfred Dunhill was to Dunhill pipes. I asked where the name Castello, which is Italian for castle, came from. "Carlo Scotti wanted a fantasy name, and castles conjure up fantasy. He also wanted a name that sounded similar in several languages, and the word castello in Italian is chateau in French, castle in English and castillo in Spanish."

Franco takes great pride in his work. He started in the factory, making pipes, and he is still very involved in designing new shapes. But like me, he prefers only slight variations on the classic shapes. "I don't like it when the pipe maker goes crazy with the designs and the pipe can hardly be smoked," he said, adding that tradition is an important part of Castello. For instance, one of his pipe makers has been with the company for 44 years and another for 36 years.

I watched a pipe maker carve a Sea Rock, which is a finish that Castello has made popular, especially because these pipes are so light in weight. The pipe maker used what looked like a small sharp spoon with a wooden handle about the size of a standard screwdriver. Using plenty of elbow grease, he very quickly, and gently, turned out tiny circles of briar wood. After he finished the carving, he brushed the wood briskly, again using elbow grease. "This job takes a lot of muscle," Franco said.

The highlight of my visit came at the end, after we entered a back room that contained a stunning wood-and-glass rack containing some of the most beautiful Castello pipes ever made. These are part of Franco's private collection -- the part where all the pipes are unsmoked. A number of different sizes and shapes are featured, including a straight-grain Hawkbill that would have made Chicago collector Chuck Rio drool. ALL of the pipes in this rack are extraordinary, and Franco said that none is for sale. However, he said that collectors can special order similar racks from any Castello dealer in America. I was afraid to ask the price.

Overall, I cannot tell you how impressive the Castello factory is -- clean, well organized, efficient, with plenty of machinery, the very best of materials and, most importantly, with a handful of experienced and skilled craftsmen, many smoking Castello pipes as they worked, turning out some of the finest pipes in the world. It is a real tribute to Franco that he has been able to carry on the tradition started by Carlo Scotti, and in many ways propel the company forward so that the pipes made in the 21st century are among the best available anywhere in the world.

Franco Coppo's wood-and-glass cabinet featuring some of the most beautiful Castello pipes ever made.

~~~~~

CHAPTER TWENTY-ONE

PAOLO BECKER -- AN EXPERT CRAFTSMAN

What interests me most as a pipe collector are the individual artisans who spend their lives making beautiful pipes by hand. While it is true that some of my favorites come from Denmark and Sweden, there are also great ones from Germany, as we have seen, as well as Japan, England, France, America and other countries. Of course, Italy has produced some of the best pipe makers in history, and without question, Paolo Becker is one of those.

* * * * *

Paolo Becker (left) and his American distributor, David Field.

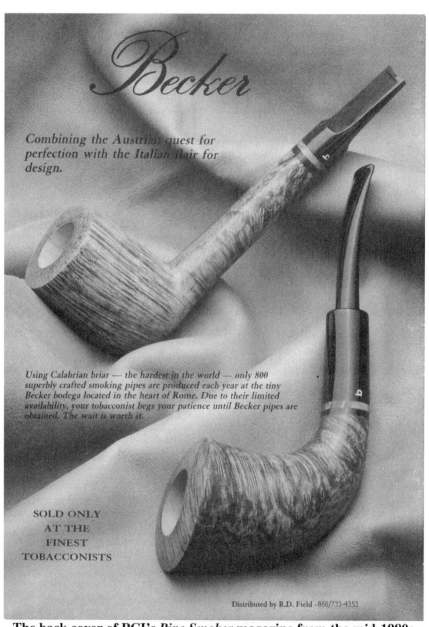

Becker

Combining the Austrian quest for
perfection with the Italian flair for
design.

Using Calabrian briar — the hardest in the world — only 800
superbly crafted smoking pipes are produced each year at the tiny
Becker bodega located in the heart of Rome. Due to their limited
availability, your tobacconist begs your patience until Becker pipes are
obtained. The wait is worth it.

SOLD ONLY
AT THE
FINEST
TOBACCONISTS

Distributed by R.D. Field -866/733-4353

The back cover of PCI's *Pipe Smoker* magazine from the mid-1980s.

Sometimes it's the little things that count most. That is certainly true when assessing the skill of a master pipe maker. By way of illustration, I was meeting with the legendary Paolo Becker at his store in Rome, Becker & Musicò, and showing Paolo a beautiful S. Bang apple-shaped pipe with a tapered mouthpiece. I separated the mouthpiece from the shank to show Paolo the enlarged air hole that I had made -- so an extra fluffy cleaner slides through the tenon end and out the lip end with virtually no resistance [See Chapter 8].

After studying the mouthpiece for a minute, Paolo put the pipe back together in one quick movement -- and the fitting was exactly perfect. I am at a loss for words in describing how quickly, smoothly -- and perfectly -- Paolo lined up the fit of the shank and mouthpiece while carrying on a conversation with me. It was almost as if he hadn't been paying attention. Talk about being able to make a pipe in your sleep!

Back in the mid-eighties, I salivated at the beautiful ads on the back covers of the old PCI's *Pipe Smoker* magazine that featured some of Paolo's gorgeous pipes. But it was not that image, nor the fact that he has been making pipes since 1974, nor the beautiful stain on his pipes that stopped me in my tracks. It was that one swift movement of putting the mouthpiece in the shank, effortlessly lining it up perfectly, that impressed me more than anything else. He is truly an expert craftsman.

I visited Paolo in early March 2003, just as the war with Iraq was about to begin. During lunch, we stayed away from politics and talked about pipes, his family, and Paolo's plan to visit Chicago for the 2003 pipe show. His American distributor is David Field, and Paolo has been very pleased with the relationship which began in 1981. Paolo makes about 400 pipes each year and sends several hundred of those to Dave, who has no trouble distributing them to tobacconists throughout America. There is a detailed list for the nomenclature on Becker pipes, which you can find on his website: www.beckerpipes.com, with the very best being the Royal Flush, which has A, B and C categories, of which C is the highest and A the lowest.

I selected a Royal Flush freehand A pipe but asked if Paolo could make a hand-cut vulcanite mouthpiece for it rather than the lucite stem he had made originally. "No problem," he said, adding that he finds vulcanite more comfortable for the pipes that he smokes himself. "But many collectors prefer acrylic, so most of my mouthpieces are made with that material," he said. I also asked if he could make the mouthpiece about one or one-and-a-half centimeters shorter than the one on the pipe, not knowing that the Becker & Musicò website (www.beckermusico.com) includes an article by Giorgio Musicò, Paolo's partner, about why he likes shorter pipes.

Paolo Becker, left, holding the Royal Flush pipe that I had just bought from him.

Paolo started making pipes when he was 22, and he makes both free hand designs and classic shapes. He was inspired by his father, Fritz Becker, who was a well respected pipe maker in his own right, though Paolo is the one known today for making super high grade pipes.

The stain on many Becker pipes frequently features a dark brown with golden highlights, showing off the straight grain and bird's eye in a dramatic way, somewhat similar to Tom Eltang's very special "golden contrast" stain. "But I am always experimenting with stains," Paolo said. "Each piece of briar is unique, so I examine a pipe carefully before I decide what color to stain it."

Paolo works with and teaches an extremely talented younger pipe maker, Massimo Musicò, whose father is Giorgio. The pipes made by Paolo and Massimo are stamped, "Becker-Musicò." I asked Paolo if there are other pipe makers, besides Massimo, whose work he admires. "When it comes to shapes," he said, "I prefer the high grade Danish. But there are many pipe makers I like and admire." He added that Castello makes good pipes with expensive briar. "They can afford the best," he said.

If you are wondering about how the name Becker, which is German, wound up in Italy, here is the story: Paolo's grandfather was a pharmacist in Vienna, Austria, who lost his drugstore from one day to the next. He was Jewish, and the Nazis seized it, so his son, Fritz, at age 18, immediately left the country, temporarily staying in Yugoslavia before finally settling in Italy. Fritz was an accomplished artist and pipe maker, he was fluent in five languages, and he eventually rose to the prestigious position of representative to the Vatican of the World Jewish Congress. His son, Paolo, has emerged as one of the premier pipe makers of all time.

If you get a chance to visit Rome, I highly recommend that you stop by the Becker & Musicò store and buy a Becker pipe. But if a trip to Rome is not in your immediate plans, then I'd suggest checking with your local tobacconist for Becker pipes, or contacting David Field to find out where you can find a selection of Paolo's masterpieces. You won't regret it.

CHAPTER TWENTY-TWO

TWO TYPES OF PIPE COLLECTORS

About the only thing pipe collectors agree on is that we like our pipes. Beyond that, all bets are off. There are countless controversies within the pipe collecting community, and the debates are lively, fun and thought-provoking. Several of us with outspoken opinions have angered a number of traditional collectors, but I believe that our disagreements add spice and variety to the hobby. The good news is that everyone wins -- because in the end we all do whatever we want to do.

* * * * *

If you ask a dozen pipe smokers the same question, you'll get a dozen different answers. This chapter raises some questions where you are bound to find dozens of different answers within the pipe collecting community. Part of it appeared as an essay in *Pipe Friendly* in 1997. I wrote that you should feel free to alter your pipes to suit your taste, regardless of the name on the pipe or the brand, and I implied that I could not care less about the nomenclature on a pipe provided it was a good smoker – concepts that most hard core collectors found appalling.

The real debating slugfest began when Dr. Fred Hanna, a psychology professor at Johns Hopkins University, wrote an article a few years later for *The Pipe Collector* called "the brand myth," in which he took my premise to the extreme by saying that collectors are deluding themselves into believing that one brand of pipe smokes better than another; in other words, he said, it's all in the briar -- and in your head. Fred wrote that the smoking qualities of a pipe are enhanced psychologically because the pipe smoker is impressed by the name on the pipe -- the brand -- but in reality, that is a myth, and no brand can guarantee that it will smoke better than any other. Fred said the key is to experiment until you find briar that has good smoking qualities -- and that is determined by nature, not the pipe maker or the brand of pipe.

From left to right, Rich Esserman, Fred Hanna, Ulf Noltensmeier and me at the 2003 Chicago Pipe Show. We might all have honest disagreements about a number of issues related to pipe smoking and collecting, but we always have fun together at a pipe show.

Personally, I think Fred makes some excellent points, and he forced me to re-evaluate my enthusiasm for high grade pipes -- and to admit that I own a few bucket pipes that smoke better than some of my fancy high grades. Still, as I have said, I believe these are flukes. But they are also facts, which I am indeed willing to acknowledge. I do think Fred takes his argument too far. However, I want to say that I admire Fred enormously -- just as I admire his critics, such as Rich Esserman -- because they both are searching for the correct answers. Is it all in the briar? Or in the way the pipe was made? Or in the brand? Or is it all psychological? If we assume it is all four, does one count more than another? If so, what are the percentages? Since we have no way of knowing for certain, our debates will probably continue forever. Also, there might be other factors involved that contribute to a good smoking pipe -- such as our mood when we smoke the pipe. The same pipe can smoke great when you're in a good mood, and terrible when you're in a bad mood. This really is a very complicated question.

To illustrate just how complicated it is, there is the story that Bo Nordh tells about Sixten Ivarsson making pipes called twins, i.e., two pipes with identical shapes made from the same block of briar. One smoked much better than the other, and Bo's theory was that it was all in the briar -- the soft wood that was sheltered did not smoke well while the wood that was forced to withstand the elements proved to be a great smoker. To support Bo's explanation -- did you know that roses grown outside, where they have to withstand the twists and turns of nature, are the ones that smell so beautiful, while roses grown in greenhouses, where they are totally protected, give off almost no fragrance whatsoever?

Having said all of this, however, you should know that when Lars Ivarsson and Jess Chonowitsch heard the story about Sixten's twin pipes, they had a completely different explanation from Bo. They said that if Sixten used the same block of briar, then the difference between the two pipes was not in the wood but in the mechanics of the way the pipes were made. Lars said that if Sixten made them, they were both good smokers, and the fact that one smoked better than the other might have been caused by a slight difference in the air stream through the mouthpiece. "Maybe my father forgot to make a sound test on one of the pipes," he said.

Lars elaborated by telling the story of the blind Danish novelist Karl Bjarnhof, who was a regular customer of Sixten's. Karl's daughter dropped one of his pipes and did not want her father to know, so she brought the broken pipe to Sixten and asked him to make an exact copy so her father would not know the difference. Sixten did just that -- to one-tenth or even one-hundredth of a millimeter -- and when her father held the pipe and first lit up a bowl, he didn't say anything. But after he smoked it for a few minutes, he said, "This pipe seems different somehow." Lars said that no matter how identical two pipes appear, they will always smoke differently -- however slight that difference is. A machine can make two identical looking clarinets, but they will always sound just a little different, because of the slightest differences in the way they are made.

Getting back to Bo's story about the twin pipes, Lars said that Sixten probably spent more time on the good smoker. "Maybe he was late for an appointment when he made the second pipe, or something like that happened," Lars said. That is why the two pipes smoked differently -- because the mechanics were different. Jess agreed 100 percent.

We will never know for sure which explanation is correct, or perhaps there is truth in both explanations. But here's the point: if some of the best pipe makers in the world cannot agree on this issue, then how can pipe collectors and pipe smokers know for sure? We can't. As the American pipe maker, Ed Jurkiewicz of E. Andrew Pipes, says, "There are mysteries about briar that we will *never* understand. That is part of what makes our hobby so interesting."

We all agree that psychology plays an important role in our enjoyment of certain pipes. But it is not all psychological, nor is it totally subjective. For instance, either a pipe is drilled dead center or it is not. The precise measurements are not a matter of opinion -- they are a matter of objective fact. Many people will argue that sex is mostly psychological, and they might be right, but it is also physical. Otherwise, it is just fantasy.

On an unrelated subject, but relevant because it raises another controversial issue within the pipe collecting community, imagine refusing to go out with Marilyn Monroe because she had one or two beauty marks on her face. That is what I thought of when I read a recent pipe article by my friend Fred Janusek, a longtime collector, who said it would be a "fraud" for a pipe maker to hide a dark spot or pinprick-sized hole in the wood. Fred says that such a pipe should be called a "second," as opposed to a "first." Fred defines a second as a bowl with a fill but says a first can have sand pits and fissures. Rick Hacker says even sand pits and fissures can make a pipe a second. Aaron Licker, pipe specialist at the original Tinder Box in Santa Monica, says that a first is whatever the factory says it is, and the same for a second. If Upshall calls one of its pipes a first, they stamp the name Upshall; if a pipe made in the same factory is deemed to be a second, for a variety of reasons, they stamp it Tilshead. The same with Dunhill and Parker and others.

What makes this Lars Ivarsson pipe great? The shape? The wood? The name? The grain? The stain? Psychology? The way it was made? My answer is "all of the above" and other factors as well.

But to me, this debate is ridiculous. Imagine the most beautifully carved pipe bowl ever made, but it has a tiny black spot, smaller than the head of a pin, in one part of the wood on the outside of the bowl. Would I want the pipe maker to discard it as a "second" or to offer it with the blemish in full view? Of course not. I would want for him to hide it as much as possible so I would never even know about it. Remember -- we are not talking about major putty fills that show up when the pipe is smoked. That clearly is a different story.

For the tiniest of flaws in the wood, however, if they can be hidden, then I want them hidden. *Remember, too, that briar wood is a natural product that once was part of a tree that was alive and growing, unlike inanimate materials such as gold or silver, and ALL blocks of briar, including Bo Nordh's $16,000 ballerina, Charatan's Summa Cum Laude and Dunhill's 9-star DR, have some imperfections and flaws, however tiny and difficult to decipher.* There are simply no exceptions. Not one. Not ever.

When I hear people say, "This is a flawless pipe," I know they are dreaming. There is simply no such thing. There never has been and there never will be a pipe that is literally "flawless," except, perhaps, in the sales and marketing departments of a few pipe companies.

Jan Andersson, who publishes the Swedish pipe magazine *Rokringar*, said it best: "I think the myth of the completely flawless pipe must come to an end -- once and for all!"

One final point, which relates directly to the traditional collector, concerns an interesting article that Robert Palermo wrote for *The Pipe Collector* in which he compared his collection of guitars over the years to his collection of pipes and said that even if alterations made improvements, they should not be made because a true collector would never tamper with the original. The people who change their pipes are pipe smokers but not true pipe collectors. I used to agree with that, but my new response is, try telling my wife that I am not a true pipe collector. With hundreds of pipes, acquired over a quarter-century of searching, including traveling thousands of miles, it would be silly to say that I am not a pipe collector.

In fact, I'm always searching for the ideal smoke, which is why I am a pipe collector in the first place.

That hardly sounds like a controversial statement, but according to most experienced collectors, I am in a definite minority. They would say that the concept of a perfect smoke is ephemeral, to say the least, and that collecting is something quite different from smoking. For instance, at a Chicago pipe show Rich Esserman once gave a fascinating talk in which he analyzed what appeals most to pipe collectors. He spoke of the rarity of one pipe or another, or the era in which it was made, or the shape, or the manufacturer, or the stamping, or a dozen other factors.

"Far down on the list," he said, "is how well the pipe smokes."

As I listened to Rich, I knew that I disagreed with him but could not put my finger on precisely why. It was only later, as I thought about his talk, that it occurred to me: there are two types of pipe collectors, and their objectives are exactly opposite. There are collectors, like Rich, who seek the ideal collection, and there are collectors, like me, who seek the ideal smoke. While we are both pipe collectors, our goals are very different.

Rich has been collecting pipes for many years, and he really knows what he is talking about. He also gives a lot of thought to collecting, and his opinions are thought-provoking for the rest of us. I admire him because he is always trying to expand his knowledge about the history of the hobby, and he retains a boyish enthusiasm that makes pipe collecting exciting and fun.

As for separating the two types of collectors, please keep in mind that we're talking about emphasis. To one collector, the most important thing might be to find a full-bent Dunhill magnum black sandblast, particularly from a specific year in the 1920s when Dunhill only made a handful of that model. Or the collector might specialize in pre-transition Barling fossils or extremely high grade Charatan free hands.

To another collector, the most important thing might be the comfort of the pipe -- a comfortable mouthpiece made of pure, soft vulcanite, an easy, open draw of smoke, the finest briar in the world, and expert craftsmanship where time is spent taking care of all the small details. For instance, the bowl needs to be turned to enhance the grain of the wood, and all centerpieces of briar and other soft parts of the wood are avoided, and the pipe is light in weight yet made so that it never develops hot spots.

See the difference?

In both cases, the collectors are extremely demanding and particular. But their objectives are quite different.

I know one collector, Ed Lehman, who is not dogmatic either way. As a trademark and patent attorney, Ed's natural inclination is to look for certain types of rare Dunhill pipes, especially those with registration and patent numbers. Ed is also an expert collector of the Red Bark series. That puts him in category No. 1 -- a collector seeking the ideal collection. But lately Ed has begun reconsidering some of his prior beliefs. It all started when he first smoked a Jess Chonowitsch oversized smooth billiard. It was such an extraordinary smoker that Ed bought two more Jess pipes. They are now among his favorites. They are so good, in fact, that Ed started questioning how open the air hole should be, and now Ed has even started opening some of his own pipes.

"I just assumed that you had to accept a pipe the way that it was made," he said. "Even if I liked everything about a pipe, except that it was a bad smoker, then I'd sell it or trade it. Now, I'll play with it a little bit, and more often than not I can solve the problem and really enjoy the pipe."

But it's that "playing with it a little bit" that drives many hard core collectors crazy. They want the old pipe kept in its original condition -- no matter what.

In the end, Ed still sides with the traditional collector. He told me he hates "tinkerers," meaning people who change the original pipe without having anywhere near the expertise of the original pipe maker. "I've seen many good pipes ruined by amateurs who thought they knew better than the pipe maker," he said. "The same goes for polishing pipes. I can't imagine how anyone could be so careless as to buff off the nomenclature, yet we see it all the time. In almost all cases where the nomenclature is faded or non-existent, it is because someone was sloppy when polishing the pipe on a buffing wheel."

Ed went on to describe the many times that he was eager to buy a pipe until he saw that the stamping was faded. "I've put my checkbook back in my pocket, and put the pipe back on the table, too many times to count," he said. We also know that collector pipes with faded nomenclature, or pipes lacking their original mouthpieces, are reduced in price by as much as 80 percent.

To understand the logic behind the traditional collector's viewpoint, I'd like to quote from an eloquent e-mail that Bob Palermo sent to Rich Esserman, which was published in the Winter-Spring 2003 issue of *The Pipe Smoker's Ephemeris*: "Pipe collecting is not just about getting a good smoke, any more than collecting pocket-watches is just about telling time, or guitar collecting is just about playing music ... Collectible pipes are our *objects d' art*, our museum pieces, our Rembrandts. And I believe for this reason, pipes that represent the best of our hobby's history should be preserved and smoked 'as is.' In fact, this concept can be extended to any pipe that cannot be replaced."

Here are two types of collectors – me with my good friend Ed Lehman. The one thing we agree on is that we have a passion for our pipes.

While writing this article I had a conversation with John Weidemann, a pipe maker who spent most of his career as an antique dealer. John said that when it comes to the traditional collectors, in any field, nearly all of them fit the description that

Rich Esserman gave. "If you find a rare old pipe, you really shouldn't touch it, other than a very careful ream and clean," John said. "Collectors are pretty fanatical about wanting to buy things in their original state. I've heard of Mustang car collectors who insist that the original paint be left untouched, even it it's faded or peeling."

I remember visiting Dunhill's London store several years ago when they had some old pipes in a display case. They were all well smoked and, to my mind, looked quite dirty. A Dunhill pipe maker was on duty at the store with a buffing wheel. He was there

Sykes Wilford of www.smokingpipes.com sells an incredible number of estate pipes, especially old Dunhills that have been professionally refurbished. His goal is to make the pipes clean and inviting, but to do so without touching the nomenclature or changing the pipes in any way.

to polish the customers' pipes and to answer questions. I asked, "Why don't you clean up those old pipes? They look pretty shabby. You could take the cake down to a thin carbon coating, run boiling alcohol through the stem and shank, re-stain the outside of the bowls and make the mouthpieces glisten."

"Yes, we could," he said. "But if we did that, then we wouldn't have museum pieces."

"Why don't you try to make them look as close as possible to the way they looked when they were first made, and not how they looked after 20 years of smoking?" I asked. "Let's say this pipe," I said, pointing to one of the pipes in the display case, "was made in 1920 and smoked until 1940. What you're doing is preserving the pipe as it looked when it was last smoked rather than making it look like it did in 1920 when it was first on the store shelf."

"That's true," he said. "And it's because these are museum pieces. Perhaps if I were allowed to take the pipe home and smoke it, I'd do as you suggest."

The Dunhill pipe maker was a very nice man and an expert craftsman. We had a pleasant conversation, but when he asked, "Where are you from?" and I replied, "Los Angeles," I couldn't help but feel that he was thinking "Hollywood," where everything, including a collectible pipe, is fantasy. He probably thought I'd want to take that old Dunhill pipe and paint it blue!

But how many of us are collecting pipes to display them in a museum? I doubt there are very many, though we all have met collectors who have certain pipes that they refuse to smoke. For example, there's Rob Cooper, a pipe collector from the Philadelphia area who is an expert at cleaning up old pipes. Rob is not afraid to use a drill bit to open a shank to get an easier draw, and he is extremely adept at staining pipes and at using a buffing wheel and a reamer. But there are certain pipes in his collection that Rob simply won't touch, and he wouldn't consider smoking them. Typically, they are very rare high grade Danish pipes. He prefers to display them and, at times, to sell or trade some when he wants to upgrade his collection. "At times I'll buy them back, too!" he said.

When asked why he doesn't smoke some of his pipes, Rob replied: "The heart of what I collect are Larsen straight grains with a 'Made in Copenhagen' stamp. They were made from the late 50s to the middle 1960s. Why should I take them down a grade or two by smoking them? I've got plenty of other good pipes to smoke."

I certainly understand and respect Rob's position, though I don't agree with it entirely. If I spend $20 or $100 or $1,000 on a pipe, I do so to smoke it -- and for no other reason. If I had a Charatan Summa Cum Laude, like Pablo Casals, I'd fire it up and smoke it regularly. I agreed with Marty Pulvers, when he wrote several years ago that if you want to make an investment to make money, then call Merrill Lynch. (You could also call Rob Cooper, who is a superb stockbroker!) Like Marty, I am looking for the ideal smoker. My goal is to enjoy a satisfying and relaxing 20 - 90 minutes with a pipe whenever I feel like it and can afford the time. I want every smoke to be a great smoke. Of all the pipes that I have owned over the years, there are about 75 that I know I can depend on enjoying each and every time. They were made by a wide variety of pipe makers, including Jess Chonowitsch, the Ivarssons, S. Bang, Bo Nordh, Paul Perri, Bertram, Dunhill, Barling, Peterson, Ser Jacopo, JHW, Savinelli, Brebbia, Sasieni, Comoy, Charatan, Ashton, Upshall and others.

Some of my all-time favorite smokers were made by Tony Rodriguez of Los Angeles. Tony has been making pipes for more than a decade, and he studied under Lars Ivarsson and Jess Chonowitsch. He buys all his briar from Jess and Bo Nordh. Tony's pipes are a perfect illustration of a brand name that is relatively unknown but smoke like a dream. "They are as good as any I have ever smoked," said collector Lalo Schifrin, the well known jazz musician and composer. One of the real advantages of Tony's pipes is that they are opened the way that I like.

In many cases, I have had the brand name pipes altered to suit my taste. This includes new mouthpieces, made by an individual craftsman who signs his work, such as Jess Chonowitsch, Tony Rodriguez, Jim Cooke, Rich Lewis or Howard Schulte, as opposed to a factory worker who was rushing to get out the door at five o'clock so he could meet his girlfriend at the pub. This includes having the top of a pipe rounded slightly so I don't get cut, or the feeling of being cut, by the sharp edges that come from chopping off the top in a straight line. In addition, it includes having the air hole re-drilled so it is open and has an easy draw. On old used pipes, if Jim Benjamin thinks the original stain has faded, and he wants to re-stain it, I always say yes. I want all of my pipes to look beautiful -- to me -- and to smoke just the way I like them. None of these things has anything to do with the stamping, or nomenclature, on a pipe, and I have never understood why that is considered so important.

This is one of my favorite pipes. It has no nomenclature whatsoever -- just gorgeous grain.

I realize that to traditional hard core collectors, this is heresy! But it's what I like. I try to find the very best craftsmen, who use the very best materials, to make the very best pipes. If they then need to be modified to suit my taste, I have them modified. *I am a pipe collector because I am a pipe smoker -- and for no other reason.*

Three types of pipe collectors: On the left is the musician Lalo Schifrin, composer of the *Mission Impossible* theme song along with hundreds of other popular musical scores, me in the middle and the legendary pipe maker, Jess Chonowitsch, on the right.

Pipe collecting is quite different from coin collecting or stamp collecting or artwork or baseball cards or the vast majority of other items that are collected. What makes pipe collecting unique is not only that we use the product, but that we smoke it, we hold it in our hands, we put it in our mouths, we go back to it over and over many hours each month for years and years -- maybe for decades -- and maybe even for a lifetime. I figure that if I'm going to spend that much time seeking enjoyment from a little wooden smoking instrument, then it needs to be exactly, precisely, 100 percent the way I like it -- regardless of the requirements of the traditional rules of collecting.

Sorry -- but I say forget those rules. Make your own. You should have your pipes altered to suit your tastes, just as you have your clothes altered to suit your body, or your food prepared the way you like it, or a hundred other things in your life that you insist be changed to suit your personality. Don't be intimidated by the purists who tell you what you are supposed to like.

Think back to when you started smoking a pipe in the first place, and the reasons you continue to pursue the hobby today. Isn't it because you see it as a source of unending pleasure and relaxation, an antidote to stress, a way of escaping from the pressures of the modern world, a satisfying hobby that promotes peace of mind, excitement, stimulation, satisfaction and serenity -- all at the same time? If your answer is yes, then you have no choice but to enjoy your pipe collecting and pipe smoking hobby your own way, and if that means having your pipes changed, then I say more power to you.

CHAPTER TWENTY-THREE

RANDOM REFLECTIONS

*This is an unusual chapter, written especially for the book,
in which I offer my thoughts on a handful of random issues.*

* * * * *

Pipe shows attract people from all walks of life from all over
the world. Invariably they are friendly and fun to be with,
such as these collectors from Europe and Asia who attended
the 2003 Chicago Pipe Show. (L-R) Rolf Osterndorff from
Germany (www.piepenhoeker.de) and, from Taiwan, Steven
Shih, Kevin Shih (www.pipes.com.tw), Tina and Chiao.

• Pipe collecting attracts all kinds of characters -- from corporate
bigwigs and prominent doctors and lawyers to unemployed
dilettantes who consider ten dollars too much to spend on a pipe ...
with the vast majority of collectors falling somewhere in between.

My favorite story illustrating who attends a pipe show involves a very successful attorney who was waiting for the doors to open at a Chicago Pipe Show a number of years ago. At that time, the shows were held at a modest hotel in what might be described as not the greatest neighborhood.

The attorney, who frequents the staid Union League Club in Chicago, settled down in a comfortable chair in the hotel lobby, reading the *Chicago Tribune* and waiting for the pipe show to start. He made the mistake of glancing up just for a second and making eye contact with a very scruffy-looking man, who instantly made a beeline straight toward him.

"Hey buddy -- where's the trucker convention?" the disheveled man asked.

"I don't know ... I don't have the faintest idea," the attorney replied, burying his head in his newspaper after waving the man off.

A few minutes later, an even more grungy-looking man entered the hotel, wearing baggy blue jeans with suspenders over a tight-fitting T-shirt that covered only half of his large and hairy stomach. Our attorney friend just happened to glance up from his paper to see -- you guessed it -- the man heading straight toward him.

"Hey buddy -- where's the pipe show?"

~ ~ ~

• There are literally thousands of choices when it comes to pipe tobaccos, and everything, absolutely everything, is a matter of personal taste. And our tastes frequently change over the years. It is not unusual for a person's body chemistry to change over time, which might explain why a certain tobacco that once tasted great now is offensive.

For the past dozen years or so, my preference has been English and Oriental tobacco blends as long as they have plenty of latakia. I especially like Dunhill tobaccos, including 965, Nightcap, Durbar, Early Morning, Mr. Alfred's Own and all of their other latakia mixtures. Another brand of tobacco that I am partial to is Peter Stokkebye, whose Proper English blend is out of this world. I also buy one pound bags of Stokkebye's English Supreme from Fred Stoker and Sons (1-800-chewers).

Greg Pease tobaccos, especially Odyssey and Charing Cross, are absolutely superb, as are several of the McClelland blends, including the original Frog Morton. Cornell and Diehl offers a wide variety of choices at reasonable prices.

It is not surprising that one of the finest selections of premium pipe tobaccos (and a large number of quality pipes, as well) can be found in South Carolina – at the beautiful Low Country Pipe and Cigar Store in the Myrtle Beach area.

~ ~ ~

• I travel a great deal, and it is always fun visiting the local tobacconists. I only occasionally look at new pipes, but I *always* buy new tobaccos.

Steve Fallon wrote an interesting article in *The Pipe Collector* in which he described how he puts his tobacco in a blender and chops it up to make it easier to smoke. I remember years ago the late Barry Levin advocated using a food processor for the same purpose.

Personally, I have done this many times and am a supporter of the practice, but my own preference is to open the lid on a tin of tobacco and transfer it to a glass or plastic jar that is closed but one in which a slight amount of air can penetrate. I might leave the tobacco like that, stored in a closet, for months or even years. When I take it out, the top part of the tobacco is crispy, but the inside still retains some moisture. It is easy to break the tobacco apart with your fingers before loading into the bowl, so there is no need for a blender or food processor.

~ ~ ~

• If the tobacco has totally dried out all the way through, you can obviously re-moisten it with water, or by placing it in a humidor with a wetted sponge or something similar that is placed inside the top of the humidor. My own preference is a little different, where I recommend one of two options:

1. Load your pipe with the dried out tobacco, then take your index finger and thumb and form a circle, similar to the way they would be if you were giving the "OK" sign. Put this circle (your thumb and index finger) over the bowl and blow hot air directly onto the tobacco. Do this two or three times, and then gently press down on the tobacco, noting how suddenly it has just the right amount of moisture.

2. Let's say I have an old 100-gram tin of 965 where the tobacco feels as dried out as Corn Flakes or Rice Krispies. I then buy a brand new 100-gram tin of 965 and combine equal amounts of the old and new tobaccos. It is amazing how the wetness of the new moisturizes the dried out old tobacco, and how the dryness of the old, helps drain some of the excess water from the new tobacco.

~ ~ ~

• After each bowl of tobacco, I use a "British Buttner" reamer, or a copy of that type of reamer, inside the bowl. This provides a very gentle scraping that will get rid of your cake but not touch the wood. As I have said throughout the book, I generally do not like a carbon cake.

But if a pipe has a "hot spot," where one part of the wood burns hotter than the rest, then I *will* build a cake. Fred Heim, the ultimate calabash collector, and I have talked about the fact that nearly all calabash pipes develop a hot spot near the bend where the shank approaches the bowl. Being a Sherlock Holmes fan, I like calabashes almost as much as Fred does, so on these pipes I have built a cake.

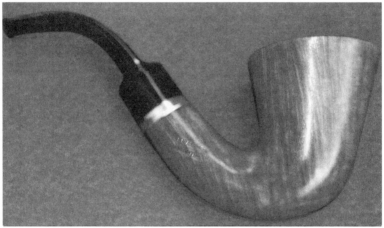

My favorite calabash -- a Ser Jacopo gem line straight grain.

One collector told me a story about one of his pipes that developed a hot spot, so he sent it back to the store that sold it to him. He got his pipe back a month or so later, with a smooth, even cake, and his hot spot was gone. He called the store to ask how they did it. The owner replied, "We sent it back to the factory and they assigned different workers to smoke the hell out of it!" Whatever works.

Are there easy ways to develop a cake quickly? You bet. There are dozens, but my favorite is to moisten the inside of the bowl. You can dip your finger into water and rub the inside walls of the tobacco chamber, or you can use a wetted pipe cleaner and do the same. Make sure you put a pipe cleaner in the pipe, and keep it there for the next step, which is to pour granulated sugar to the top of the bowl. Then dump out the sugar. You'll see that plenty of the grains of sugar are stuck to the side of your bowl. Just fill it up with tobacco and enjoy your smoke, and you won't believe how quickly you can build a smooth, even cake using this method. If the cake is uneven, use your finger to rub it down gently so it becomes even again.

~ ~ ~

• There are so many individual pipe makers throughout the world, and I admire each and every one of them. It takes a special skill and dedication to become a pipe maker. One of the more interesting individuals is Julius Vesz, who is based in Toronto, Canada.

Collector Marke Beale, M.D., has written a number of items in *The Pipe Smoker's Ephemeris* about Julius Vesz' skill at repairing old pipes and about how much he enjoys smoking Vesz pipes. I have one Vesz pipe, and I like it very much. The shape makes it easy to keep in your mouth. Of course, I try not to keep a pipe clenched between my teeth, but there are times when it is unavoidable, or a real nuisance to have to put the pipe down repeatedly, such as when I am writing or otherwise working with my hands.

But what I find most intriguing about Julius Vesz is his commitment to freedom, and the fact that in his youth in Eastern Europe he was confronted first by Nazism, which he escaped, and then by Communism, which he escaped. The truly scary part is that he compares the anti-smoking movement today to those two totalitarian systems. It is one thing for me, having lived in the United States all my life, to pontificate about the threat to freedom that the prohibitionists appear to represent. But it is quite another for Mr. Vesz, having *lived* under both Nazism and Communism, to make the comparison. I take that as genuinely frightening, and I hope you do too.

~ ~ ~

• If you want to know more about the anti-tobacco movement, I highly recommend two books: *For Your Own Good* by Jacob Sullum (The Free Press), and *Tobacco* by Iain Gately (Grove Press). Both books are thoroughly researched, well written, lively and informative. Just to give you a flavor of their styles, I will quote from each:

"If you think the legal tobacco industry is sinister, imagine the sort of people who will be attracted to the business after prohibition. They will be aggressive risk-takers with no compunction about breaking the law or using violence to settle disputes. They will have experience in smuggling, deception, and bribery. And they will be fighting each other for shares of a very lucrative business."
--Jacob Sullum, p. 266

"Although the No Smoking signs going up everywhere showed a red circle enclosing a cigarette with a red line through it, they did not imply that other forms of smoking were permitted. Indeed, pipes and cigars were banned on many forms of public transport long before cigarettes were prohibited. The bans were usually on the grounds of smell as opposed to health. While the human nose was unchanged, the category of odors considered offensive had expanded. The industrialized world had developed a fascination for personal hygiene. Although it was acceptable to spew vast quantities of complex and toxic chemicals into the environment ... "
--Iain Gately, pp. 306-307

Sullum is an American magazine editor and syndicated columnist, while Gately is a journalist and novelist who lives in London. Both men are brilliant, and reading their books provides insight into the deceptions and half-truths used by the anti-tobacco crusaders.

~ ~ ~

• One of the most interesting essays I have read about tobacco was written by Dennis Prager, the popular radio show host based in Los Angeles. It was included in the May and June, 1998, issues of his newsletter called *The Prager Perspective*, and the essay was entitled The War Against Tobacco and America's Broken Moral Compass.

"The joy and relaxation that cigars and pipes have brought me are very great," he wrote. "Life does not afford us an unlimited number of daily pleasures that are largely as innocuous as cigar or pipe smoking."

Prager objects to the demonization of smokers by the government, and I want to add that this is especially true in California. I was watching television recently with my 21-year-old son, Jack, and a commercial came on implying that parents who smoked in front of their children, which I had done for many years, were in fact *killing* them. I was ready to throttle the people who made that commercial (in a manner of speaking), but it is what we have come to expect from the anti-smoking movement. As I have said before, this is official hate speech from the state. It is nothing more than pure propaganda.

As Prager pointed out, "Aside from common sense culled from our own experience -- for example, nearly all of us over 40 years of age grew up with at least one smoking parent and are perfectly healthy -- there are many scientists and scientific studies that reveal the lie behind the claims made about secondhand smoke's dangers:

> • "In 1981, prior to realizing that secondhand smoke was the key to getting the American public behind anti-smoking laws, the American Cancer Society told a different story about secondhand smoke. An analysis of 75,000 women by the Cancer Society's Lawrence Garfinkel concluded that 'compared to nonsmoking women married to nonsmoking men, nonsmokers married to smoking men showed very little, if any, increased risk of lung cancer' ...

- "Three of the most comprehensive studies on secondhand smoke ever undertaken were excluded from the EPA risk assessment. *None of the three showed any statistical link between spousal smoking and lung cancer ...*"

Prager also criticizes the government for saying that tobacco is worse than alcohol and that smoking is as addictive as heroin or cocaine. He asks, which pilot would you rather fly with -- the cigarette smoker or the drug addict?

~ ~ ~

- I have used a thousand different pipe racks for storing my pipes over the years, and today I am finally satisfied with the ones in my den. They were custom built, and, in my opinion, worth every penny. I can look at my pipes whenever I want; they get plenty of air, yet there is no direct sunlight on them. Each cabinet has a Plexiglas cover (I'd use real glass except we have too many earthquakes in California!), and I put a covering over the Plexiglas of the material used to darken car windows. This tinting prevents my pipes from being exposed to sunlight, which can damage the stain on your pipe bowls and totally oxidize your vulcanite mouthpieces.

I believe it is important that pipes be allowed to "breathe" when they are at rest, so I had a half dozen holes cut into the wood, on each side and on the top and bottom, of my pipe cabinets. I have seen collections where the pipes are hidden away in drawers, or kept in boxes in storage closets, but I don't think that is wise. I think the open air between smokes helps the pipes smoke better. I really don't know why, but I am almost positive this is the case.

~ ~ ~

- Ever since I started praising the high grade pipes, I have found myself having to deny charges that I am elitist or that I am on the payroll of the high grade pipe makers. I really am not an elitist, as evidenced by the fact that I have said repeatedly in this book that some of my no-name pipes that cost less than $50 smoke better than some of my elegant high grades. At the same time, I don't think elitism is all bad. I would rather be an elitist than a communist. High standards are important to me, and it would be ridiculous to say that all pipes are equal. They are far from it. But there is no place for intolerance when it comes to pipe collecting. *Vive la difference!*

That is why I am so adamant about the precise airflow that I like. Although I sound a little dogmatic on the subject, I always do back off in the end and say that it is strictly a matter of personal opinion. For instance, Jim Cooke is a phenomenal pipe maker, and his customers are intensely loyal to him. There is no way Jim would open one of his pipes to my dimensions, so that means that his repeat customers such as Vic Griseta, obviously like the smaller opening. Who am I to say that they are wrong? It would be preposterous for me even to try, so I won't.

Three of the smartest, and nicest, distributors of high grade pipes. (L-R) Mike Glukler (www.briarblues.com), Marty Pulvers of Sherlock's Haven in San Francisco, and Steve Richman of Piedmont Tobacconist in Oakland, California.

But what about my saying that Bo Nordh's pipes (and Jim Cooke's pipes) don't smoke well unless they are opened the way that I like? That's life. Of course, it *clearly* shows that I'm not on anyone's payroll! But that is my honest opinion after years and years of trial and error and experimentation and drawing my own conclusions. Am I right and are they wrong? Of course not. We just have our own opinions. The good news, from my point of view, is that the pipes can be "fixed" easily, and once opened, there is nothing like them! They are the best in the world ... *in my opinion.*

Which leads me to apologize in advance to any reader who interprets any part of this book as being dogmatic. I avoid like the plague anyone who writes about pipes as if they are offering the Ten Commandments of Pipe Collecting, and if I fall into that trap in any of the pages of this book, please tear them out.

One of the main attractions of pipe collecting is that a dozen of us can get an equal amount of pleasure and satisfaction from the hobby, and yet not agree on what pipes we like, what shapes, what types of tobacco, and a hundred other basic issues. Isn't that great?

I realize that individualism is becoming a lost art these days, but we should cherish the extent to which we can preserve it, and pipe collecting, dating back to the 19th Century, allows us to express ourselves in the 21st Century like nothing else. There is something that is quite special, extraordinary and completely unique about this hobby, and each of us should embrace it with our own individual preferences and opinions.

~ ~ ~

• When I wax poetic about the beauties and smoking qualities of high grade pipes, I do not mean to imply that you will reach an instant epiphany the moment you take your first puff. There is nothing magical or psychedelic about these pipes. You won't get a sudden rush after you light up.

No, what these pipes do is call you back for more -- night after night. They are the ones you naturally gravitate toward. They are the ones you enjoy smoking over and over.

That is the test of a great pipe. Do I reach for it again and again?

One corner of the tobacco bar at Sherlock's Haven in San Francisco. The store's owner, Marty Pulvers, was one of the first American distributors to recognize the value of high grade pipes. Since closing the store, Marty has developed a thriving online business.

~~~~~

CHAPTER TWENTY-FOUR

PIPE SMOKING AS AN ANTIDOTE TO STRESS

This final chapter appeared as an article in Pipes *and* tobaccos *in 1998, and I believe it contains many valuable suggestions to help you minimize any possible health risks associated with pipe smoking. I refer once again to Ed Kolpin, who has spent his entire life surrounded by secondhand smoke, and who continues to enjoy his pipes today at age 94. I also refer to the philosopher Bertrand Russell, who smoked his pipe non-stop until he died at age 98. I plan on living as long as Russell did, and I will do it by following the advice given by the experts quoted in this article.*

I would like to relate an extraordinary anecdote about this pipe-loving academic; it involves a terrifying experience that very nearly curtailed the sage's longevity. Ultimately, it was his love of tobacco and his pipe that saved the day. I read about this in an old Pipe World *letter-to-the-editor by Sir Alexander Haddow, an eminent medical scientist who was a professor at the Institute of Cancer Research at London's Royal Cancer Hospital. Sir Alexander wrote about Bertrand Russell:*

"A good many years ago -- I think he was in his seventies -- he was about to fly home from Oslo. Before boarding the plane, he asked the stewardess, could he smoke his pipe during the flight? In deference she seated him at the tail end where he might smoke to his heart's content. Not long after take-off, the plane dived nose first into the fjord. Several of the passengers in the forward end were

drowned, while others in the tail, including Russell, made their escape and swam about for half an hour before being rescued. This extraordinary experience greatly impressed Russell as showing: 1. that tobacco can save life; 2. that a philosopher can speak the truth without knowing it at the time: before boarding the plane, he had said to the stewardess: 'If I don't smoke I shall die.'".

Bertrand Russell, who credited his pipe with saving his life.

* * * * *

During the past decade, it has been impossible to escape the steady drumbeat decrying the "evils" of tobacco, particularly the claim that cigarette smoking cuts short the lives of more than 400,000 Americans each year. There are so many anti-tobacco messages emanating from the media that it seems far-fetched, or even dangerous, to assert that moderate pipe smoking in a relaxed setting actually promotes good health and longevity.

But those of us who enjoy our pipes that way don't need to be told that pipe smoking is an ideal antidote to stress -- because we already know it. "Our pipes help us unwind, they let the air out, they release the pressure and they are extremely soothing," said Ed Kolpin, who founded his Santa Monica pipe store in 1928 and who still enjoys at least two or three pipe bowls a day. "There are immense psychological benefits from pipe smoking. Pipes help you relax. You live longer with a pipe." Ed will turn 90 on his next birthday [written in 1998], and he was smoking a Barling Guinea Grain while making these comments.

Some photos from the wall in my den, including Arnold Schwarzenegger (left) enjoying a large canadian and David Ogilvie ("Confessions of an Advertising Man") next to Michael Jordan (right). I love to relax with a pipe in this room.

Remember, stress kills. It has been linked to strokes, many types of cancer, heart attacks and a thousand other ailments. We're all living such fast-paced lives these days, full of pressure, strains, demands and tension, that it's not unusual for many health care professionals to recommend slowing down and relaxing as the most important steps toward good health.

Very few studies have been conducted to determine the longevity of pipe smokers, and not a single study has concluded that moderate pipe smokers suffer fatal consequences because of their enjoyment of the pipe. In earlier chapters I have mentioned the one study conducted by the American Cancer Society and the American Heart Association, among others, to find out just how dangerous pipe smoking could be, where the research showed that pipe smokers on average live two years longer -- yes, longer -- than non-smokers. While those results are encouraging, I must confess to being suspicious of *any* study of pipe smokers.

The problem is that there are so many different ways to enjoy a pipe -- and some are a lot safer than others -- that it is impossible to conduct an apples-to-apples type of comparison. For instance, we all know pipe smokers who inhale every puff, and obviously, that is *not* a safe way to enjoy a pipe. Since most of us do not inhale, we would want those pipe smokers excluded from any study of the health effects of our hobby. Otherwise, they would make pipe smoking appear to be far more dangerous than it is.

Another problem with a study of pipe smokers is that there is a great variety in the amount of time each individual pipe smoker actually spends smoking. Many collectors are very strict about limiting their smoking to one or two bowls per day, and there are others who only smoke on weekends. But then there are those who smoke their first pipe practically before they're out of bed in the morning and proceed to smoke all day and all night until they go to sleep. How does a study differentiate the weekend puffer from the chain-smoking addict?

Then, there are the differences in the size of pipe bowls. Back at the turn of the century, the average pipe bowl was smaller than it is today. The best way to illustrate this is to study the writings of Christopher Morley, who said that he basically lived to smoke his pipe. "I define life as a process of the Will-to-Smoke; recurring periods of consciousness in which the enjoyability of smoking is manifest, interrupted by intervals of recuperation," he wrote in 1916. Morley strongly recommended a minimum of 16 pipe bowls per day! But he also said he never smoked during the day at work. Well, clearly, those 16 bowls must have been very small, probably like a Dunhill Group 2, because he simply would not have had time to smoke 16 large-bowl pipes, especially if he abstained while at the office.

Another reason that a study of pipe smokers would almost certainly lead to erroneous conclusions is that the *style* of smoking varies so much among individuals. We all know the Type A pipe smokers who puff, puff, puff, and then come up for air just for a second before returning to puff, puff, puff. Contrast them with the veterans who have mastered the art of keeping their pipes barely smoldering so they just take an occasional puff, what author Paul Gallant called a "kiss puff." The Danish pipe maker Lars Ivarsson once pointed out that the term "cool smoke" is a contradiction in terms, and of course, he is correct, but there are degrees of heat when it comes to pipe smoking. The temperature inside the mouth of our Type A smoker is going to be a whole lot hotter than the temperature inside the mouth of the veteran who enjoys an occasional puff.

So let's say that our goal as pipe smokers is to be relaxed, moderate and stress-free. We want to get the maximum enjoyment from our pipes, and we know that if we only have one or two bowls a day, we'll obviously enjoy and savor each one more than if we have 16 bowls a day. Nearly all the books and magazines on pipe smoking, including this one, recommend moderation. I think we can all agree that when problems occur, they are caused by excess.

But I don't think we should leave it at that -- for a number of reasons. Personally, I find it offensive when one pipe smoker scorns another for not adhering to some arbitrary definition of moderation. Excess for you might be moderation for me, or vice versa. Also, what good does it do to advocate moderation, as pipe books do, without offering concrete tips to make it easy to incorporate into your lifestyle? Or if you want to continue smoking heavily, the least these publications can do is to offer practical suggestions that will help you minimize the risk.

While I do indeed advocate moderation, however that is defined, I believe there is much to be said in favor of those people who are never without their pipes. Remember, I'm talking about your friends and mine. For one thing, they're likely to be a lot more knowledgeable than the rest of us. If one person smokes one bowl per day and another person smokes 10 bowls per day, assuming the bowls are the same size, then the heavy smoker will have 10 times more experience than the moderate pipe smoker. After 12 months, the moderate smoker will have one year's worth of experience as a pipe smoker, while the heavy smoker will have the equivalent of a decade's worth: We're talking about experience in loading his pipe, keeping it lit and probably in trying different pipes and tobaccos, among other things.

Assuming he doesn't inhale, the only likely danger to the heavy pipe smoker is in his mouth -- his palate, gums and lips, the lining of his cheeks and his throat. Unlike our lungs and arteries, everything in the mouth is visible to the naked eye, and any problems in the mouth are extremely slow-growing and easy to detect long before they become serious. Hence, if the 16-bowl-a-day pipe smoker gets two or three teeth cleanings each year, which I believe is a must for cosmetic purposes if for no other reason, then his dentist will be able to detect any problems in their earliest stages. If he has an annual physical exam, he can ask his doctor to look at his vocal chords -- again, this is all with the naked eye.

Now let's say he does have a problem. There are still plenty of options for even the heaviest of pipe smokers -- besides giving up the pipe. Of course, he can always cut down. This is one of the beauties of the pipe. Cutting back from 10 bowls a day to two is nowhere near as difficult as reducing from a two-pack-a-day cigarette habit to five cigarettes a day, especially using some of the suggestions that various experts offer in this article.

Pipe collector Ben Rapaport, who sells what is called "antiquarian tobacciana" literature, once got into trouble from smoking at a non-stop pace. "I had 13 stitches in my tongue," he said. "The problem was that I kept a pipe in my mouth all day. The surgery was four years ago, and I have never had a problem since. Now, I either hold the pipe in my hand or put it down. I never just leave it in my mouth. My doctor is an ear, nose and throat specialist, and he said the problem came from the heat. If you keep the pipe in your mouth all the time that you're smoking, the constant heat can destroy the protective coating on your tongue that you're born with."

In addition to holding the pipe in your hand, and smoking slowly, you can also drink water to keep your mouth cooler. Many health care professionals recommend drinking at least eight 8-ounce glasses of water a day anyway. Some pipe smokers also suck on lozenges, hard candy or cough drops. My personal favorites are sugar-free black currant pastilles, which contain glycerine. My doctor advises against mint or menthol because they actually dry your mouth. Biotene toothpaste and mouthwash are also excellent products because they are designed to increase moisture in the mouth.

Several years ago, I visited Johannesburg, South Africa, and met one of that country's most enthusiastic pipe collectors, an attorney named Carl Witte-Vermeulen. He told me that he had developed what felt like a blister on the roof of his mouth, which he had surgically removed. "I was determined not to give up the pipe," he said, adding that his dentist was also a good friend. "We came up with the idea of creating a plastic cover for my palate, similar to the type that holds a retainer. Since then, I've never had a problem, and I have continued to enjoy my pipes. In fact, my dentist told me that I have the mouth of a non-smoker."

I was so impressed by Carl's story that I asked my dentist to make a retainer-type of covering for my palate as well. It took a few days to get used to it, but it was worth the effort because my dentist, who took photos before and after, says that he sees such a big difference in the roof of my mouth. "The tissues are moist and pink, like they are supposed to be," he explained as he showed me the most recent photos. Pipe collector Jimmy Booth also uses a covering for the roof of his mouth, and he said, "My dentist used to give me a hard time, but now, he says I have the mouth of a non-smoker." That's three out of three.

You can also do the same if you have trouble with your gums or with keeping your teeth white. People who grind their teeth very often are given plastic "night guards," which can be worn over the bottom teeth to cover the lower gums, or over the upper teeth to cover the upper gums. If you have a problem with your gums, or with keeping the inside of your lower teeth clean, I don't see why you couldn't have your dentist make you a night guard that you could wear when smoking your pipe.

Most of your taste buds are on your tongue, so none of these suggestions for using plastic to cover various parts of the mouth will impede your enjoyment of the pipe. Of course, I am not recommending that every pipe smoker arm himself to the teeth, so to speak, with plastic. I am only offering these suggestions if you have a trouble spot in your mouth and yet want to continue enjoying your pipe.

Dr. David Boska, my personal physician, is a pipe smoker, and he recommends moving the pipe around each time you smoke. "People get into trouble when they just leave the pipe in the same spot in their mouths all day long," he said. "If you normally smoke the pipe from the left side of your mouth, then try it from the right side. After a while, smoke from the middle, then the left side, and then the right again. The whole point is to avoid having any one irritant over and over without any let up."

But let's say that you are one of those 10-to-16-bowl-a-day pipe smokers, you really do want to cut down but you don't know how. Or maybe you're contemplating switching to a pipe as a way to quit cigarettes, yet you're concerned about smoking just as much as before. Are there any proven suggestions for these smokers that work and make it easy? "Yes," says Dr. Brad Rodu, an oral pathologist at the University of Alabama at Birmingham. "There are plenty of ways to get nicotine without smoking, especially now with all the replacements like nicotine gum, patches, lozenges and so forth. Unquestionably, the most effective way is with smokeless tobacco such as Skoal, Skoal Bandits, Oliver Twist or Swedish snus [www.snusworldwide.com], and I strongly recommend these products as substitutes for cigarettes."

Rodu is one of the country's leading cancer researchers, and his specialty is mouth cancer. I expressed surprise at his answer because the media presents smokeless tobacco as being almost as harmful as cigarette smoking. I remember once seeing an old baseball player interviewed on television by Joe Garagiola and half of the man's face was carved away because of the effects of a lifetime of chewing tobacco.

"Yes, that can happen," Rodu said. "But it is extremely rare. In fact, it is only 13 smokeless users out of every 100,000, after five or six decades of continuous use, who suffer negative consequences like you are describing. That research was reported in the prestigious *New England Journal of Medicine*. Compare that with auto travel, where the death rate due to accidents is 17 per 100,000 people each year. Nothing is risk-free, but research shows that smokeless tobacco is literally 98 percent safer than cigarette smoking. I have not studied pipe smoking per se, but I do know that smoking one or two cigars a day carries almost no risk, and I suspect the same is true with pipes."

Rodu is convinced that the reason some pipe smokers inhale or smoke continuously all day, exactly like cigarette smokers, is because they want the nicotine. The good news, according to Rodu, is that nicotine has been studied up one side and down the other and, in the end, has been found to be relatively harmless. Addictive, yes, but it doesn't cause cancer or emphysema. "Nicotine is the captor, but smoke is the killer," is how Rodu puts it. Nicotine elevates your pulse a little and aids in mental alertness. In fact, Rodu says it is very much like caffeine. In his book, *For Smokers Only*, he provides a chart comparing nicotine to caffeine, which is reprinted here. If you are a 10-to-16-bowl-a-day pipe smoker and want to cut back to two or three bowls a day, I strongly recommend that you read Dr. Rodu's book. *(For*

Smoker's   Only.   For   more   information,   see www.uab.edu/smokersonly.)

So the two doctors are making similar suggestions, where Dr. Boska recommends moving the pipe around, changing position, while Dr. Rodu recommends changing the nicotine delivery system around, mixing the nicotine source. I want to add that these are two of the most brilliant and accomplished doctors in their respective fields, and it takes great courage for them to deviate in any way from the conventional wisdom that all tobacco is bad no matter what. Rather than being moralistic, they are focused on harm reduction strategies.

Similarities of Nicotine and Caffeine		
	Nicotine	**Caffeine**
Brain:	Stimulant	Stimulant
	Enhances concentration	Enhances concentration
	Enhances performance	Enhances performance
	Sense of well being	Sense of well being
	Mood elevation	Mood elevation
	Addictive: Psychic dependence	Addictive: Psychic dependence
	Withdrawal	Withdrawal
	Tolerance	Tolerance
	Stimulates breathing center	Stimulates breathing center
Circulatory:	Increases heart rate	Increases heart rate
	Increases blood pressure	Increases blood pressure
	Constricts blood vessels	Constricts blood vessels
Other:	Increases: Free fatty acids	Increases: Free fatty acids
	Catecholamine release	Catecholamine release
	Saliva and lung secretions	Stomach acids
		Urine flow

A chart from Dr. Brad Rodu's book, *For Smokers Only*.

During a recent Chicago Pipe Show, I met Charles "Chip" Dull, who is trying to bring snuff back into popularity. By snuff, I mean the old-fashioned kind that you snort through your nose. In fact, Dull was so enthusiastic that he earned an advanced degree in history from the University of Sheffield in England writing his master's thesis on snuff. Dull's company is importing snuff to the United States from two of the United Kingdom's oldest and highest quality firms in the field, Wilsons and the legendary Fribourg & Treyer. "A lot of the snuff users are executives who can't smoke in the office," he said. Dull agrees with the theory that it is best to mix it up to avoid smoking a pipe all day long. "I have three or four pipe bowls a day," he said. "But I also use snuff, and I like cigars, too. I just try not to do too much of any one thing."

Chip Dull, left, enjoys a snuff break with Ric Glaubinger of BR Tobacco in Austin, Texas.

Dr. Garret Annofsky, a retired dentist who is also a pipe collector, takes a holistic approach to good health. "If people are content in their lives, if they are satisfied and fulfilled, their general health will be better," he said. "I find that pipe smoking gives me pleasure and fulfillment. It supports an attitude of contentment and reflection, and that contributes to my overall well-being, which obviously includes my health." The pipe maker Jess Chonowitsch told me that the chief health officer in Denmark takes exactly the same position as Annofsky. And *The Economist*, which says that "America has taken leave of its senses over smoking," is convinced that the treatment is worse than the transgression. "The intolerance of the anti-smoking movement is a greater threat than smoking," it said in an April editorial.

Writer-philosopher Bertrand Russell lived to be 98, and he was never without his pipe. He was once asked if he really liked to smoke, and he answered, "No, but I dislike not smoking." Maybe he was speaking for the 10-to-16-bowl-a-day crowd. If you are in that group, and you'd like to cut back to a more moderate number so that you can savor each pipe that you smoke, then try some of the suggestions offered by Brad Rodu, D.D.S.; David Boska, M.D., Charles Dull and the other experts cited here. All you need is for one or two of them to work, and it could change your entire pattern of pipe smoking enjoyment.

Russell lived in a very different world from today's high-tech, sanitized and frantic society that has become mindlessly intolerant of anything to do with tobacco -- except for taxing and regulating it. Today's scientists would denounce Albert Einstein for his pipe just as modern-day psychiatrists would demand that Sigmund Freud extinguish his cigar. "If Freud were living today," says Dr. Boska, "he would live a longer life and enjoy his smoking more by taking advantage of the simple precautions now available."

Fortunately, Einstein and Freud were fiercely independent thinkers, and I have no doubt that if they were alive today, they would continue to enjoy their pipes and cigars, respectively. But as we approach the 21st century, we are increasingly being told how to live and what to do by the government, the media, the academics -- all the elitists whom syndicated columnist Thomas Sowell calls "the anointed." Technology is advancing so rapidly that it is exhilarating, breathtaking, unrelenting and confusing all at the same time.

How can you slow down? When can you relax? Where can you find some peace and quiet? I think the answer is obvious: whenever you can settle into your favorite easy chair, load up a beautiful old briar pipe with a tobacco specially blended for your taste, relax, savor the moment, and just puff and tamp, puff ... and tamp ... and puff ... and unwind ... and feel all the tension and stress leave your body. What a great way to live a long and healthy life!

How's this for an antidote to stress? The above photo was taken in Iceland, and the photo below shows me relaxing in a hotel in Cologne, Germany.

EPILOGUE

by Albert Mendez

When Mr Rick Newcombe first asked me to write the introduction to *In Search of Pipe Dreams* I accepted without hesitation. I've always enjoyed his essays, written in that easy, distinctively American style—so full of common sense and good humour—which has, over the past three decades, very nearly vanished. Afterwards, upon sober reflection, insidious doubt did privily assail me, and for a space I thought I should have to decline the honour in favour of some more suitable person. After all, I reasoned, Mr Newcombe is a doughty champion of the Danish School of pipe making, as personified by such luminaries as Messrs Ivarsson, Nordh, and Chonowitsch, whereas I am a devotee of the humbler examples of the English Pipe. Why, I don't own one single, solitary example of the Danish pipe-maker's art, and what's more, being a very private man who finds all communal activities somewhat distasteful, I don't attend 'pipe shows', so I've never even had the opportunity of examining any examples of the superior sort of Danish pipe. In view of all this, I calculated that there must be hundreds of pipe-smokers far better qualified to write these lines. Then I remembered that this is the twenty-first century, when in most cases a lack of knowledge or experience is considered an advantage, as it virtually guarantees that one is not burdened with any pre-conceived notions or tiresome principles.

But then even my credentials as a pipe-smoker are somewhat suspect. I grew up in pre-1959 Cuba, where the very finest of the best cigars in the world were within easy reach of the poorest of men, and consequently the number of pipe-smokers was infinitesimal. What's worse, my maternal grandfather was a part-owner of the cigar house founded by my great-uncle, Francisco Farach, in the early years of the twentieth century. My grandfather, Jaime Farach, was a scrupulous-minded man, and by the fifties, he had distanced himself from the trade. My great-uncle (known as 'Pancho' to all and sundry) was not so fastidious. He continued to manufacture *Flor de Francisco Farach*(no connexion with the cigars now made under this name in Nicaragua) at 156 Arsenal Street, across the way from the central railway station in Old Habana, until the rapid succession of political and economic upheavals forced him to close in 1960.

My father, I am happy to say, smoked pipes as well as cigars. He was an army officer who—like so many other men of the sword— found pipes a more practical, elegant, and suitable method of enjoying tobacco. All of his pipes were large Barlings with straight stems and smooth finishes; I still have two of them that were in his jacket pocket when he flew into exile. His favourite tobacco was the Craven Mixture, which he purchased three tins at a time, from a taciturn and melancholy Yorkshireman who kept a shop in Habana. This is where most of the Barlings came from as well, even though the Army commissariat at San Ambrosio barracks could supply them at cost, because my father felt that it behoved him—*noblesse oblige*—to support honest, hard-working tradesmen.

So it was only natural that I should turn to pipe smoking, and that I should be drawn to smooth-finished, straight-stemmed English pipes, and that I should prefer the Craven mixture, the aroma of which was so familiar to me. However, there was a point in my life, shortly after I first began smoking a pipe, when I was very nearly seduced away from the unexceptionable ideal of the English pipe, by the voiceless siren song of the frankly foreign Danish pipes.

Railways—both full-size and miniature—were one of my many youthful interests, and I regularly visited the New York City shops that stocked model railway supplies and publications. One of these was (until quite recently) located on West Twenty-Second Street, and specialized mainly in large-scale, flying model aeroplanes. One chilly Saturday afternoon in March of 1965, I walked west from Seventh Avenue to find a Bentley S1 Continental crouching by the kerb in front of this shop. The

Mulliner 'Sport Saloon' coachwork was a deep Ivory Black (with the luminous transparency that requires fourteen coats of paint, each one carefully rubbed down with pumice before the next one is applied), and the glossy Connolly leather upholstery was a consummately elegant blue-grey. In these stultifying days, when our sensibilities have been blunted (to a greater or lesser degree) by the concerted and relentless bombardment of visual and aural ugliness, and when motoring is—at best—a bore, it is difficult to understand the effect that such machines had upon us.

The pavements in the older commercial districts of New York City are dotted with 'standpipes' to which—in the event of a fire—the firemen connect water hoses, thereby insuring an unfailing supply to the building sprinklers and to the hose connections on the upper floors. These fixtures were—in fine weather—the favourite outdoor seating of real New Yorkers, from where they watched the passing of the world in precarious comfort. There was one outside the shop, its brass 'Siamese' fitting polished to a lovely golden glow by the caress of many thousands of trouser seats. I dropped on it and sat awhile, dreaming of *La Grande Corniche*, for which the Bentley was plainly intended.

After a few minutes, a coltish blonde with geometrically sculpted hair, pale-pink lips, and black-and-white Op-Art earrings, emerged from the shop carrying a long box with a coloured label depicting a Mk II Spitfire. She was wearing the shortest skirt that I had ever seen—the hem-line was a hand's breadth above the knees—and shiny, white, ankle-length boots. Her ensemble was the height of youthful London fashion, but nothing short of remarkable in the dingy meanness of New York City. Noting my scrutiny, she gave me the disdainful, meant-to-wither look that fashionable young women reserve for impertinent men a year or two younger than themselves. She walked haughtily to the car and stood there waiting, studiously ignoring me. After a few seconds, the shop door opened again and out stepped the young man that she was waiting for.

He was probably only three or four years older than me (an enormous difference, when one is under twenty-one years of age), slightly built, with curly, light-brown hair. He was wearing a genuine, pre-war Irvin jacket[i] over one of those crew neck sweaters in off-white wool (which the R.A.F. described as an 'aircrew frock'), with a carelessly knotted, blue-and-white, birds-eye scarf to complete the Battle of Britain look. Even his tan suede, Clarks desert boots and fawn-coloured cavalry twill trousers, would not have looked out of place in the cockpit of a Spitfire. The flat hat on his head, however, was one of those patchworks of heavy tweed, which are worn only by the most dissolute of Sloane rangers.

In his mouth was an extraordinary pipe, the likes of which I had never before seen. To begin with, it was huge, perhaps one-third larger than the Barlings my father smoked, and then there was the colour; a soft, golden honey, slightly darker than a topaz. The grain was symmetrically spicular and—thanks to the cool, deep polish—perfectly defined. The shape too, was excitingly different from the mundane forms that I was familiar with. The bowl was an exaggerated Dublinesque affair, tapering out of a long, solid stem cut with those precise chamfers, which so delighted mediæval craftsmen. In fact, the overall appearance of the pipe suggested nothing less than a gently curved hammer beam in some eccentric Great Hall.

He gave me a curious look—I suppose I *was* staring—and taking the pipe from his mouth, said 'Hullo.'

We struck up one of those spontaneously friendly conversations—far more common in those relatively innocent days—and spoke of cars and aeroplanes while his chic friend sat impatiently in the Bentley. I finally asked him about the pipe.

'Oh, this?' he said, holding it at arm's-length. 'It is rather nice, isn't it? I got it from a man in Copenhagen.' He glanced at his restless companion and then at his watch. 'I must be off,' he said, 'but I expect I'll see you again.'

During our brief conversation, he had mentioned that he collected Bentleys, and that the S1 Continental was only his town car. He didn't mention his name and I didn't ask (for I had been taught that it was bad form to ask strangers anything about themselves, even their name), so I mentally labelled him 'The Bentley Collector'.

I did meet him again, outside of the shop on two consecutive Saturday afternoons; both times, he was driving the S1 and we chatted about aeroplanes and motor-cars. He also told me a series of awful stories, the protagonist of which was an R.A.F. pilot named 'Lord Chauncey'. The best of these narratives concerned a talk given to a girl's school by this gentleman, about his flying experiences during the Battle of Britain. The 'punch-line' depended upon the similarity of the name 'Fokker' (a German aircraft manufacturer of the pre-1919 era) to a vulgar English noun.

Each time we met, he was smoking a different pipe, all made by 'a man in Copenhagen'. If I saw them again today, I might be able to say who the maker was, but back then, with my limited experience, they were simply beautiful *objets* with the strong appeal that the artefacts of different cultures once had, before we were inundated with offensively inferior examples from every corner of the globe. Forced to guess, I would say that they were probably Larsens.

Our acquaintance had reached a point where I felt that we could introduce ourselves properly, but then that spring—with the precipitiousness and irrevocableness which mark events in our youth—I turned one of life's crucial corners and nothing was ever the same again. I no longer visited the shop on Saturdays (I wouldn't do so again for more than twenty years), so I lost sight of The Bentley Collector, and I never did learn his name. Neither could I ever be certain whether he was an American pretending to be an Englishman, or an Englishman trying to sound like an American. His conversations were peppered with forties-vintage R.A.F. slang (he always spoke of motoring accidents as 'Wizard Prangs', and of his stylish friend as 'The Blonde Job') and for the most part, he spoke good English. Yet, even my young, inexperienced ear could detect a suspicion of the unpleasant nasal whine characteristic of New York City and the suburban wastelands around it. I thought no more of him until one day, six years later, when I was visiting a vintage-car establishment in Brook Mews and I was introduced to Alan Clark[ii]. He was still a private person then, eking out his slender means by writing elegant little books on military history, which were—like the man himself—unorthodox, sagacious, and incisively honest. Needless to say, the 'well-respected' hacks and critics hated them, as did the inane defenders of the propaganda-film version of England.

I told him how much I admired his landmark book on the B.E.F. in 1915 (*The Donkeys*, 1961), and we spoke of the Great War, finding ourselves in complete agreement about the true significance of that pivotal conflict, and the identity and nature of its architects. Quite naturally, we moved on to his other great (and emotional) interest, The Battle of Britain. He related an anecdote of how Bader[iii], when flying home over the English Channel, would remove his oxygen mask, slide open the cockpit of his Spitfire, and—propping the stick between his one knee and a tin leg—light his pipe and puff away contentedly. The pilots on either side would endeavour to get as far away from him as possible, in case he blew himself up, or absent-mindedly veered into their flight path. Then he told me the talking-to-the-schoolgirls-about-Fokkers story, except in his version *Bader* was the speaker. I described The Bentley Collector to him, and asked if he had ever encountered the gentleman. He recalled having seen my nameless acquaintance at vintage-car events, but he didn't know his name or anything about him. Some time later I recounted the story to Rivers[iv], who also remembered the man from the occasional *concours d'élégance* but once again, knew nothing of the fellow's identity or antecedents.

My wife was of the opinion that the man was nothing more than 'your typical New York *comédien*'. Then one dazzling morning in May of 1975, we were viewing the paintings displayed along the park and gardens, when a magnificent two-tone khaki, 4 $\frac{1}{4}$-litre Park Ward coupé detached itself from the traffic on the Bayswater Road and drew up at the kerb. Inside was The Bentley Collector, accompanied by an elegantly dressed woman 'of a certain age'. He was still wearing the Irvin jacket, and a huge and ugly freehand pipe was clenched between his teeth. He greeted me warmly and asked me how I liked the car, which he had quite recently purchased from the original owner. I expressed my admiration for it, and was just about to introduce my wife to him and thereby have a polite pretext for asking him his name, when a pugnacious-looking Traffic Warden came striding purposefully over, and my friend quickly slipped the Bentley into gear and drew silently away with a careless wave of the hand.

I've never seen the man again, and his identity remains a tantalizing mystery, but our meeting had a profound effect on the formation of my pipe tastes. The lingering memory of that Danish pipe, with its crisp, clean lines, gem-like grain, and flawless polish—so different from the dark, blurred lineaments of the typical English pipe of that period—attracted me to the Charatan pipes, which were—in the sixties and seventies—quite clearly influenced by Scandinavian design.

Albert Mendez

If anything in *Somewhat Introductory* has given the reader an uneasy feeling that I am Against Collectors, let me hasten to explain that this is not the case, and that in fact, I have been a collector myself. My main interest lay in the pipes of the nineteenth century — meerschaums, briars, clays, and even porcelain examples. In the beginning, most of the briars that I was able to find from this period originated with one of the well-known English firms, and they were, without exception, remarkably small pipes, rather shoddily-made from inferior briar.

Then one day a friend in Nice handed me a well-worn black morocco case. Inside was a magnificent *cou de gygne* briar, with a breathtaking, flame-like straight grain, and a translucent amber mouthpiece. The bowl was large and gracefully proportioned with good, thick walls, and inlaid into the bottom of it was an oval gold cartouche engraved with an inscription in French, identifying the pipe as a gift to a Captain de Solages, from his fellow officers, in September of 1871. There was no maker's name, and my acquaintance explained that this was customary with continental artisans of the period, who respected the prevailing opinion that a visible maker's name was in bad taste, and marred the appearance of the article[v]. This is the reason why watches were invariably marked inside the rear case cover, the outside of the case being elegantly plain, or reserved for varying forms of decoration.

I was not able to persuade the owner to part with this exceptional pipe, so I set off in search of similar examples, and I was fortunate enough to find a few. I also started making inquiries into the original tools and techniques employed in making briar tobacco pipes, as I felt that a thorough understanding of the craft was essential to a complete appreciation of the finished products. I found that in nineteenth-century continental Europe, the vast majority of pipes were made entirely by hand, using hand-tools instead of steam-powered, belt-driven machinery (as in England, and the United States). Indeed, it became apparent that the methods used for making briar pipes were virtually identical to those used when the material was meerschaum.

The craftsman began by sawing the *ébauchon* into a rough shape with a small bow saw, then further reducing it with a fine-toothed pad saw blade (in later years, both of these were largely replaced by treadle-operated jig saws), after which the shape was further refined with a drawing knife, of a pattern similar to those used by gunstockers. Using a brace fitted with a gimlet bit, a small pilot hole was bored into the centres of the bowl and stem, to accept the taper screw chuck of a pole lathe (although some rustic craftsmen dispensed with the use of even this ancient implement). Turning chisels were then used to bring the bowl and stem very close to the desired shape.

The next step was to bore the draught hole, and the cylindrical mortise, using shell bits in a brace (which was always a wooden one). It is worth noting that one-sixteenth of an inch (1.588mm) was the smallest diameter bit made, and that in the vast majority of the nineteenth-century European, artisan-made pipes that I have examined, the draught holes were bored to either two *lignes* (4.52mm), or three-sixteenths of an inch (4.763mm), which is precisely the diameter that Mr Newcombe has fixed upon as ideal.

Only after the small holes were finished, was the tobacco chamber bored with a spoon bit[vi]. This is why the thin walls that detract from the smoking qualities of so many pipes are rarely seen on *good* nineteenth-century pieces. Modern pipes always have the tobacco chamber turned or drilled *before* the bowl is completely shaped, and in most cases this forces the craftsman to remove far more wood than is desirable, in his efforts to eliminate major defects, and keep the pipe in the 'first' category.

After all of the holes were properly bored, the mouthpiece (of amber, horn, or boxwood) was fashioned on the pole lathe, using turning chisels, and the short, double-ended rasps known as wax files in the jewelry trade. After the pipe and mouthpiece were joined (by threading the peg to the mortise) and matched to each other, the complete piece was ready for its final finishing, which was done with small cabinet-maker's scrapers of various shapes. These 'scrapers' are actually cutting tools, with razor-sharp edges that are 'turned' (with a hardened-steel burnisher) so that they remove nearly transparent shavings from the surface of the work. This accounts for the clear grain and perfect surfaces of very old, high-grade pipes. Even the finest grades of glass-paper (known here as sandpaper) 'blur' the grain by removing the softer material between the canals more rapidly, leaving a soft, fuzzy, uneven surface, which is clearly visible under a powerful glass. Heavy glass-papering also tends to fill the pores (no matter how much water or alcohol is used during the process), which affects both the ability of the wood to take a fine finish, and the smoking qualities of the pipe.

Finally the pipes were polished with a hard felt block charged with a polishing paste mixed from pumice and olive oil, then covered with hardwood dust (to soak up the oil), and given a final polish with rottenstone and olive oil. After a second treatment with hardwood dust, the finished pipe received an application of white beeswax in benzene (with an added infusion of alkanet for a reddish finish, or of Cassel brown for a mahogany finish), and polished with linen rags.

The sources for the methods described above are the notes taken by me during lengthy conversations that I had with two different French artisans in the early seventies. The youngest of these gentlemen was eighty-two years of age, and had been apprenticed to a small maker in Saint-Claude in 1904, at the age of thirteen. He served as an infantryman in the Great War, and later travelled to London, where he briefly worked for Barling, before returning home in 1928.

For the past eighty-five years, most pipes have been made on machinery, by persons who cannot truly be called craftsmen, since they are responsible for only one or two separate steps in the making of a pipe. They are paid hourly wages, and are expected to perform a specified number of these identical actions every single day, with the inevitable result that boredom, fatigue, and disgust set in, and the worker loses any interest in the quality of his work.

Even genuine craftsmen use electrically powered machine tools for much of their work, including the ubiquitous large-diameter abrasive disk chucked in the headstock of the lathe, which is used for most of the shaping. This particular implement is largely responsible for the mediocre quality of many (if not most) modern pipes, as it softens contours that should be sharp, and wastes away the fibers unevenly, instead of shearing them cleanly. No subsequent amount of wet glass-papering with successively finer grades can eradicate the initial damage. One sees so many high-grade pipes, made by reputable craftsmen, where the stem gently undulates along its entire length; this is not the result of artistic exuberance, but merely a sign that the craftsman was not fully in control of his tools and material.

One relatively recent development in pipe making, which I am not at all in favour of, is that of extending the stems with materials other than briar. Charatan was doing this in the seventies, using vulcanite to salvage superb bowls that had developed fatal flaws in the stems. Where plain black vulcanite was used, some very satisfactory effects were achieved (I own an example of this, an 'Extra Large Special Crown Model', which is one of my favourite pipes), but many were done with that hideous mock amber of a particularly disagreeable yellow colour. One of the most common materials now used for this purpose is bamboo, which apart from its flexible strength and relatively low cost has the added virtue of appealing to the depraved middle-class taste for *chinoiserie*.

I offer up the preceding paragraphs as a partial justification for my oft-expressed disdain of modern pipes, lest some *soi-disant* analyst be moved to decide that it stems solely from ill-informed prejudice, or mere caprice. In closing, I must confess that the pipes of the past eighty-five years cannot arouse in my breast the same affection and admiration as their truly hand-made predecessors. There are modern pipes that are very good, and I do smoke them, but I cannot *love* them, as I once did the products of a gentler age.

This is where I had intended to end this rather long-winded commentary, containing much that many will find unpalatable, but it proved necessary to continue, because at some point during the process of reading these essays twice or thrice over, I found that a dusty mental corner had been disturbed. Then when Mr Newcombe kindly sent me copies of some of the photographs in the book, I found amongst them one (which appears on the bottom right of the rear cover) of a superlative pipe by Bo Nordh, which is virtually identical to the one The Bentley Collector was smoking when he first hove in sight.

A few days later, on a wet and windy Saturday morning, I travelled into Manhattan and walked down Seventh Avenue to Twenty-Second Street. There are no Dolphin Passages in this wretched city, so when I turned the corner there was no Bentley S1, no leggy blondes, and no breezy young men in sheepskin jackets. The building occupied by the shop was recently torn down, and the foundations of a larger replacement are being excavated, but there was no one working there on that rainy Saturday, and except for the occasional passerby, the street was deserted.

The standpipe is still there, hard by the hoardings, and I dropped on it as I did on that other Saturday, thirty-eight years ago, and sat there smoking *London Blend* in the gentle drizzle. By a curious coincidence, the pipe that I had with me is a 'Free Hand Relief' Charatan billiard (the only rusticated pipe that I then owned) with the flue and mouthpiece altered according to Mr Newcombe's system. Having over the years spent a great deal of time smoking pipes in the rain, I can testify that very few of them are wholly satisfactory under these conditions, but that one Charatan smokes perfectly dry and easy on the wettest of days.

As I smoked, I mentally reviewed everything that I had read and written in the past few weeks—the contemplative state induced by pipe smoking is ideal for an exercise of this sort—and I became aware of a vague sense of general dissatisfaction. How could I write laudatory remarks about the work of the Danish craftsmen without owning any examples of their work? Then, too, it seemed improper to embrace Mr Newcombe's *Luftströmungtheorie*[vii] based upon my experience with a single example, and that a Charatan, of which make I own many that are excellent smokers without having been modified in any way.

Consequently, I acquired two pipes to assist me in my cogitations. One is a very handsome saddle-stem Pot (with a singularly attractive 'flame' grain) by Mr Jess Chonowitsch. This piece has had the draught hole increased to eleven sixty-fourths of an inch, and the mouthpiece relieved to provide an unobstructed draw. The other is an apple of striking appearance, finished in beautifully executed rippled striations. This perfectly balanced rustication sweeps back to a Petersonesque mouthpiece that combines the best features of both the 'military' push bit and a conventional one. The maker is Mr Tony Rodriguez, a disciple of the Danish school of pipe making. Although a relative newcomer, his work has already attracted wide attention, and he enjoys two unparalleled advantages; he has studied the methods of Mr Lars Ivarsson and Mr Jess Chonowitsch in their own workshops, and he obtains all of his briar from these two great craftsmen, and from Bo Nordh. As far as I know, Mr Rodriguez is the only maker that bores all of his pipes according to Mr Newcombe's specifications.

The workmanship on both pieces is superlative, although the elegant, traditionally shaped Chonowitsch pipe — with its exquisite details that bespeak lavish attention — is closer to my nineteenth-century ideal. Both pipes have moderate tobacco capacities, and over the years I have found that — with the mixtures that I favour — a proportionately smaller tobacco chamber (not necessarily a smaller pipe) affords me a superior smoke. This is only one of many minor points in which I find myself at variance with received form. The smoking qualities of both of these pipes are quite extraordinary. The Rodriguez pipe was new when I got it and I have been smoking *965* in it. The Chonowitsch is second-hand but nearly new, having been smoked only a few times by the previous owner, and I am smoking the current, rather rough-edged version of Craven Mixture in it. The first pipeful in the Rodriguez was delightful, without the need for any arcane preparation, and it continues to smoke excellently. The Chonowitsch is a revelation; the only other pipe that I have ever smoked, which could come close to matching it, is a fifties-vintage Dunhill ODA 837 that is unluckily no longer in my possession. One of the most remarkable properties of that ODA—which the Chonowitsch shares—was the way that the outside of the bowl was never more than slightly warm, even after the pipe had been smoked for forty-five minutes. I sat on my balcony with that Chonowitsch the other day, and smoked a pipeful of the harsh, new Craven in a stiff wind; after twenty minutes, the exterior of the bowl was just perceptibly warm.

Now, after smoking English pipes for thirty-eight years, and heaping scorn upon modern pipes for thirty of them, I find myself smoking and enjoying an American pipe, and a Danish pipe, both newly-made. One is never too old to learn.

---

[i] Flying garment, made from thick, short-pile sheepskins, which became the hallmark of R.A.F. fighter pilots in the second war, although after 1943 they were only authorized for issue to bomber crews. Named for the original maker, Irving Air Chute of Great Britain LTD.

[ii] Alan Clark, military historian, Member of Parliament and Minister of State for Defence.

[iii] Group Captain Douglas R. S. Bader, CBE, lost both legs in an aeroplane crash in 1931, but returned to active service in 1939, and led a squadron during the Battle of Britain.

[iv] A. F. Rivers Fletcher, motor racing driver, author and Bentley salesman. He was one of the Bentley Boys, when the marque dominated the 24-Hour Le Mans, in the twenties and thirties

[v] When a maker's name was present, it was usually found stamped in gold in the lining of the case.

[vi] As early as 1880, the standard practice in England (and the United States) was to turn the tobacco chamber first. This was done on the lathe, with the roughed-out pipe held in a wooden spring chuck.

[vii] Airflow theory.

An American Pipe, and a Danish Pipe

A straight grained pipe by Los Angeles-based Tony Rodriguez, who is becoming recognized as an outstanding pipe maker.

A beautiful Jörn Micke pipe -- made in 1963. Micke, who is Danish, worked with Sixten and Lars Ivarsson and is still making pipes today. He is considered one of the best of all time.

INDEX

Aaron, Hank, 33
Abi-Fadel, Eva, 193
Ali, Muhammad, 66
American Cancer Society, 19, 228
American Heart Association, 19
Amorelli, 195
Amrom, George, 134, 175
Anderson, Steve, 161
Andersson, Jan, 117, 211
Anima Pipes, 147
Annofsky, Garret, 243
Apitz, Michael, 187
Ardor, 195
Ashton, 11, 14, 161, 217
Astley's, 23, 25

Bach, Johann Sebastian, 69,124, 126, 179
Balkan Sobranie, 187
Balleby, Kurt, 90
Bang, S., vii, 27, 29, 32, 38, 58, 67, 69, 73,
    76, 78, 87, 88, 89, 93-98, 101, 117, 120,
    123, 124, 130, 133, 134, 135, 138, 157,
    171, 173, 191, 193, 203, 217
Bang, Svend, vi, vii, 32, 96
Barbi, Rainer, xi, 173, 174, 184-194
Barbie, Klaus, 190
Barling, ii, iv, 14, 59, 83, 106, 125, 161,
    212, 217, 235, 256
Barrie, J.M., 161
BBB pipes, v
Beale, Mark, 226
Becker & Musicò, 203, 204, 205
Becker, Fritz, 204
Becker, Gitta, 175, 176, 177
Becker, Paolo, xii, 201-205
Becker, Wolfgang, xi, 174-177
Beethoven, Ludwig von, 64, 69, 159, 179
Behrens, Heiko, 187
Benjamin, Jim, 49, 50, 55, 56, 59-61, 70, 71,
    80, 84-88, 94, 106, 109, 110, 112, 146,
    160, 167, 218
Bentley, Paul, 25
Berle, Milton, 7, 20
Berry, Chuck, 124
Bertram, xi, 107, 164-172
Bertram, Sid, 168, 169
Bertram, Sydney, 166-168
Bilhall, Per, 134
Biotene, 239
Bjarnhof, Karl, 208
Blake, David, 152
Bonaquisti, Paul, 161, 171
Bonfiglioli, Alberto, 107

Booth, Jimmy, 240
Boska, David, 240, 244
Botter, Paul, 28
Brebbia, 195, 217
Briar Blues, 230
Briar Rose, 103
British Buttner Reamer, 114, 224
Burak, Ed, 155
Burla, Frank, 174
Burns, George, 7, 20
Butch Cassidy and the Sundance Kid
    (movie),185
Butera, Mike, 28, 111, 190
Butz Choquin, 56
Byrd, Larry, 33

Campbell, Ken, 80, 89
Captain Black, 2
Casals, Pablo, 217
Castello, xii, 57, 87, 133, 161, 195-200, 205
Cellini, 51
Chamberlain, Wilt, 33
Chan, Andy, 5
Charatan, ii, x, xi, 11, 14, 47, 65, 67, 75, 83,
    103, 133, 144, 161, 182, 211, 212, 217,
    253, 257-259
Chicago Tribune, 81, 222
Chonowitsch, Bonnie, 23, 45, 70, 77
Chonowitsch, Emil, 32, 37, 44
Chonowitsch, Jess, ii, 5, 6, 23, 27, 29, 32,
    34-45, 55, 58, 59, 67-70, 78, 82, 83, 85,
    86, 87, 89, 102, 113, 116, 117, 119, 123,
    124, 128, 133-138, 148, 156, 157, 160,
    171, 173, 182, 208, 213, 217, 219, 244,
    259
Churchill, Winston, 20
Cigar Aficionado (magazine), 19
Cigarettes Are Sublime (Richard Klein), 8
Clinton Health Plan, 11
Cobb, Ty, 33
Colter, Ron, 68, 117
Colwell, Tom, 51, 85
Comoy, 11, 47, 57, 83, 161, 170, 217
Compleat Smoker, The (magazine), 19
Confessions of an Advertising Man (David
    Ogilvie), 235
Cooke, Jim, 102, 111, 112, 154-156, 171,
    217, 230
Coolidge, Calvin, 16
Cooper, Rob, 68, 103, 117, 132, 216, 217
Coppo, Franco, 197-200
Corn Flakes, 224

INDEX

Cornell and Diehl Tobaccos, 223
Corona pipe lighters, 187
Cosby, Bill, 20
Cox, John "Duke", 104
Cronkite, Walter, 16
Crosby, Bing, 16, 108
Custombilt, 48, 51

da Vinci, Leonardo, 118, 119
Dan Pipe, 28, 187, 188
Davis, Jody, 28, 161
Di Maggio, Joe, 33
Dill's pipe cleaners, 111
Domenico, Romeo, 197
Don Carlos, 195
Dorsett Knotty, 84
Doyle, Arthur Conan, 16
Dr. Sheehan On Running (George Sheehan),
   1
Dudleigh of Hollywood, 47, 51
Dull, Charles "Chip", 243-244
Dunhill, ii, iii, ix, xi, 2, 11, 13, 26, 28, 29,
   47, 55, 57, 60, 65, 67, 83, 84, 122, 123,
   125, 133, 144, 156, 158, 159, 161, 170,
   172, 196, 198, 210-213, 215-217, 222,
   237, 260
Dunhill, Alfred, 13, 82, 112, 198
Dunn, Tom, I, 160

E. Andrew Pipes, 209
Economist, The (magazine) 244
Edison, Thomas, v, 62, 65
Eells, John, 28, 51, 161, 168
Ehrmantraut, Jack, 23, 33
Einstein, Albert, xvi, I, 7, 16, 22, 244
Ellis, Lowell, 55
Eltang, Tom, 26, 27, 191, 205
Erickson, Ken, 51
Erskine, John, 22
Esserman, Rich, 106, 154, 155, 167, 207,
   212, 214, 215
Ezrati, Moty, 14, 23

Fader, Bill, 2, 100
Fader's Tobacconist, 100, 150
Fallon, Steve, 223
Farr, Joel, I, 146, 155, 160
Field, David, 183, 190, 201, 203, 205
For Your Own Good (Jacob Sullum), 227
Ford, Gerald, 16
Former, 26, 27
Fortune, Angela, 150

Frank, Hans Joachim, 105
Fred Stoker and Sons, 223
Freud, Sigmund, 244
Fribourg & Treyer, 243
Frickert, Holger, 187

Gaddis, Bob, 190
Gallant, Paul, 237
Garagiola, Joe, 241
Garbe, Ingo, 27, 75
Garfinkel, Lawrence, 228
Gately, Iain, 227
Georgetown University, 18
Getty, J. Paul, 154
Glaubinger, Ric, 243
Glukler, Mike, 230
Godbee, Brian, 25
Great Danes, The (video), 24, 173
Griseta, Vic, 230
Guards' in London, ix
Guizot, 17
Gus' Smoke Shop, 137, 149

Hacker, Richard Carleton, 18, 19, 33, 48, 54,
   57, 65, 68, 141, 166, 210
Haddow, Sir Alexander, 233
Hamlin, Bob, 106, 168, 195, 196
Hanna, Fred, 206, 207
Hansen, Per, vii, 32, 88, 93-98, 101, 136, 191
Hayek, F.A., 16
Heim, Fred, 131, 225
Heinrichs, Peter, 26, 27, 29, 30, 31, 137,
   181, 183
Herbruck, Andy, 104
Hermann, Per, 134
Hitler, Adolf, I, 7, 8, 9, 22
Holm, Preben, 32, 97
Holmes, Sherlock, 75, 150, 175, 195, 225
House of 10,000 Pipes, 26, 181
Howdy Doody, iii
Humphrey, Gary, 102, 103, 147

Iacocca, Lee, 20
Il Ceppo, 195
Illustrated History of the Pipe, The, 63, 68
Ilsted, Poul, 26, 90
Ivarsson, Annette, 77
Ivarsson, Camilla, 77
Ivarsson, Lars, v, vi, 27, 31, 32, 58, 62-79,
   82, 87, 88, 106, 120, 121, 123, 133-136,
   138, 146, 157, 167, 173, 176, 193, 208-
   210, 217, 237, 259, 261
Ivarsson, Nanna, 27, 32, 63, 65, 76, 77

INDEX

Ivarsson, Sixten, v, 26, 27, 29, 31, 32, 36, 37, 42, 44, 51, 58, 62-65, 67-70, 74, 76-78, 83, 98, 120, 121, 123, 130, 132-134, 139, 157, 173, 208, 209, 261
Iwan Ries, 36, 51, 63, 67, 115, 117, 127, 137

Janusek, Fred, 130, 131, 209
Jim Benjamin, 218
John Barleycorn (Jack London), 11
Johns Hopkins University, 206
Johnson, Magic, 33
Johnson, Todd, 28
Jones, Barry, 14
Jordan, Michael, 16, 33, 235
Joura, Coco, 181
Joura, Fabian, 181
Joura, Chini, 181
Joura, Karl Heinz, xi, 66, 174, 178-184
Julie, Anne, 28, 29, 32, 37, 97
Jung, Carl, 1
Jurkiewicz, Ed, 161, 209

Kaywoodie, 51, 170, 172
Kenny, Joe, 151, 152
Kessler, David, 11
King James I, 11, 13
King Louis XIV, 22
King, Martin Luther, 164
Klein, Richard, 8
Knudsen, Mette, 27
Knudsen, Sven, 27
Knudsen, Teddy, 27
Kolpin, Ed, 16, 17, 233, 235

L.J. Peretti, 169
Lankford, Joe, 105
Larsen pipes, 54, 58, 216
Larsen, Niels, 54, 61
Larsen, W.O., 23, 29-31, 37, 41, 54, 58, 61, 103, 216
Learned, Sam, 161
Lee, Christina, I
Lehman, Ed, 84, 94, 197, 213, 214
Levi, Chuck, 115
Levi, Stan, 67
Levin, Barry, 33, 65, 67, 102, 113, 223
Levine, Brian, 25
Lewis, Jerry Lee, 124
Lewis, Rich, 161, 217
Liberty Tobacco, 137
Licker, Aaron, 210
Liebaert, Alexis, 68
Limbaugh, Rush, 20

Little Richard, 124
Lives of the Saints (book), ix
London, Jack, 11
Long's pipe cleaners, 111
Loring, John, 18
Los Angeles Times, 20
Low Country Pipe and Cigar Store, 223

McClelland Tobaccos, 223
McNulty, Brian, 147, 161
MacArthur, Douglas, 166
Mantle, Mickey, 33
Marks, Andrew, 28
Marx, Groucho, 20
Marx, Harpo, 124
Marxman, 51
Mastro de Paja, 195
Maszynski, Felizitas, 193
Matisse, 33
Matlick, Dayton, I, 70-72, 146, 160
Maya, Alain, 69
Mays, Willie, 33
Memories of a Cuban Kitchen (Mary Urrutia Randelmann), ii
Michaelangelo, 33
Micke, Jörn, 261
Mincer, Tracy, 51
Mission Impossible (television show and movie), 219
Monet, Claude, 33
Monroe, Marilyn, 209
Mont Blanc, 159
Montreal Pipe Smokers Club, 9
Morley, Christopher, 18, 236, 237
Mountain Village Evening Standard, 187
Mozart, Wolfgang Amadeus, 69
Museum of Modern Art in New York, 42
Music City Marketing, 13, 23
Musicò, Giorgio, xii, 204
Musicò, Massimo, 205
Mustang, 215
My Lady Nicotine (J.M. Barrie), 161
My Own Blend, 30

Napoleon, 22, 168
Nation, Carry, 12
Neubert, Regina, 182
New England Journal of Medicine, 241
New York Times, The, 11, 19
Newcombe, Carole, 2, 4, 6, 77, 174, 175, 178, 193
Newcombe, Jack, 228
Newcombe, Sara, 77

INDEX

Nielsen, Hans, 26
Nielsen, Tonni, 27
Noltensmeier, Ulf, vii, 32, 88, 93-98, 124,
  136, 191, 207
Nordh, Birgit, 118, 120, 123-125
Nordh, Bo, viii, 6, 26, 38, 57, 67, 69, 73, 78,
  87, 99, 105, 106, 116-129, 130-136, 138,
  139, 157, 159, 171, 173, 181, 182, 191,
  208, 209, 211, 217, 230, 258, 259
Nording, Eric, 29
Northwestern Pennsylvania Lung
  Association, 21
Novelli, 196
Nunnelly, Bill, I, 23, 24

Ogilvie, David, 235
Oliver Twist, 241
Ostermann Pipes, 137, 193
Osternforff, Rolf, 221

Palermo, Robert, 211, 214
Palmer, Tom, 149-153
Pappas, Shane, 103
Parascenzo, Marco, 196, 197
Parker, 210
Patton, George, 166
PCI, 202, 203
Pease, Greg, 223
Peretti, Robert, 169
Perri, Margaret, 143, 144, 148
Perri, Paul, ix, 51, 101, 143-148, 217
Peter Pan, iii
Peterson, ix, 149-153, 158, 161, 217
Peterson, Charles, 150
Phi Beta Kappa, 18
Piaget, 159
Picasso, 33, 183
Piedmont Tobacconist, 230
Pipe Collector, The (newsletter), I, 80, 130,
  132, 133, 206, 211, 223
Pipe Collector's Club of America, 106, 168
Pipe Dan, 28, 133, 191
Pipe Friendly (magazine), I, 23, 34, 36, 62,
  66, 116, 143, 146, 149, 154, 155, 160,
  206
Pipe Lovers (magazine), 67, 105, 168
Pipe Smoker, The (magazine), 25, 68, 93,
  117, 155, 164, 173, 202, 203, 226
Pipe Smoker's Ephemeris, The, i, vi, I, 214
Pipes and tobaccos (magazine), I, 10, 70,
  72, 73, 80, 88, 99, 108, 140, 146, 155,
  157, 160, 174, 223
Pipesmoke (magazine), 154, 157, 159, 160

Poggenpohl, Rex, 115
Postrel, Virginia, I
Prager Perspective, The, 228
Prager, Dennis, 228, 229
Pulvers, Marty, 69, 143, 177, 183, 184, 190,
  217, 230, 232

Quindlen, Anna, 11

Radice, 195
Ram, Sydney P., 101, 102, 166-168
Randelmann, Mary Urrutia, ii
Rapaport, Ben, 239
Rasmussen, Kent, 90
Rasmussen, Poul, 36, 37, 44, 83
Rattray's No. 7 Reserve, 30
Reason (magazine), I, 7
Reich, Robert, 11
Rembrandt, 33, 119, 214
Reschke, Mike, 174
Reston, James, 19
Retail Tobacco Dealers Association, 2, 115,
  196
Rice Krispies, 224
Richman, Steve, 230
Rio, Chuck, 199
Ritz Hotel, 159
Robinson, Edward G., 61, 166
Rockwell, Norman, 16
Rodriguez, Tony, 28, 84, 87, 141, 146, 156,
  217, 259, 261
Rodu, Brad, 240, 242, 244
Rokringar (magazine), 211
Rolls Royce, x, 159
Roosevelt, Franklin Delano, 166
Rose, Fran, 28
Roush, Larry, 28, 161
Russell, Bertrand, xv, 233, 234, 244
Ruth, Babe, 33
Rutzen, Rolf, 54, 88

Sandburg, Carl, 16
Sasieni, 11, 51, 59, 83, 85, 86, 161, 217
Savinelli, xi, 21, 156, 195, 217
Schifrin, Lalo, 217, 219
Schrire, Robert, vii, 130-139
Schulte, Howard, 217
Schwartz, Alan, 154, 157, 158, 160
Schwartz, Joan, 158
Schwarzenegger, Arnold, 15, 16, 24, 235
Schweitzer, Albert, 16
Scotti, Carlo, 198, 199
Ser Jacopo, 75, 195, 217, 225

INDEX

Sermet, Beth, 142
Shakespeare, William, 159
Sheehan, George, 1
Sherlock's Haven, 131, 143, 230, 232
Shih, Kevin, 221
Shih, Steven, 221
Shropshire, Mark, 88, 130, 131
Silbereis, Jean Luc, 106
Skelton, Red, 166
Skoal, 241
Skoal Bandits, 241
Smoke (magazine), 157
Smoker's Den, 50
SMS Meerschaum, 142
Soladar, Gordon, 36, 51, 117, 144, 158
Sowell, Thomas, 244
Stalin, Joseph, 28, 166
Stanion, Chuck, I, 55, 88, 160, 174, 197
Stanwell, 29, 40, 74, 84, 133
Stokkebye, Peter, I, 10, 55, 223
Stone, W. Clement, 7, 20
Stradivarius, 36, 44
Sundqvist, Wille, VI
Sugawara, Marianne, I
Suits, Julia, I
Sullivan, Basil, 103, 104
Sullum, Jacob, 227

Tabak-Lädeli, 6, 58, 89, 136, 137
Talbert, Trever, 161
Ten Commandments of Pipe Collecting, 231
Tesch Pipe Store, 186
Three Nuns, iii
Tilshead, 210
Time (magazine), 8
Tinder Box, 16, 150, 210
Tinsky, Mark, 161
Tobacco (Iain Gately), 2, 196, 227, 228, 243
Tolle, John, 132
Trinity College, 152
Tsuge, 59, 70
Twain, Mark, 16

Ultimate Cigar Book (Richard Carleton Hacker), 19
Ultimate Pipe Book (Richard Carleton Hacker), 8, 18, 68
Ultimate Pipe Video, 141
Unger, Bill, I, 132
Union League Club, 222
United Press International, 2
University of Chicago, 18
Upshall, James, 11, 14, 23, 65, 156, 161, 210, 217
Uptown's Smoke Shop, 23, 34, 127, 137
USA Today, 81

van Gogh, Vincent, 33
Vatican, 205
Vesz, Julius, 226
Vogt, Corinna, 105

W. Curtis Draper, 104
W.C. Demuth, 51
Wagner, Rachel, 89
Wagner, René, v, 6, 58, 136, 137
Wall Street Journal, The, 81
Waxman, Henry, 10, 11
Weber Pipes, 51, 169
Weidemann, John, 47, 48, 51, 214
Weinberger, Jack Henry (JHW), 49, 51, 145, 217
West, Tim, 28, 111, 161, 171
What's My Line? (television show), 192
Whelan, Tony, 151
White Dot (Dunhill), 112, 190
Wiley, Randy, 102, 106
Wilford, Sykes, 215
Williams, Ted, 33
Wilson's Snuff, 243
Winslow, Paul, 29, 30
Witte-Vermeulen, Carl, 239
Wohrle, Ulrich, 57, 58
World Cup, 178
World Gym, 15
World Jewish Congress, 205
World Series, 178

Yager Hand Made, 47-51
Yagerlehner, C., 47, 50-51